# STRATEGIES FOR ASIA-PACIFIC SHIPPING

# Strategies for Asia-Pacific Shipping

JEFF HAWKINS
*Asia Pacific Maritime Institute, Launceston, Australia*

RICHARD GRAY
*Institute of Marine Studies, University of Plymouth*

**Ashgate**

Aldershot • Burlington USA • Singapore • Sydney

Published by
Ashgate Publishing Limited
Gower House
Croft Road
Aldershot
Hampshire GU11 3HR
England

Ashgate Publishing Company
131 Main Street
Burlington , VT 05401-5600 USA

Ashgate website: http://www.ashgate.com

**British Library Cataloguing in Publication Data**
Hawkins, Jeff
    Strategies for Asia-Pacific shipping. - (Plymouth studies
    in contemporary shipping and logistics)
    1. Shipping - Asia 2. Shipping - Pacific Area
    I. Title II.Gray, Richard, 1943-
    387.5'095

**Library of Congress Control Number:** 00-135323

ISBN 0 7546 1492 1 ✓

Printed and bound by Athenaeum Press, Ltd.,
Gateshead, Tyne & Wear.

# Contents

# Figures and Tables

# Acknowledgements

Many people and organisations have provided help in producing this book. The authors would like to acknowledge the contribution of their respective organisations, the Asia Pacific Maritime Institute and the Institute of Marine Studies at the University of Plymouth, in the research and preparation of this book.

The Asia Pacific Maritime Institute funded this project as part of its ongoing efforts to produce quality research for the Asia Pacific maritime industry. Special thanks must also go to Luz Hawkins of the Asia Pacific Maritime Institute whose professional expertise and personal support has been highly pivotal to the success of this project.

At the University of Plymouth, special mention should be made of Harry Churchill, Kevin Cullinane, Michael Roe and Harry Heijveld for the expert advice and assistance they so willingly gave. Thanks also to Marie Bendell for secretarial support.

Finally, our deep gratitude to all the participants in the survey, interviews, and simulations without whom this work would not have been possible.


Jeff Hawkins, Launceston, Australia
Richard Gray, Plymouth, UK

# 1 Introduction

**Background**

Over the past several decades, the rapid globalisation of the market place has intensified competition within the already competitive shipping industry. This is particularly true in the Asia-Pacific region, which is predicted to dominate international trade in the twenty-first century. It is a certainty that with this dynamic growth in trade will come an increased demand for shipping services. Asia-Pacific shipowners intent on taking advantage of this growth and successfully competing in the market place will require a strategic approach to the way they manage their organisations. Research suggests that strategy is the single most important factor leading to a firm's success or failure. A shipowner's choice of strategies, therefore, will be critical to its long-term market success.

The strategic management literature offers a wide range of strategy selection models but serious doubts have been raised over the applicability of these models to shipowners in general and Asia-Pacific shipowners in particular. Much of what is known about strategy is drawn from manufacturing industries; very little comes from the service industries, and even less from the maritime industry. Shipping-based research on strategy selection is limited, and very little is known about shipowners' strategic decision making behaviour. Practical tools to guide and inform shipowners in their strategy selection are also seriously wanting.

Criticism of existing strategy selection models highlights the general lack of empirical support for such models. Most have not undergone any empirical testing to establish their utility and reliability in enhancing an organisation's strategic decision making. Furthermore, although most models assume a generic nature, claiming broad applicability across businesses and industries, there is very little empirical evidence to support this claim. Indeed, there is growing evidence to the contrary.

These limitations to our current knowledge of strategy selection require greater scrutiny and examination. If we are fully to understand the application and effectiveness of strategy in a service industry like shipping, particularly in the context of a rapidly growing economic region like the Asia-Pacific, then it is critical that we learn more about how shipowners in the region actually make strategic choices. What factors do they consider when making strategic choices? What process do they follow to select and evaluate strategies? How does this behaviour compare with current theory on strategy selection? These are questions that this book aims to answer. Based on the results, a strategy selection model applicable to Asia-Pacific shipping is developed.

## The importance of strategy

The study of strategy lies within the domain of strategic management, which has emerged as an important new discipline within the general field of management. In the last two decades, there has been a steady build-up in our knowledge of the subject, both in terms of theory and empirical evidence. Literature reviews conducted during that period (Snow and Thomas, 1994; Lyles, 1990; Morris, 1986, 1987; Thomas, 1984) show a steadily maturing field where conceptual and methodological debates continue to enrich and advance current understanding of strategic management. After more than two decades of research, there is now a substantial body of evidence to show that organisations practising strategic management tend to outperform those that do not (Collis and Montgomery, 1997; David, 1997; Hussey, 1994; Miller and Cardinal, 1994). The groundwork was laid by a number of studies conducted in the 1960s and 1970s (e.g. Wood and La Forge, 1979; Karger and Malik, 1975; Herold, 1972; Schoeffler *et al* 1974; Ansoff *et al* 1971; Eastlack and McDonald, 1970; Thune and House, 1970).

Thune and House (1970) carried out a study in 1965 to examine the performance of a number of companies over a 7-15 year period (i.e. since the introduction of formal planning in each company). They found that those who planned outperformed those that did not on three counts: earnings per share, earnings on common equity, and earnings on total capital employed. They also found that planners outperformed themselves based on records prior to the introduction of planning. Herold (1972) extended the study and also found that companies that planned outperformed those that did not. Other studies have provided further supporting evidence. Eastlack and McDonald (1970) studied 211 companies, 105 of which were among the Fortune 500. They concluded that CEOs who used strategic management concepts headed companies with the fastest growth rates. The following year, Ansoff *et al* (1971) examined the strategic decisions made by 93 companies regarding acquisitions over a 19-year period (1946-65). They found that on many financial and sales measures, as well as ability to predict the outcomes of planning activities, companies that used a strategic management approach performed better than those that did not.

Further proof was provided by Schoeffler *et al* (1974) whose study became popularly known as the Profit Impact of Marketing Strategy (PIMS) study. This study involved 57 firms in 620 different lines of business and analysed the relationships of a wide range of strategic activity variables and profitability. Results showed that the appropriate use of strategic management resulted in increased profitability. Similar results were obtained by Karger and Malik (1975) who studied 273 companies in the chemical, drug, electronics and machinery industries. They found that on a number of financial measures, firms which used strategic management methods outperformed those that did not. Wood and La Forge (1979) got similar results: their study of 60 large US banks showed that banks using comprehensive long-range planning methods had significantly better financial performance than those that had no formal planning system.

From these promising beginnings, knowledge of strategic management continued to advance. Studies not only focused on monetary variables but on more intangible organisational factors. Based on a review of the literature, Greenley (1986) identified fourteen benefits of strategic management, which David (1993) has summarised as follows:

1.  It allows for identification, prioritisation and exploitation of opportunities.
2.  It provides an objective view of management problems.
3.  It represents a framework for improved co-ordination and control activities.
4.  It minimises the effects of adverse conditions and changes.
5.  It allows major decisions better to support established objectives.
6.  It allows more effective allocation of time and resources to identified opportunities.
7.  It allows fewer resources and less time to be devoted to correcting erroneous or ad hoc decisions.
8.  It creates a framework for internal communication among personnel.
9.  It helps to integrate the behaviour of individuals into a total effort.
10. It provides a basis for the clarification of individual responsibilities.
11. It gives encouragement to forward thinking.
12. It provides a co-operative, integrated and enthusiastic approach to tackling problems and opportunities.
13. It encourages a favourable attitude towards change.
14. It gives a degree of discipline and uniformity to the management of a business (p. 19).

Yoo and Digman (1987) further add that because the strategic management process results in increased employee satisfaction and provides more timely information to key decision makers, decision making becomes faster, more reliable and less costly to the organisation.

Simply applying the strategic management concept is no guarantee for success, however. As a number of reviews and research studies point out, not all companies using strategic management have achieved significantly higher financial performance. However, they attribute this failure to errors in the application of the concept, rather than in the concept itself (Miller and Cardinal, 1994; Fredrickson, 1984; Fredrickson and Mitchell, 1984; Schellenberg, 1983; Kudla, 1980; Grinyer and Norburn, 1975).

Overall, there has been a significant increase in the popularity and usage of strategic management over the years (Porter, 1980). About a decade ago, it was estimated that 75 per cent of all companies in the United States were using strategic management techniques, compared to less than 25 per cent in 1979 (Allen, 1985). Today, application has become more global, with strategic management concepts continuing to be applied to a widening range of businesses and industries in various parts of the world, and new models developed or old ones refined as a result of ongoing research in the area.

## Limitations of strategy selection models

Leading management thinkers agree that strategic management is particularly essential to those industries subject to higher levels of uncertainty and risk, and that if applied well, it can help such industries adapt to their environments more effectively (Ansoff, 1984; Simon, 1976; Drucker, 1974). As reviews of the literature show, research into the area largely substantiates this argument (Miller and Cardinal, 1994).

Shipping is one industry, which clearly falls under the high-risk, high-uncertainty category (Lorange and Norman, 1972; Hope and Boe, 1981). As Frankel (1989) points out, this is even truer today than in the past:

> Shipping and ports are today affected by larger uncertainties and risks than ever before. These risks include not only market risks, but uncertainties in terms of financing, ship and port technological and operational restrictions, terms of business, competition, control, and many more. On the other hand, commitments of financial or other assets and resources to ports and shipping remain long term and are usually very large in relation to cash flow turnover. As a result, it is more important than ever to [select and] evaluate alternative strategies for the determination of tactics which maximise the chances of success (p. 123).

Unfortunately, Frankel's call for more effective ways of selecting and evaluating strategies remains largely unanswered in the shipping literature.

Research in various industries shows that strategy is a major, if not the most major, determinant of a firm's success or failure (e.g. Rumelt, 1991; Kruger, 1989; Robinson and Pearce, 1988). However, there is very little evidence of the practical application of strategic management concepts to shipping, much less of conceptual models specifically designed to guide the industry in its choice of strategies (Hawkins, 1993).

This is not to say, however, that there is a dearth of strategy selection models. The general literature on management and business offers a wide range of models (see, for instance, Pearce and Robinson, 1997), but the applicability of many of these models is under serious question. An increasing number of researchers and practitioners have cast doubt on the generic nature of these models, questioning the validity of the assumption that they can be uniformly applied to all industries. Criticism has tended to focus on four problem areas: lack of research drawn from the service industries in general and commercial shipping in particular, lack of empirical support for strategy selection models, problems with methodological rigour, and lack of a global/international research focus.

Most strategy models are based on manufacturing industries, whereas research suggests that what applies to manufacturing does not necessarily apply to service industries (Schellenberg, 1983; Hambrick, 1983; Thomas, 1979). Schellenberg (1983) notes that

> applying some supposedly all-purpose or universal [concepts] to the whole range of entirely different types of companies in entirely different industries is virtually destined to result in a list of business strategy failures; indeed, universal concepts of strategic management have to be tailored to each industry and organisation type. Blanket application can only result in less than optimal results (p. 4).

There is some empirical evidence that shipping sectors do use strategy selection models (Wong, 1991; Harvey, 1987), but it is not known whether such models have been used 'as is' or modified to fit individual needs, and whether usage has led to better performance.

Another major criticism is the lack of empirical data to validate models. Many models have been built from conceptual constructs which have little supporting empirical evidence to demonstrate whether they do work and how effectively. In their review of typologies of strategies in the early 1980s, Galbraith and Schendel (1983) noted that:

> in general, ... classifications of strategy types have been conceptual constructs derived from appropriate dimensions taken from theory without much empirical support beyond perhaps some grounding in case studies and anecdotal accounts of competitive activity. Although important insights regarding strategic behaviour have been gained in this manner, the validity of any typology is enhanced if empirical support could be provided (p. 155).

Since then, other empirical studies have been conducted to validate typologies of strategies across different business settings (Herbert and Deresky, 1987) and industries (Schellenberg, 1983). However, empirical support from the maritime industry has yet to be provided.

A third area of criticism revolves around methodological problems. Citing Hambrick (1980), Herbert and Deresky (1987) attribute the lack of empirical support for strategy selection models to 'methodological difficulties in identifying and measuring business-level strategy, for which no generally accepted approach has been developed' (p. 136). The same is true with corporate-level strategies. Referring to portfolio models in particular, which are used to evaluate corporate-level strategies, Wind and Mahajan (1981) argue:

> [Although the] importance of the measurement aspect of portfolio analysis is evident from a cursory examination of the diverse dimensions and definitions various approaches use ... surprisingly, most of the literature on portfolios has focused not on the fundamental issues of definition and measurement but on the selling of one approach over another and on the strategic implications of, for example, the 'dog' or 'cash cow' status of a certain product (p. 157).

More recent reviews of the literature (Snow and Thomas, 1994; Lyles, 1990) also point to the minimal attention paid to the development of valid and reliable measures of key strategy constructs. In addition, they also highlight a growing concern over the dominance of quantitative approaches to the study of strategy and the need for a better balance in the choice of research topics, methods and perspectives. While quantitative approaches may provide greater objectivity and reliability, they have not been able to explain many important, more complex organisational realities. Within the field, therefore, there are now calls for multi-method approaches, where quantitative and qualitative methods can be used in the same study to facilitate a fuller and richer examination of complex and dynamic strategic issues.

Another problem inhibiting strategic management research has been a lack of an international or global research emphasis. Such issues as international competition and global strategies, although considered critical in today's world, did not become a research focus until recent years. For example, Hamel and Pralahad (1985) wrote:

> The threat of foreign competition preoccupies managers in [various] industries ... [but] corporate response to this threat is often misdirected and ill timed—in part because many executives don't fully understand what global competition is. [Unfortunately, they] haven't received much help from the latest analysis of this trend ... [The] current perspective on global competition and the globalisation of markets is incomplete and misleading. Analysts are long on exhortation—'go international'—but short on practical guidance (p. 139).

6

Five years later, after reviewing articles published from 1986-89 in leading management journals and interviewing established researchers in management in the US, Lyles (1990) concluded that although global competition was the 'top issue of the day', little research had been done on the area. She found that international competition and multinational strategies were the topics identified as being the most relevant to practising general managers. They were also the topics having the most impact on strategic management research in the 1990s and beyond. However, none of the recent major research studies, which were widely regarded as having the most impact on strategic management thought in the 1990s, applied to international or global strategies. Further, very few of the experts surveyed were actually involved in this research area.

During the 1990s, there was a growing effort to rectify this lack of a global or international research perspective, as evidenced by an increasing number of publications on the topic (see, for instance, Chryssochoidis·et al, 1997; Hibbert, 1997; Alkhafaji, 1995; Lasserre and Schutte, 1995; Yip, 1995; Rugman and Verbeke, 1992). However, because research interest and work on global or international strategies is relatively recent, much of the discussion is still at the conceptual level. Studies focus on individual cases, and integrative reviews and syntheses of available literature are not much in evidence.

## Objectives of the book

In view of the identified gaps in current knowledge about strategy selection, the applicability of existing strategy selection models to an international service industry such as commercial shipping requires careful scrutiny and examination. This book, therefore, aims to:

- analyse the strategic choices that Asia-Pacific shipowners pursue at the corporate level;
- compare actual shipowners' behaviour with strategic management theory on strategy selection; and
- develop a strategy selection model that is applicable to Asia-Pacific shipowners and consistent with strategic management theory.

If the general literature on corporate strategy selection is correct, it can be assumed that Asia-Pacific shipowners will:

- change/modify their corporate strategies in response to changing environmental conditions;

- base strategic changes and the time frames for these changes on their future expectations of environmental conditions;
- pursue a 'grow' strategy when internal and external environmental factors are favourable;
- pursue a 'stabilise' strategy when internal environmental factors are favourable but external environmental factors are not;
- pursue a 'develop' or 'turnaround' strategy when external environmental factors are favourable but internal environmental factors are not; and
- pursue a 'harvest' strategy when internal and external environmental factors are both unfavourable.

But how valid are these assumptions? Since not much is known about the strategic choices that Asia-Pacific shipowners make, it is necessary to establish if these assumptions do reflect what Asia-Pacific shipowners actually do. If theory and practice do not match, where do the differences lie? And if there are differences, what should a strategy selection model that is specific to Asia-Pacific shipowners look like? These are the questions that the book aims to answer. The different types of strategy mentioned above are described in detail later in the book.

A brief comment on nomenclature needs to be made at this stage. The internal and external environmental factors mentioned earlier represent the two dimensions on which strategy selection is examined. In the strategic choice model developed for this work, these variables are formally called 'organisational competitive factors' and 'market factors' to define clearly the parameters being studied. The first includes an organisation's strengths and weaknesses vis-à-vis its competitors; the second includes opportunities and threats in the markets in which the organisation operates. For ease in reference, these variable names are often replaced by the terms 'internal' or 'external' environmental conditions or factors. Any succeeding reference to such terms, therefore, should be made in relation to the more narrow definitions given here.

**Focus of the book**

The focus of this study is on one geographical and economic area (the Asia-Pacific region), one type of decision-makers (commercial shipowners), and one type of strategy (corporate-level strategy).

*Geographical focus: Asia-Pacific*

The last three decades have seen the remarkable growth of the Asia-Pacific region into an economic power (World Bank, 1993). The financial crisis of the late 1990s dramatically put a halt to this rapid growth and the euphoria that has accompanied it. However, predictions continue that once past this painful crisis, which has seen the severe erosion of many achievements such as the reduction of absolute poverty, the region will continue to build its dominance in international trade in the coming century (World Bank, 1997). Within this region, of particular interest to the study are twelve countries that have been responsible for much of the region's economic growth: Australia, China, Hong Kong, Indonesia, Japan, Malaysia, New Zealand, the Philippines, Taiwan, Thailand, Singapore, and South Korea. Although Hong Kong is now back in China's hands after more than a century of British rule, for the purposes of this book it will continue to be treated as a separate entity. These twelve countries are discussed in further detail in chapter two when discussing Asia-Pacific shipping. Figure 1.1 shows a map of the 12 countries.

*Maritime focus: commercial shipowners*

Within these 12 countries, the targeted group of maritime decision-makers is commercial shipowners. With all the rapid changes that have occurred in the region, shipowners are now faced with the challenge of meeting increased demands amidst more intense competition and under highly uncertain conditions. How well they rise to this challenge, and how effectively they are able to maintain a competitive edge, depend a lot on their ability to think and act strategically. To develop a comprehensive picture of strategic choice patterns among Asia-Pacific shipowners, all major shipowners in the liner and bulk trades are considered in this book.

**Figure 1.1 Focus on twelve countries**

Strategies can be grouped into three levels: corporate, business and functional. At the top are corporate strategies, which govern all strategic choices within an organisation. Before any lower level (i.e. business and functional) strategy can be pursued, corporate strategies must first be in place. In this sense, therefore, corporate strategies can be regarded as 'master' strategies. They set the strategic direction that an organisation should take: what mix of businesses (services, markets, or industries) the organisation should go into, and how resources should be allocated to these businesses. Once established, they then set the parameters within which business and functional strategies should be made. They determine what specific business strategies an organisation should take to ensure each of its businesses is competitive; and what specific functional strategies each business should pursue to support its business strategy or strategies.

Of these three strategy levels, this book focuses on corporate-level strategies. There are two reasons for this. First, the study is concerned with strategic choices that enhance the overall competitiveness of major shipowners, most of whom operate a mix or portfolio of businesses. Their main concern is to ensure that the businesses all contribute to the organisation's overall competitive position, and this is clearly the domain of corporate-level strategies. Second, although both corporate and business strategies are primarily concerned with keeping a firm competitive, research on business strategies already outweighs work done on corporate strategies, particularly in relation to shipping and a region like the Asia-Pacific. An examination of corporate strategies in a relatively un-researched area like Asia-Pacific shipping should, therefore, help broaden our understanding of strategy selection. Strategies are discussed in detail in the following three chapters.

## Definition of key terms

Defining strategy has always been problematic. The review of the literature conducted for this book reveals two main reasons. The first stems from fundamental differences in people's perspectives, in the way they view the world and how it operates; the second stems from mere semantic sloppiness.

The strategic management field has drawn on a wide range of disciplines for its theories, concepts and methods. Within the field there is a good representation of disparate academic disciplines (e.g. economics, management science, psychology, sociology), theoretical leanings (e.g. microeconomic theory v. behavioural theory, logical positivism v. process orientation), re-

11

search foci (e.g. content v. process, formal planning variables v. organisational or behavioural variables), and methodological approaches (e.g. quantitative v. qualitative, snapshot v. longitudinal).

Even among those who share the same theoretical perspective, major differences exist. Within the dominant formal analysis school, for instance, which espouses the use of rational and logical models, some quarters define strategy in broad terms, including in the definition both the goals (variously called 'objectives', 'plans' or 'missions') of a firm and the means to achieve these goals. Those belonging to this group include, among others, Chandler, Andrews, Katz, Steiner and Miner, Rumelt, Porter and other writers associated with the Harvard Business School. Others within the same school see strategy in a narrower sense, preferring to limit its scope to the means by which a firm can achieve its goals. In this second sense, goal setting is seen as a closely related but separate activity. Those who belong to this group include, among others, Hofer and Schendel, Ansoff, and Cannon and Glueck.

There is no easy answer to this aspect of the strategy debate; ultimately, choices are left to individual convictions and preferences. Empirical evidence cannot be the ultimate arbiter in this regard because research to date provides all sides of the debate with enough justification to support their respective positions. What makes the literature unnecessarily confusing is the looseness with which certain key terms are used and the contradictory uses to which they are put. Some prime examples are 'corporate' versus 'business', 'generic', and 'goals' versus 'objectives'.

In the literature, four levels of strategies are universally cited: enterprise or societal, corporate, business, and functional. This classification is based on the organisational structure of a complex firm: top management, single business units, functional departments. Of the four strategy levels, corporate and business strategies get far greater attention in the literature because they represent the competitive areas of the firm. In spite of this attention, there is no consistent differentiation applied between levels of strategy, particularly between 'corporate' and 'business'.

The confusion lies in the fact that the term 'business strategy' is typically used in different semantic contexts. In one sense, it may refer to a specific course of action that aims to improve a firm's profitability and market share. In this case, a 'business' strategy can be contrasted with an 'organisational' strategy, which focuses on structure and organisational processes, or a socio-political strategy, which focuses on the dynamics of human behaviour. In another sense, 'business strategy' is used to refer to the organisational level at which the strategy is used, that is, the single business unit level. Where a firm is engaged in a single business, then the term 'corporate', as typically used in business (that is, as having the nature of a corporation, which is defined as a group of people authorised to act as one individual, with legal rights, powers and privileges), becomes irrelevant. Instead, the term 'business' is used in place of, or as a synonym for 'corporate'. Used in this second sense, 'business' acquires a broader meaning, probably closer to its traditional use as an umbrella concept, akin to the concept 'business policy', for any commercial enterprise, regardless of size and type.

Since all these definitions are valid, the field offers no standard definitions. The task of defining key strategy terms is typically left with individual authors. Unfortunately, not all do so and readers are thus left to infer, from the flow of the discussion, the intended meaning attached to such fundamental concepts as 'corporate' or 'business' strategy.

Another term that is sometimes misused is the word 'generic'. The dictionary defines 'generic' as 'referring to a whole kind, class, or group' or 'inclusive or general'; therefore, a generic strategy would mean a broad grouping of strategies that share common characteristic or that have general applicability. In most cases, the word 'generic' is used in this sense, but there are occasions when it is given a totally different meaning. In a discussion of strategy evaluation, for instance, a leading writer in the field talks of a 'generic' and a 'competitive' aspect of strategy, where the generic aspect is concerned with the 'basic mission or scope of the business' and looks 'at changing economic and social conditions over time' (Rumelt, 1980, as cited in Quinn *et al.*, 1988, p. 52). While it is likely that a strategy can indeed manifest these characteristics, nonetheless, to use 'generic' in this sense is misleading. It merely adds confusion to a literature that is already littered with confusing jargon.

A third area where confusion continues to surface, even when there is no longer any need to, involves the distinction between goals and objectives. Older disciplines in the social sciences make clear-cut distinctions between goals and objectives. Goals are broadly couched statements that attempt to encapsulate an organisation's 'ideals' or 'vision'. In this respect, goals are broad and fuzzy, and often unmeasurable. Objectives transform these goals into specific, measurable and attainable statements of intent. These objectives, in turn, can be categorised or ordered into a hierarchy, with each level supporting the next higher level until the terminal or long-term objectives are achieved. Although these distinctions are in standard use in other research areas, such is not the case in strategic management, where confusion between goals and objectives still continues.

To avoid the semantic confusion discussed above, the following definitions are used in this study:

- *Strategy* The means by which an organisation achieves its goals and objectives (Ansoff, 1965; Hofer and Schendel, 1978). The word is used here in its most generic sense, that is, regardless of scope, level, etc.

13

- *Generic strategy*  A broad group of strategies which share common characteristics and are applicable across a variety of situations.
- *Corporate strategy*  The overall means by which an organisation can remain competitive in the market(s) where it operates. It is designed to help the top management determine the mix of businesses the organisation should be in, how these businesses should be run, and how resources should be allocated to them. Corporate strategy sets the general strategic direction that an organisation should pursue, as well as the parameters within which lower-level strategies (business and functional) should be made.
- *Business strategy*  The means by which each individual business that a organisation operates can be competitive. Business strategies should support corporate strategies.
- *Grand strategy*  The overall strategy of an organisation, regardless of size or type. For a complex organisation engaged in several businesses, its grand strategy is synonymous to its corporate-level strategy. For an organisation engaged in a single business, its grand strategy is a combination of strategies that a complex organisation may delineate as 'corporate' and 'business'.
- *Organisation*  Any business company, whether unincorporated or not. In this study, the words 'organisation,' 'company' and 'firm' are used interchangeably and refer to commercial enterprises only.
- *Multinational/global*  These words are used in this study to mean either of two things. When used to describe a strategy, as in multinational or global strategy, they mean the same thing: a strategy that is used across national borders, i.e. world-wide.  Another term used interchangeably with global strategy is *international* strategy. When used to describe an organisation, as in multinational company and global company, they assume very specific meanings. A multinational company has one or a limited range or products made and sold in a specific set of countries; a global company uses resources wherever they are located and sells products/services wherever there is a market.
- *Typology*  A system of classifying similar items on the basis of explicitly stated criteria; synonymous to taxonomy or to what Miller and Minztberg (1983) call 'configuration'.

These definitions will underpin all succeeding discussion and should, therefore, be used as frame of reference for the entire study.

**Structure of the book**

In this initial chapter, the objective has been to present the subject of the study, the rationale for choosing it, the objectives that the study aims to achieve, and the key questions it seeks to answer. The chapter also provides a definition of key terms used in the book.

The remainder of the book is organised into nine other chapters. Chapter two documents the economic growth of the Asia-Pacific in the last three decades, discusses Asia-Pacific shipping and the strategic challenges shipowners must face to take advantage of the region's dramatic growth. It also highlights the lack of information on strategic decision making in general and strategy selection in particular that can assist Asia-Pacific shipowners in their pursuit of a competitive advantage.

Chapters three to five then examine the literature on strategic management to analyse and synthesise what is currently known about strategy selection. Chapter three provides a backdrop to the discussion by tracing the development of strategic management as a field of inquiry, highlighting major trends in strategic management theory and practice, and identifying current areas of research. Chapter four focuses on various types of strategies that organisations can use and synthesises the discussion with a comprehensive typology of strategies for use at the corporate, business and functional levels of an organisation. Chapter five extends the discussion on strategy by reviewing a range of models used for strategy selection and analysis, and then presents a composite strategic choice model that reflects the common features and strengths of these models.

In chapter six, the strategic management process and the typology of strategies and the strategic choice model are integrated into one conceptual framework to provide a strategy model for Asia-Pacific shipping. Key aspects of the framework are explained and defined, as is the general approach to data collection and analysis, and specific methodological techniques and procedures are identified.

Research findings are presented in the next three chapters. Survey and interview data are discussed in chapter seven; simulation data in chapter eight, and a synthesis of research findings, which leads to a shipping-specific strategic choice model, in chapter nine. In the final chapter ten, major conclusions about corporate strategy selection by Asia-Pacific shipowners and the applicability of the strategic choice model to Asia-Pacific shipping are drawn.

# 2  Asia-Pacific shipping

## Introduction

The last three decades have seen the phenomenal growth of the Asia-Pacific region into an economic powerhouse. Behind this growth is a small band of countries located along the western rim of the Pacific. They are primarily responsible for the intensification of trade within the region, as well between the region and the rest of the world, particularly the United States and Europe. Because most of these countries are maritime countries, their economic growth and burgeoning trade have significant implications for shipowners operating in the region. If shipowners are to compete effectively in this dynamic market, they must know, and be prepared to pursue, those strategies that will optimise their chances of gaining a desired competitive position. Further, since strategy choice is predicated on a knowledge of the environment, it is imperative that shipowners have a good understanding of what is going on in the Asia-Pacific region and where strategic opportunities, as well as threats, lie.

In subsequent chapters, discussion will focus on strategy selection and its implications to Asia-Pacific shipowners. To put this discussion in perspective, it would be useful to begin with a profile of the Asia-Pacific region and commercial shipping in the region. In this chapter, therefore, a summary of key growth trends and trading patterns in the region in general and commercial shipping in particular is presented. Against this background, the competitiveness of Asia-Pacific shipowners is then examined, and the extent to which the current shipping literature on strategy and strategic management is able to lend practical advice to shipowners is assessed.

## The Asia-Pacific region: defining its scope

The term 'Asia-Pacific' is used widely in the academic and professional literature and in the mass media, but its precise geographical configurations remain in contention. In its broadest sense, the Asia-Pacific region is said to encompass all countries located on both sides of the Pacific Ocean: from Asia on one side to North America and Latin America on the other. This grouping is reflected in the composition of the Asia-Pacific Economic Cooperation (APEC) forum, whose 18 members make up half the total world economy (for a detailed discussion of APEC, see Rimmer, 1997; Garnaut and Drysdale, 1994; Higgott, *et al*, 1991; Elek, 1991). Writers also refer to this broad grouping of nations as the Pacific Rim (Rimmer, 1997).

In its narrower sense, the term Asia-Pacific is used to refer to those countries located along the western rim of the Pacific Ocean, but even within this limited version, different interpretations exist. A popular view includes China, South (and North) Korea, and Japan in the north all the way down to Australia, New Zealand, and Papua New Guinea in the south. All these countries belong to APEC, but some writers prefer to call them the 'Western Pacific' to distinguish them from the broader Asia-Pacific (Kunkel, 1995). Other geographical configurations either broaden or reduce this grouping. Some writers start further north to include Russia and Mongolia; others go further east to include the smaller Pacific island nations; still others restrict their coverage to East Asian countries only, from China and Japan in the north to Burma in the west and down to Indonesia in the south (Lasserre and Schutte, 1995; Shibusawa, *et al*, 1992; Park, 1991). The uncertainty of the region's geographical boundaries is reflected in the various names given to the region. Some retain the name 'Asia Pacific' even if they mean the East Asian countries only (Lasserre and Schutte, 1995); others use alternatives like 'Pacific Asia' (Shibusawa, *et al*, 1992; Park, 1991) or more traditional nomenclature like 'Far East' (Fitzgerald, 1994).

This book has adopted the narrower definition of the Asia-Pacific region, that is, only those countries located along the western rim of the Pacific Ocean. However, the term 'Asia-Pacific' will be used, rather than 'Western Pacific', because it is the more widely used terminology. Within this region, of particular interest to the study are those countries that are inter-linked by strong trade and investment ties (Garnaut and Drysdale, 1994). These include ten countries in East Asia (China, Hong Kong, Japan, Indonesia, Malaysia, South Korea, Singapore, the Philippines, Taiwan, and Thailand) and two in Australasia (Australia and New Zealand).

In terms of geographical distribution, these ten East Asian countries can be grouped into Northeast Asia (China, Hong Kong, Japan, South Korea, and Taiwan) and Southeast Asia (Indonesia, Malaysia, Singapore, the Philippines, and Thailand). Because the Southeast Asian countries are members of the Association of Southeast Asian Nations (ASEAN), they are also referred to as ASEAN countries.

Questions may be raised about the inclusion of Australia and New Zealand in any Asia-Pacific grouping, largely on the argument that these countries have always viewed themselves more as part of the Western world, rather than of Asia. While this sentiment may still be predominant (not only in the countries involved but throughout Asia as well), geographical proximity offers a persuasive argument for inclusion; so do current trading patterns. Already, a big majority of the trade conducted by Australia and New Zealand takes place within the region. As the cause of intra-regional cooperation, through such mechanisms as APEC, is furthered, the fact that both countries are stable high-income economies can only be a boon to the entire region. For these reasons, Australia and New Zealand are included, with East Asia, in the category 'Asia-Pacific region'.

Throughout the book, any reference to the Asia-Pacific region will be limited to countries on the western side of the Pacific Ocean, and more specifically, to the 12 countries covered by the study. Because the purpose of this chapter is to present an overall picture of the Asia-Pacific environment, particularly as it relates to shipping, no attempt is made to discuss individual country performance. Instead, the region is treated in aggregate terms, much akin to broad brushes on a canvas. However, this should not be taken to mean that this book views the region as a homogenous mass. Far from it. Within the region, significant differences in economic performance exist (Garnaut and Drysdale, 1994; World Bank, 1993; Shibusawa, et al, 1992; Ariff, 1991), as do equally significant social, cultural and political differences (Fitzgerald, 1997; Chow et al, 1997; Chu, 1995; Adler et al, 1995). Providing some telling comparisons, Lasserre and Schutte (1995) note:

> Asia Pacific [excluding Australia and New Zealand] by no means represents a group of homogeneous economic or political systems. National and business cultures vary significantly and macro-economic data show extreme differences. In 1993 Indonesia had 187 million people with an income per capital of US $370; neighbouring Singapore had a population of less than three million with an average income of US $19310. Japan represents 16 per cent of the global economy, but has only 2.3 per cent of the world's population; China's population, on the other hand, makes up more than a fifth of the world's population but contributes only 2.2 per cent to the world's economy. Officially, at least, government socialist principles still determine the fate of the Chinese economy, while Hong Kong's *laissez faire* policies have turned its economy into a capitalist's paradise. In no other part of the world does one find such variations, whether in Europe, Latin America or Africa ... (p. 3).

Country-specific information such as this, while critical to effective strategy selection at the individual shipowner level, lies outside the scope of this chapter. Instead, attention is directed toward a general picture of the Asia-Pacific environment, particularly on general growth trends and regional trading patterns that have direct relevance to Asia-Pacific shipowners.

## The Asia-Pacific region as an economic power

Although the region has sustained remarkably high growth rates since the 1960s, and often at a time when all other regions were either stagnating or in recession (World Bank, 1993), world-wide interest in the region's growth, particularly at the academic and policy-making levels, is of relatively recent origin. Indeed it was not until the late 1980s that the region's economic record was subjected to more widespread scrutiny. Since then, there has been an explosion of writings, both academic and popular, all intent on analysing the reasons behind the region's economic success and whether this success will continue well into the new century.

The substantial literature on the subject bears strong proof of the region's growth as an economic power over the last 30 years, but there is less agreement, indeed there is intense debate, over the nature, causes, and sustainability of this growth. The specific details of this debate will not be covered in this chapter, as their full treatment goes far beyond the scope of this book. However, as part of the backdrop to the study, it will be useful to identify the main streams.

On the one hand are those who firmly believe in the region's ability to maintain a healthy pace and lead the world in economic development (Garnaut, 1997; Rimmer, 1997; Tan and Wee, 1995; Garnaut and Drysdale, 1994; World Bank, 1993). Many writers refer to the region's success as a 'miracle', and the primary contributors to this growth (i.e. Japan, Hong Kong, Singapore, South Korea, Taiwan, and more recently, Indonesia, Malaysia, and Thailand) as 'miracle' economies that are predicted to lead the region into what is being dubbed as the 'Asian' or 'Pacific' century. There are those, however, who contend that this miracle is but a myth (e.g. Krugman, 1994). They argue that because the region's growth has been due more to substantial foreign capital and investment inflows, rather than to improvement in overall technical efficiency and domestic productivity, which are essential for long-term competitiveness, the sustainability of this growth is doubtful (Lingle, 1997; Ignatius, 1996; Krugman, 1994). These two opposing views serve as the main themes around which current discussions of Asia-Pacific growth now revolve.

The debate has intensified in the last few years, fuelled by the region's slowing growth rates, fiercer global competition, and more recently, a financial upheaval that has had devastating effect on the region's national economies. This market upheaval, which started in mid 1997, saw a steep and sudden drop in currency values and a subsequent massive flight of capital out of the currency and shares markets in Thailand initially, and then in Indonesia, Malaysia, the Philippines, and South Korea. Subsequent government action— or inaction—merely exacerbated the problems, and the crisis deepened as national governments failed to implement hard-nosed economic structural reforms that would have helped restore market confidence. The continuing crisis has raised grave doubts about the financial and political stability of the region, especially Southeast Asia. Prospects, at least in the short term, are bleak. For 1997 and 1998, the anticipated annual growth rates of 5–8 per cent for Indonesia, Malaysia and the Philippines were pushed back to 4–6 per cent; more pessimistic estimates go even lower, to about 1-2 per cent. For Thailand, which averaged a nine per cent growth rate from 1986-1995, the most optimistic forecast was 3-4 per cent; conservative analyses talk of negative growth or even a probable recession. Market recovery in these countries is expected to take some time, as foreign investors take their money elsewhere, notably China and Latin America, while warily awaiting further developments in Southeast Asia. It is argued that unless confidence in the markets and Southeast Asia's political leadership is restored, foreign investors are likely to stay away, which in turn will further dampen economic growth.

Does this mean then the end of the Asian 'miracle'? While some analysts and commentators are quick to agree, noting dismissively the 'rise and fall of the Asian century', the more broadly accepted view is that in spite of current market and political uncertainties, as well as a region-wide slowdown in growth rates, the long-term prognosis for the region remains optimistic. A World Bank assessment (World Bank, 1997) shows that the countries in the region are economically strong enough— [they have] 'comparatively high savings ratios, low debt burdens, historically strong fiscal positions, and a history of market-friendly policies' (p. 2)—to recover from the currency crisis and regain healthy growth rates, especially if needed economic, fiscal and policy changes are quickly put into effect. To be certain, tough economic decisions have to be made by East Asian countries to strengthen their economies, but overall the region is still expected to maintain healthy growth rates, albeit at a more subdued pace, but that will keep them well ahead of other regions in the world. Trade will continue to intensify, particularly within the region, to meet the consumption needs of the region's growing middle class which, given current demographics, is poised to become the world's biggest (Rohwer, 1996). Given all these driving forces, the region is predicted to emerge 'as an independent engine of growth [that]... in the longer run ... may even evolve into a powerful trading region that can propel itself with less and less reliance on the US and Europe' (Tan and Wee, 1995, p. 51).

## Major trading patterns in the Asia-Pacific region

What major trade patterns characterise this growing economic power? There are several that are particularly noteworthy. Since the 1960s, when the countries in the region began to advance economically, there has been a significant flow-on of benefits from the wealthier countries to their poorer neighbours. With economic growth has come a significant increase in people's incomes and educational levels, and a subsequent rise in purchasing power and consumer spending. Today, the region's exports account for about a quarter of total world exports. It is also becoming its own biggest market. Initially, trade between countries was underwritten for the procurement and supply of cheap labour and land; today, it is to satisfy the growing needs and demands of the region's growing middle class. Whereas before, manufactured goods made in the region were mostly exported to countries outside the region, notably the United States and Europe, today these goods are increasingly kept within the region. While the United States remains a major player in the region, the region's leading economies are taking on a more significant role. Today they provide a big majority of the investments flowing into the region's newly industrialising economies. These major trends are expected to continue into the twenty-first century, particularly as China, with its more than a billion people, gradually transforms itself into the world's biggest economy.

*The flying geese of East Asia*

East Asia's economic growth is often likened to the flight formation of geese: Japan at the head, followed by the Four Tigers (Hong Kong, Singapore, South Korea and Taiwan), and then by the region's newly industrialising economies (NIEs) notably, Indonesia, Malaysia, Thailand and more recently, China and the Philippines. The 'flying geese' analogy is drawn from the way the East Asian economies have developed their economies within a relatively short period of time. Japan started the growth momentum, first by industrialising and, when it prospered as an exporter nation, by moving its high capital and labour intensive industries to the less-developed countries in the region, whose low labour and production costs allowed Japan to maintain its competitive edge. Since then, the momentum has been maintained, with the countries in the region growing together. The advancement of a country has typically led to the advancement of others, as all have closely followed Japan's overall strategy for growth. This pattern of development has allowed the region to grow rapidly, as the following market trends reflect.

*World market share*

Largely because of the economic success of the East Asian countries, the trade controlled by the Asia-Pacific region has grown at an unprecedented rate over the last three decades. It is now 26 per cent of total world trade, compared to the European Union's 37 per cent and NAFTA's 19 per cent. When the region's share is added to the other members of APEC (i.e. Canada, Chile, Mexico, and the United States), the total APEC share jumps up to almost half of the entire world trade (Bergsten, 1997). A significant proportion of the region's exports include higher-value manufactured goods, while most imports are relatively low-value raw materials or energy (Drewry, 1993).

*Intra-regional trade*

One striking aspect of Asia-Pacific trade has been the increase in intra-regional trade (Menon, 1996; Kunkel, 1995). The region is now its own biggest market, with intra-regional trade estimated in 1991 to account for 40 per cent of total trade, up from 30 per cent in 1986 (Drewry, 1993). The value of trade among these countries is now greater than their trade with the US. About a decade ago, for instance, Japan's trade with the US was about 40 per cent of its total trade; now it is less than a third. During the same period, Japan's trade with its neighbours rose to around 40 per cent, from less than 25 per cent (Leger, 1995). This trend is reflected throughout the region, particularly between the Four Tigers and the five NIEs (Kunkel, 1995).

*Intra-regional investments*

The rapid market integration within the Asia-Pacific region has been fuelled by the massive inflows of investment from the wealthier nations of the region to their newly industrialising neighbours. Major foreign investors in the NIEs have been Japan and the Four Tigers, displacing the US and Europe. As a group, the Tigers have been the largest investors in the NIEs: 44.7 per cent in Thailand, 40 per cent in the Philippines, 47.8 per cent in Malaysia, and 29.3 per cent in Indonesia. They also hold the biggest share of the NIEs' exports, and are the biggest market for China's exports. (Tan and Wee, 1995; Leger, 1995). While for a number of countries these huge inflows dramatically came to a stop in the wake of the 1997 financial crisis, the investment pattern outlined here is nonetheless expected to continue.

*Growth triangles*

Another significant aspect in the growing intra-regional trade has been the development of 'growth triangles' within the region. Growth triangles are economic zones that involve two or more countries but not necessarily these countries' entire national economies. Two very successful growth triangles now attracting world interest and attention are the Singapore-Johor-Riau

(SIJORI) triangle, which comprises Singapore, the state of Johor in Malaysia, and the Riau province in Indonesia; and the Great South China Economic Zone, which includes Hong Kong, Macau, Taiwan, and the southern coastal provinces of Guangdong and Fujian in China (Yue and Yuan, 1994). Massive investments by the Tigers (and to a lesser extent by Japan) into Guangdong and Fujian in China, Johor in Malaysia and Riau in Indonesia have led to a dramatic economic transformation in these areas. From being areas of poverty, they have become major industrial and investment centres, whose high incomes contrast sharply against national averages (Yue and Yuan, 1994). Major industrial restructuring is also being undertaken, as investments allow the construction of superhighways, power generators, communications systems, and similar infrastructure programs critical to the sustenance of an industrialising economy.

The concept behind the growth triangles is similar to the flying geese pattern of national development. Wealthier nations invest in their poorer neighbours, whose cheap labour and land allow the former to keep manufacturing costs down and thus remain competitive. With growth triangles, however, the areas involved are physically close to each other to allow (with government approval) a relatively easy movement of goods, people and capital across national borders. As with the flying geese pattern, there is growing evidence that the economic benefits from the growth triangles are spreading beyond the original boundaries; as wages rise and labour becomes in short supply, and as real estate prices soar, investors go further in search of fresh supply of cheap labour and land (Yue and Yuan, 1994).

Mindful of these successes, various countries in the region are now in different stages of negotiation to establish more growth triangles. At the most advanced stage of negotiations is the Northern Growth Triangle, proposed by Malaysia, and designed to comprise fifteen southern provinces of Thailand, four states in Malaysia and two provinces of Sumatra in Indonesia (Yue and Yuan, 1994). The Association of Southeast Asian Nations (ASEAN) has also agreed to establish a free trade area (to be called ASEAN Free Trade Area, or AFTA) within 10-15 years, commencing 1 January 1993. Since its meeting in 1992, when the AFTA concept was approved, ASEAN member nations have been negotiating on timetables for tariff reductions of ASEAN products, covering all manufactured and capital goods, processed agricultural products and other items that do not meet their definition of agricultural products (Menon, 1996). Three others in the offing are the Tumen River Delta Area project (eastern Russia, China, Mongolia, South and North Korea), the Yellow Sea Economic Zone (Japan, South Korea, northern China), and the Japan Sea Economic Zone (Japan, eastern Russia, northeastern China, South and North Korea).

*Growth of consumer power*

Companies initially began investing in East Asia to take advantage of low-cost labour and then export their products outside the region. While this trend continues today, a growing proportion of manufactured products now remains within the region to serve a fast-growing middle class. Sustained economic growth has led to a substantial rise in incomes, educational levels and purchasing power, making possible the rapid emergence of this middle class, whose sheer numbers make their purchasing potential formidable. The ten East Asian economies covered by the study that forms the basis of this book account for about 30 per cent of the world's population, more than 60 per cent of whom are between 25 to 65 years old and with some consumer spending power. If growth trends are sustained, the region is expected to have about one billion consumers during the early 2000s, whose consumption needs and demands would have to be met (Rohwer, 1996; Tan and Wee, 1995).

*The Chinese network*

Another critical aspect of intra-regional trade in the Asia-Pacific is the presence of the so-called Chinese network. There is actually no single network; rather, there are numerous networks that span national boundaries, crisscrossing the Asia-Pacific region and over to North America and Europe. These networks are made up of Chinese who have resettled throughout the Asia-Pacific and the rest of the world; they are estimated to be about 50 million strong in East Asia alone (6 million in Hong Kong, 21 million in Taiwan, 30 more million spread out from Korea to Indonesia). Not much research has been conducted into these Chinese networks, but the accepted wisdom is that their ties are strong and extensive, and that they work largely on the basis of personal, family, school, and/or business connections. They control much of the banking, finance and trade in East Asia and are involved in major investments throughout the region, including Australia and New Zealand (Fitzgerald, 1997). They are principally responsible for massive investment inflows into China, accounting for about 70 per cent of the country's total investments (Tan and Wee, 1995). These investments are expected to continue, giving China the strength and resilience it needs to transform itself into a major economic force.

*Future prospects*

Trade in the Asia-Pacific region is expected to follow the region's overall pattern of economic development. Although short-term prospects are gloomy due to the continuing financial crisis, the long-term prognosis for the region remains positive. From all indications, countries will continue to industrialise and liberalise their economies, which will enable intra-regional trade to grow in importance (Menon, 1996). Intra-regional cooperation and competition will also be maintained as countries work together to establish free trade areas and more growth triangles, and as they maintain regional consultations through various mechanisms, notably APEC and ASEAN. While the idea of a 'Pacific or Asian century' may not be widely shared—indeed, is hotly contested—the prevailing view is that the Asia-Pacific region will grow into a strong economic region in the 21st century, particularly if individual countries implement much-needed economic and structural reforms.

## Asia-Pacific shipping

The performance of the Asia-Pacific region over the last several decades finds close parallel in the performance of commercial shipping in the region, which should come as no surprise since shipping is a derived demand and the region's geography virtually demands heavy reliance on maritime transport.

### The role of maritime transport

The region is highly archipelagic, which means trade within the region, as well as within individual countries, almost always implies the use of water transport (Peters, 1986). Contiguous land links to mainland Asia and beyond do not necessarily provide an advantage. In their discussion of the influence of geography on the use of maritime transport in Asia, Leinbach and Sien (1989) point out that 'the high mountains to the north and east create formidable barriers which effectively render the region highly dependent on water transport' (p. 98). A further complication, reports Lloyd's Maritime Asia (May 1997), is the lack of reliable and extensive land-based infrastructure links to facilitate transport of goods, forcing fast-growing Asia-Pacific countries with manufacturing bases to significantly increase their use of maritime transport.

Trade has not been the only reason for the region's dependence on maritime transport; the improvement of communication and the need for greater administrative and political control, to name a few, have also been major factors behind the growing demand for shipping (Rimmer, 1997; Leinbach and Sien, 1989; JAMRI 1987). Neither is the region's reliance on maritime transport merely a late 20th century phenomenon. It goes back in time, long before western countries made their presence felt in the region.

26

In the last two decades, the reliance on maritime transport has grown significantly to keep pace with the rapid economic growth of the region. Recent studies on Asia-Pacific shipping highlight a remarkable record of growth in shipping activity from the 1970s to 1990s, with the 1980-90 period recording the most significant growth (OECD, 1997; UNCTAD, 1996b; Lee, 1996; Drewry, 1993; Xingyuan, 1991; Thanopoulou, 1995; JAMRI, 1987; Peters, 1986). In 1980, the region controlled eighteen per cent of the total world volume in bulk imports and 29 per cent in container throughput. By 1991, this share had grown to 33 per cent and 40 per cent, respectively (Drewry, 1993). In terms of annual growth rate, the Asia-Pacific has been leading the way (OECD, 1997).

*Asia-Pacific seaborne trade*

Shipping is not one homogeneous market; rather, it is made up of several important sectors. There are three main sectors (also called markets or trades): liner (also called general cargo), tanker (also called wet bulk), and dry bulk (Stopford, 1993). The tanker and dry bulk markets are normally grouped together as bulk trades. Because the industry norm is to organise the shipping market into these three sectors, this typology will be used for the remainder of the chapter. Further, because the characteristics of each shipping market is well documented in the shipping literature (e.g. Spruyt, 1994; Farthing, 1993; Stopford, 1988; ESCAP, 1986; Branch, 1982), no attempt will be made here to replicate previous efforts. The reader is asked instead to refer to these sources for an extensive discussion of shipping markets.

Forecasts for world seaborne trade from 1996-2005 show growth is expected to be an average of 4.1 per cent per annum, specifically from 3,865 million tons in 1995 to an estimated 5,454 million tons in 2005 (Fearnleys Review, 1996a; UNCTAD, 1996b). As shown in Table 2.1, the highest growth rate is expected from the liner sector (6.4 per cent), mainly from containerised and general cargo, followed by the dry bulk sector (4.5 per cent), and the tanker sector (2.6 per cent).

**Table 2.1**
**Growth forecasts for world seaborne trade (1996-2005)**

| Industry Sector | Growth Rate (base year = 1995) | Estimated Volume million tons (2005) |
|---|---|---|
| Dry bulk | 4.5 | 1,685 |
| Tanker | 2.6 | 2,168 |
| Liner | 6.4 | 1,601 |

Source: DRI/McGraw-Hill (1995) as cited in UNCTAD (1996b)

Growth rates in seaborne trade for the Asia-Pacific region were not as great in the 1990s as those achieved in the previous two decades. The main growth drivers (China, Taiwan, Hong Kong, Korea, Malaysia, Singapore, and Thailand) started slowing down after years of rapid unprecedented growth (OECD, 1997) and the financial crisis gripping the region further dampened this growth. In terms of differential trade requirements, JAMRI (1987) predicted that as countries continue industrialising, trade in raw materials will decrease while trade in semi-finished products will increase. Drewry (1993) also predicted higher growth rates for liner shipping, especially containerised cargoes, but a much slower growth for the bulk trades. In spite of this slowdown, however, the bulk trades are still predicted to grow not only in volume but also in world importance. More specific trends in each sector are discussed below.

*Bulk trades* The three largest commodities in world seaborne bulk trades are crude oil, iron ore, and coal, all of which have had a dominant impact on demand patterns (ISL, 1997). Comparative figures for these and other bulk commodities are presented in Table 2.2.

**Table 2.2**
**World seaborne trade of main bulk commodities (billion of ton-miles)**

|                   | 1985    | 1990    | 1995    |
|-------------------|---------|---------|---------|
| Crude oil         | 4 007   | 6 261   | 7 375   |
| Iron ore          | 1 702   | 1 978   | 2 287   |
| Coal              | 1 473   | 1 849   | 2 176   |
| Grain             | 1 004   | 1 073   | 1 160   |
| Bauxite & alumina | 166     | 205     | 199     |
| Phosphate         | 156     | 154     | 136     |

Source: Fearnleys (1996b)

The Asia-Pacific region already commands a significant share of this trade. Drewry (1993) predicted a 25 per cent growth by 2000, which would put the region's share to about 34 per cent of total world trade. Tables 2.3 and 2.4 provide some comparative figures.

**Table 2.3**
**World and regional share in bulk trades* (million tons)**

|       | World   | Asia-Pacific | %    |
|-------|---------|--------------|------|
| 1992  | 3 014   | 1 025        | 34.0 |
| 2000  | 3 422   | 1 170        | 34.2 |

* excluding LNG

Source: Drewry (1993)

**Table 2.4**
**Asia-Pacific trade as a percentage of world trade**

|                  | 1991 | 1995 | 2000 |
| ---------------- | ---- | ---- | ---- |
| Crude oil        | 24.6 | 26.9 | 28.3 |
| Oil products     | 25.9 | 22.7 | 17.3 |
| LNG (1)          | 73.3 | 76.4 | 65.8 |
| Iron ore         | 53.5 | 51.3 | 53.0 |
| Coking coal      | 57.3 | 60.3 | 58.1 |
| Steaming coal    | 40.5 | 41.5 | 42.3 |
| Grain            | 35.9 | 38.7 | 39.8 |
| Forest products  | 39.0 | 41.0 | 43.9 |
| Cement           | 55.6 | 54.5 | 53.5 |
|                  |      |      |      |
| Total (2)        | 33.6 | 34.0 | 34.2 |

(1) billion cu.av of low/high forecasts
(2) excluding LNG

Source: Drewry (1993)


*Container trades* The region's container trades have followed similar growth patterns as the bulk trades, with the last three decades showing increased container traffic in and out of the region. From a negligible one per cent of world container traffic in the early 1970s, it jumped to 28 per cent in 1982 (Peters, 1986). Since then the region has continued on its exponential growth pattern, growing at a much faster pace than any other region, more than twice that of Western Europe and four times more than North America. As of 1990, the region controlled nearly 40 per cent of world container traffic. By 1995, this had risen to 46 per cent and by 2000 it was predicted to rise to 50 per cent. Regional growth trends are summarised in Tables 2.5 and 2.6.

## Table 2.5
## Global container activity (million TEU)
(Total throughput at regional ports)

|  | 1980 | 1990 | 1995 | 2000 |
|---|---|---|---|---|
| Asia-Pacific | 11.2 | 34.9 | 63.4 | 99.1 |
| W. Europe | 11.7 | 22.4 | 30.5 | 39.9 |
| N. America | 9.5 | 16.7 | 20.8 | 24.1 |
| L. America | 2.3 | 4.8 | 8.0 | 11.7 |
| Mid East | 1.9 | 3.5 | 6.8 | 10.5 |
| Africa | 1.5 | 2.7 | 4.2 | 6.2 |
| S. Asia | 0.2 | 1.8 | 3.4 | 5.8 |
| E. Europe | 0.4 | 0.6 | 0.6 | 1.0 |
| World Total | 38.7 | 87.4 | 137.7 | 198.2 |

Source: Drewry (1996c)

## Table 2.6
## World and Asia-Pacific container activity

|  | World Total (million TEU) | Asia-Pacific Percentage Share |
|---|---|---|
| 1980 | 38.7 | 28.9 |
| 1990 | 87.4 | 39.9 |
| 1995 | 17.7 | 46.0 |
| 2000 | 198.2 | 50.0 |

Source: Derived from Table 2.5 Drewry (1996c)

Individual country performance within the region is predicted to vary. ASEAN countries are expected to lead the way, with an annual growth rate of 9.5 per cent, closely followed by Hong Kong, Taiwan, South Korea and

China, which are expected to grow at an average of 6.1 per cent per annum. Both groups will exceed the world average of 4.6 per cent, while Japan, Australia, and New Zealand are expected to fall below it.

*Intra-regional seaborne trade*

One striking aspect in the growth of seaborne trade in the Asia-Pacific has been an extraordinary increase in intra-regional trade. In the last several decades, intra-regional seaborne trade has expanded much faster than trade with countries outside the region (Drewry, 1993; Xingyuan, 1991). In 1991, it accounted for 40 per cent of its total trade, and in 1995, for the first time it exceeded the region's trade with the rest of the world. Like regional economic growth in general, the growth in seaborne trade has been spurred by regional co-operation networks (e.g. APEC, ASEAN) and the establishment of economic zones, or more colloquially known as 'growth triangles' in the region (Rimmer, 1997; Lee, 1996). As noted earlier in the chapter, such regional co-operative schemes have significantly boosted trade within the region either through increased dialogue and consultation among the countries in the region or through joint ventures between nationals or governments of two or more countries. Most analysts agree that this growth in intra-regional trade will continue well into the future, which augurs well for the region's maritime industry (Containerisation International, 1997b; Lloyd's Maritime Asia, 1997; Lloyd's Shipping Economist, 1997; OECD, 1996; Lee, 1996; UNCTAD, 1995; Drewry, 1993; Xingyuan, 1991; JAMRI, 1987).

For Asia-Pacific shipowners, the implications of this trend are immense. Greater intra-regional trade will require a major shift in the way shipping is conducted. From being mainly feeder service providers, shipowners will increasingly serve as longer haul operators and providers of direct service routes to Asia. Changes will also be inevitable, as the promise of greater profits will attract more competitors into the area. Lloyd's Maritime Asia (1997) offers a hint of the lurking potential:

> Intra-regional trades, are, in comparison to transpacific routes, lucrative. One account has it that the cost of running a TEU from Shanghai to Rotterdam has flattened from $1,800 two years ago to less than $800 today. By way of contrast, a TEU from Shanghai to Manila earns $1,200, the same as it did two years ago. The trades offer other comparative cost savings as well. For example, on short-haul, port-to-port services, containers do not generally need to be relayed from one ship to another en-route to final destinations, so transhipment costs are limited. These port-to-port services also translate into relatively low inland transportation costs compared to long-haul carriers, for which rail and trucking costs represent almost 20 per cent of operating costs (p. 44).

Of the region's shipping markets, container trades are predicted to show the most significant increases (Rimmer, 1997; Containerisation International,

1996c; Drewry 1993); and their growth is expected to be a major determinant in the development of world shipping (ISL, 1996). By 2000, the region was expected to account for about a quarter of total world box movements (Containerisation International, 1997c). This growth in the region's intra-regional containerised cargo flows is summarised in Table 2.7.

As can be seen from the table, the region's containerised cargo leapt by 63 per cent from 1991 to 1996, with the Philippines, Malaysia, and Indonesia showing the most significant increases, closely followed by Singapore, Thailand, and Hong Kong. By the year 2000, the region's share was expected to rise by another 52 per cent, with Malaysia, Indonesia, and Singapore expected to show the highest increases.

**Table 2.7**
**Intra-regional Asia-Pacific containerised trading volumes***
**(TEUs, 1991-2001)**

|  | 1991 | 1996 | % change | 2001 | % change |
|---|---|---|---|---|---|
| Japan | 1 703 098 | 2 407 654 | 41.4 | 3 288 194 | 36.6 |
| South Korea | 705 497 | 1 103 844 | 56.5 | 1 755 552 | 59.0 |
| Taiwan | 967 849 | 1 339 826 | 38.4 | 1 970 373 | 47.1 |
| Hong Kong | 832 740 | 1 402 177 | 68.4 | 2 308 549 | 64.6 |
| Philippines | 184 748 | 400 901 | 117.0 | 664 042 | 65.6 |
| Indonesia | 492 084 | 962 353 | 95.6 | 1 647 277 | 71.2 |
| Singapore | 762 509 | 1 337 456 | 75.4 | 2 245 544 | 67.9 |
| Thailand | 533 033 | 922 372 | 73.0 | 1 487 487 | 61.3 |
| Malaysia | 573 811 | 1 131 603 | 97.2 | 1 941 940 | 71.6 |
| Total | 6 755 369 | 11 008 186 | 63.0 | 17 308 958 | 57.2 |

* Data based on import customs reports; revenue terms converted to tonnes and then into TEU.

Source: DRI/Mercer (1997), as cited in Containerisation International (1997c)

As of December 1995, a total of 35 maritime nations controlled the majority (93.8 per cent) of world tonnage, as measured by number of vessels and deadweight tonnage. As Table 2.8 shows, all Asia-Pacific shipowners except New Zealand made it to this elite group of maritime nations, controlling over a third (32.8 per cent) of the world fleet. Japan, with its 12.9 per cent share, dominated, but even with considerably smaller shares, China, Hong Kong, South Korea, Taiwan, and Singapore all made it to the top fifteen countries. The Philippines, Indonesia, Australia, Thailand, and Malaysia were positioned closer to the bottom of the list.

**Table 2.8**
**Distribution of the Asia-Pacific fleet**

| World Fleet Rank | Country | % of World Fleet |
|---|---|---|
| 2 | Japan | 12.93 |
| 5 | China | 5.25 |
| 6 | Hong Kong | 4.67 |
| 8 | South Korea | 3.12 |
| 11 | Taiwan | 2.14 |
| 13 | Singapore | 1.94 |
| 25 | Philippines | 0.70 |
| 27 | Indonesia | 0.61 |
| 32 | Australia | 0.51 |
| 33 | Thailand | 0.49 |
| 34 | Malaysia | 0.49 |

Source: Adapted from UNCTAD (1996a)

In terms of ship types, those that dominate world shipping today are oil tankers (tanker trades), bulk carriers (dry bulk trades), and general cargo ships and containerships (liner trades). The collective strength of these ship types can be described in a number of ways, one of which is by gross tonnage (gt). If all ship types above 100 gt are considered, then the four ship types can be said to make up 86.3 per cent of the 1997 world fleet. If the cut-off point is above 1,000 gt, then the percentage jumps up to 99.2 per cent for the same period. The distribution of the world fleet according to ship types using these two measures is shown in Table 2.9.

**Table 2.9**
**Determining world fleet distribution by ship type (1997)**

| Major Ship Types | over 100gt | over 1,000 gt |
|---|---|---|
| Oil tankers | 36.5 | 42.0 |
| Dry bulk carriers | 32.3 | 37.2 |
| General cargo ships | 11.0 | 13.3 |
| Container ships | 6.5 | 6.7 |
| Total % of world total | 86.3 | 99.2 |

Source: Lloyd's Maritime Information Service (1997)

For commercial shipowners operating in major trades, which excludes those providing feeder services, the 1,000gt basis is more appropriate because it provides a better representation of major commercial ship types and the tonnage size used on major shipping routes (Lloyd's Maritime Information Service, 1997; ISL, 1997). This higher gt level is used as the basis in Table 2.10, which shows the Asia-Pacific's share of the world fleet by ship type, gross tonnage, and deadweight tonnage. As the table shows, the four ship types account for 99.2 per cent of the world fleet, with oil tankers and dry bulk carriers representing almost 80 per cent of the total. Of this fleet, 37.6 per cent is controlled by the Asia-Pacific region. In terms of gross tonnage (gt), container ships (43.8 per cent) and dry bulk carriers (43.6 per cent) represent a slight majority, with oil tankers (33.3 per cent) and general cargo ships (31.7 per cent) not far behind. In terms of dead-weight tonnage (dwt), bulk ships, which account for nearly 80 per cent of the total world fleet, dominate Asia-Pacific shipping, with dry bulk carriers comprising the largest group (47.1 per cent), followed by oil tankers (32.8 per cent). The liner sector is smaller due to the prevalence of small semi-container ships (8.8 per cent) and even smaller general cargo ships (11.2 per cent) in the region (Drewry, 1993).

**Table 2.10**
**Regional fleet distribution by gross (gt) and deadweight (dwt) tonnage**
**(1997)**

| Major Ship Types | % of World Fleet (Over 1,000 gt) | % of Asia-Pacific share (Over 1,000 gt) | (Over 1,000 dwt) |
|---|---|---|---|
| Oil tankers | 42.0 | 33.3 | 32.8 |
| Dry bulk carriers | 37.2 | 43.6 | 47.1 |
| General cargo ships | 13.3 | 31.7 | 11.2 |
| Container ships | 6.7 | 43.8 | 8.8 |
| Total % of world total | 99.2 | 37.6 | 37.6 |

Source: Lloyd's Maritime Information Service (1997)

In terms of geographical distribution, Europe and the Asia-Pacific account for almost 82 per cent of the world fleet, with the first holding 44.1 per cent and the latter 37.6 per cent. North America holds the next largest share (seven per cent), followed by Latin and South America (2.4 per cent), and Africa (one per cent). Between 1994-1997, the Asia-Pacific region registered the highest growth rate (4.2 per cent), followed by Africa (2.9 per cent). The rest—Europe, North America, and Latin and South America—all declined. Regional fleet distribution and growth rates are summarised in Table 2.11. The geographical location of 8 per cent of the world fleet cannot be ascertained and hence are grouped under the category 'unknown'.

The national fleets of the Asia-Pacific have grown considerably over the last three decades (Lloyd's Maritime Information Service, 1997). Their most significant growth period was between 1960-1970, when they grew by 250.5 per cent; however, as world fleet size increased and shipping demand slumped, the growth rate slowed down, to 104.4 per cent between 1970-1980 and then to a low 30.9 per cent between 1980-1990. Between 1990-1996, however, the growth rate picked up again, reaching 61.3 per cent. At these growth rates, the national fleets of the region have been able to increase substantially their share of the world fleet, from only 6.9 per cent in 1960 to 23.4 per cent in 1996. If foreign flag vessels are included, which means a further 16.2 per cent added to the world total, the region's share will rise to over one third. Behind this remarkable growth are six countries: Japan, China,

Hong Kong, South Korea, Taiwan, and Singapore (Lloyd's Maritime Information Service, 1997).

**Table 2.11**
**Regional fleet distribution and growth rates, 1997**
(% share of world fleet by dwt for ships of 1000gt and over)

| Regions | Oil Tankers | Bulk Carriers | Container Ships | General Cargo Ships | Total % | Growth Rate* |
|---|---|---|---|---|---|---|
| Europe | 46.0 | 41.3 | 40.2 | 46.8 | 44.1 | - 0.1 |
| Asia-Pacific | 33.3 | 43.6 | 43.8 | 31.7 | 37.6 | 4.2 |
| North America | 11.9 | 2.8 | 8.1 | 2.6 | 7.0 | -3.7 |
| Latin & South America | 2.5 | 2.3 | 1.5 | 2.5 | 2.4 | -3.5 |
| Africa | 0.9 | 0.9 | 0.9 | 1.9 | 1.0 | 2.9 |
| Unknown | 5.3 | 9.1 | 5.5 | 14.4 | 8.0 | ---- |

* Average yearly growth rates from 1994-1997

Source: Lloyd's Maritime Information Services (1997)

Since container shipping has had and will have the most dramatic impact on world shipping (Rimmer, 1997; JAMRI, 1987), it is worth exploring the growth of this fleet at this point. Container carriers were introduced to the maritime industry in the 1970s, and in the short span of 10 years, many had made their presence felt on world shipping markets. Evergreen (Taiwan), NOL (Singapore), and MISC (Malaysia) were all formed in 1968, followed by Yang Ming (Taiwan) in 1973, Hyundai (Korea) in 1976, and Hanjin (Korea) in 1978. Table 2.12 traces the development of the leading Asia-Pacific container operators over a 15-year period (1975-1990). By 1990, Evergreen of Taiwan had the largest number of TEUs carried, followed by three Japanese companies (NYK, MOL, K Line), Cosco from China, and OOCL from Hong Kong.

As a result of this growth, many of the region's leading container operators improved their world ranking within a relatively short period of time (Rimmer, 1997; Tanaka, 1993). Table 2.13 compares their performance vis-à-vis other leading world container operators over a 10-year period (1980 and 1991).

**Table 2.12**

**Number of TEUs carried by leading Asia-Pacific container operators**

|  | 1975 | 1980 | 1985 | 1990 |
|---|---|---|---|---|
| Cho Yang | - | 564 | 3 033 | 10 742 |
| Cosco | - | 474 | 28 752 | 71 046 |
| Evergreen | - | 18 100 | 74 132 | 130 498 |
| Hanjin- | - | 5 948 | 7 028 | 46 943 |
| Hyundai | - | - | 6 841 | 16 048 |
| Japan Line | 4 684 | 5 992 | 7 209 | - |
| K-Line | 7 967 | 8 906 | 22 851 | 58 290 |
| KSC | - | 7 776 | 9 650 | - |
| MISC | - | 4 900 | 10 734 | 10 442 |
| MOL | 13 373 | 18 952 | 35 967 | 66 838 |
| NLS | - | - | - | 17 809 |
| NOL | 1 100 | 8 323 | 13 874 | 35 943 |
| NYK | 15 330 | 21 664 | 33 963 | 73 062 |
| OOCL | 18 267 | 21 701 | 33 825 | 56 629 |
| Showa | 2 795 | 5 190 | 5 780 | 228 |
| Y-S Line | 5 413 | 6 584 | 9 950 | - |
| Yang Ming | - | 7 344 | 23 409 | 46 817 |

Source: Containerisation International Yearbooks, various dates

Between 1980 and 1991, Evergreen moved from 9th to the top position; NYK, from 6th to 4th; and MOL from 12th to 7th. While OOCL of Hong Kong and NOL dropped from 5th to 8th and 8th to 14th respectively, they still remained in the top 15. In contrast, seven leading operators, mainly from Europe and the US (OCL, CGM, APL, Wilhelmsen, US Line, and Farrell Lines), did not make it to the 1991 list. A more recent analysis provided similar results (Containerisation International, 1996c). In 1983, six container operators from the Asia-Pacific made it to Containerisation International's Top 20 league; collectively they accounted for 27 per cent of the total. By 1995, half the list was made up of Asia-Pacific shipowners, representing close to 50 per cent of total world container capacity. These changes clearly reflect the shift of the centre of power within container shipping to the Asia-Pacific region (Rimmer, 1997).

**Table 2.13**

**Top 15 container operators (1980-1991)**

| Rank | Operator | Capacity (000s TEU) | Rank | Operator | Capacity (000s TEU) |
|------|----------|---------------------|------|----------|---------------------|
| | **1980 Rank** | | | **1991 Rank** | |
| 1 | Sea-Land (USA) | 58 | 1 | Evergreen (TWN) | 115 |
| 2 | Hapag (GER) | 43 | 2 | Maersk (DEN) | 104 |
| 3 | Maersk (DEN) | 34 | 3 | Sea-Land (USA) | 95 |
| 4 | OCL (GBR) | 29 | 4 | NYK (JPN) | 83 |
| 5 | OOCL (HK) | 27 | 5 | COSCO (CHN) | 69 |
| 6 | NYK (JPN) | 26 | 6 | APL (USA) | 61 |
| 7 | CGM (FRA) | 24 | 7 | MOL (JPN) | 60 |
| 8 | APL (USA) | 21 | 8 | OOCL (HK) | 55 |
| 9 | Evergreen (TWN) | 19 | 9 | Hapag (GER) | 54 |
| 10 | Wilhelmsen (NOR) | 18 | 10 | Hanjin (KOR) | 53 |
| 11 | Nedlloyd (NTH) | 18 | 11 | K-Line (JPN) | 53 |
| 12 | MOL (JPN) | 17 | 12 | Yang Ming (TWN) | 49 |
| 13 | US Line (USA) | 16 | 13 | P&O (GBR) | 44 |
| 14 | Farrell Lines (USA) | 12 | 14 | NOL (SNG) | 40 |
| 15 | NOL (SNG) | 8 | 15 | ZIM (ISR) | 40 |

Source: Tanaka (1993)


## Competitiveness of Asia-Pacific operators

The shipping literature cites four main reasons why Asia-Pacific shipowners have succeeded in gaining significant headway into world shipping within a relatively short period of time: cost advantage, government support, access to a vibrant maritime infrastructure, and aggressive growth strategies.

*Cost advantage*

In their early stages of development, the main competitive advantage of Asia-Pacific shipowners was easy access to a relatively inexpensive and committed workforce, which meant lower vessel operating costs (Holste, 1993; Drewry, 1993; Leinbach and Sien, 1989; Peters, 1986). This cost advantage over the traditional maritime nations of Europe has been maintained over the years as the fleets of the Asia-Pacific have continued to expand. A typical example of the lower operating cost differentials between Europe and the Asia-Pacific is provided in Table 2.14. A 30 per cent lower operating cost structure is a significant competitive advantage in freight markets, especially during times of depressed freight rates and long periods of over-tonnaging. This difference would be even more pronounced if compared to the even cheaper South East Asian shipowner (Leinbach and Sien, 1989).

### Table 2.14
### Operating cost differentials for an 800 TEU containership
### (1992, US$ per day)

|  | N. European Operator | Asia-Pacific Operator | % Difference |
|---|---|---|---|
| Operating costs* | 10,315 | 7,915 | 30.3 |

*manning, insurance, stores, ship management

Source: Drewry (1992)

Cheaper labour costs, both at sea and ashore in shipping management, have not been the only cost advantages of Asia-Pacific shipowners. As their share of the world fleet increased, the use of more modern and efficient ships and equipment, particularly in container trades, gave them another competitive advantage (Holste, 1993). Drewry (1993) sums up the situation very well:

> During the last 20 years, there has been a tremendous expansion in the merchant fleet owned and operated by interests located within the Asian Pacific Rim. In recent years attention has focused on the growth of its container carrying services but throughout the whole period there has also been substantial growth in the number of other vessel types operated by regional interests (by both domestic and foreign flag holdings), most notably the dry bulk carrier and tanker fleets. Undoubtedly a major factor encouraging the penetration of Pacific Rim fleets into the world scene was cost advantage. The region is the centre of the world shipbuilding industry and close relationships have been built up between local ship operators, cargo interests and shipbuilders. But more than this has been the large differentials in operating costs - particularly crew costs, which (with the exception of Japan) have given local ship operators a significant cost advantage - more so in periods of depressed freight levels (p. 6).

In the tradition of the 'flying geese' model of development, discussed earlier in the chapter, as operating costs increased, many Asia-Pacific shipowners initially flagged out their national fleets to other cheaper Asian national flags (e.g. from Japanese to Hong Kong registry). This was an attempt to maintain their cost advantage over Europe and North America (predominantly the US). These regions in turn tried to narrow the cost advantage of the Asia-Pacific by flagging out their national fleets to open registries, offshore flags, and the creation of second registries. Many also formed joint ventures and tended to specialise in the more advanced areas of shipping like containerisation in an attempt to be competitive. The Asia-Pacific retaliated through imitation, flagging out their national fleets mainly to open registries, thus still maintaining their cost advantage (Thanopoulou, 1995; Sletmo and Holste, 1993; JAMRI, 1987).

**Table 2.15**
**Asia-Pacific fleets under foreign flags (December 1995)**

| World Rank | Country | Foreign flag as a % of total controlled fleet |
|:---:|:---|:---|
| 2 | Japan | 73.00 |
| 5 | China | 34.28 |
| 6 | Hong Kong | 77.70 |
| 8 | South Korea | 53.55 |
| 11 | Taiwan | 47.02 |
| 13 | Singapore | 39.48 |
| 25 | Philippines | 3.34 |
| 27 | Indonesia | 31.39 |
| 32 | Australia | 8.84 |
| 33 | Thailand | 41.18 |
| 34 | Malaysia | 5.20 |

Source: UNCTAD (1996b)

This trend is reflected in Table 2.15, which shows what percentage of the Asia-Pacific fleet are under foreign flags. It is interesting to note that, with the exception of China, the countries with the highest world ranking are those with the highest percentage of fleets under foreign flags, namely, Japan, Hong Kong, South Korea, and Taiwan. These countries have mainly used the open registries of Liberia and Panama (and Vanuatu for Japan and Hong Kong) and to a lesser extent Cyprus and the Bahamas (Lloyd's Maritime Directory, 1997). In the case of China, where the fleet is owned and operated by the state, it is reasonable to expect the majority of its fleet to be under its national register. The main reason why 34 per cent of its fleet is under foreign flags is to gain access to shipping markets and commercial finance (Drewry, 1993).

In summary, cheaper crewing costs, the use of more modern ships and technology, and the move by many of the leading Asia-Pacific shipowners to open registries led to a fundamental shift in the comparative advantage of the industry players. The result was that Asia-Pacific shipowners were able to maintain a cost advantage over their competitors.

*Government support*

The Asia-Pacific's rise to power in world shipping has been greatly assisted by individual national governments whose maritime and industry policies have been instrumental in developing and promoting the industry. In the bulk sector, the expansion into tankers and dry bulk carriers has been encouraged to meet the increasing demand for bulk imports so that the domestic economy could achieve the maximum benefit from such trade. In the liner sector, the development into containerisation has likewise been encouraged to meet the export and intra-regional trade growth in semi-finished products (Lee, 1996; Thanopoulou, 1995; JAMRI, 1987; Brooks, 1985). Peters (1986) explains the rationale behind government support:

> One reason the developing countries [of the Asia-Pacific] moved so aggressively into the shipping markets was their concern about invisible trade. The contention was—and largely still is—that substantial and avoidable payments of scarce foreign exchange were going to foreign carriers and their insurers. Officials decided the solution was to acquire their own tonnage. In some cases, the decision was also influenced by strategic considerations. Often, easy export credit financing was available from foreign shipyards, further encouraging such decisions (p. 11).

The economic 'infant industry' argument contends that shipping should be protected until strong enough to compete on its own. Applying this argument, many Asia-Pacific governments used a range of measures to restrict foreign competition and assist national shipowners. Assistance was both direct (operating, construction, credit and loan subsidies) and indirect (taxation allowances, cargo/flag preference and reservation, cabotage, moratoria and loan guarantees). Other measures that guaranteed preference for national flags over foreign flags were carrier licensing, discriminatory pricing (giving national flags a subsidised rate), support given to ancillary industries (e.g. funding maritime training institutions, shipbuilding, research and development), operation of government-owned national carriers, tight government control on foreign investment, joint ventures and business restrictions, and additional bureaucratic requirements imposed on foreign operators. Such measures have significantly helped expand the fleets of the

Asia-Pacific into their current carrying power (Lee, 1996; Thanopoulou, 1995; Goss and Marlow, 1993; Holste, 1993; Leinbach and Sien, 1989; Hawkins, 1989; Brooks, 1985).

Shipping market analysts have argued and debated the merits of this assistance given to Asia-Pacific shipowners. Many claim that such government intervention is unfair and discriminatory, arguing that the benefits of this assistance to Asia-Pacific shipowners have been at the expense of international shipping, contributing to overtonnaging and over-investment and creating market inefficiencies and economic distortions by undercutting more efficient international competitors. Others also argue that over-investment in shipping hurts national productivity because it shifts scarce resources away from other well-deserving economic areas. Underlying these criticisms is the view that Asia-Pacific shipowners have been given an unfair advantage, which in turn is fuelling the growing calls for a more 'level playing field' in international shipping (Thanopoulou, 1995; Goss and Marlow, 1993; Sletmo and Holste, 1993; Kim, 1992; Hawkins, 1989; Peters, 1986; Jon, 1986; Yui and Nakagawa, 1985).

On this issue, however, the traditional maritime countries of Europe and North America can hardly stand on high moral ground. As one of the authors found in his study of shipping subsidies, similar measures were followed by many of these traditional maritime countries in their efforts to consolidate the position of their national fleets during the early stages of their maritime development(Hawkins, 1989). Rightly or wrongly, subsidisation has always been viewed as the primary method of assisting national fleets:

Shipping subsidies have always been the classical method of assistance to national shipowners. Their origins go as far back as the seventeenth century when England started providing subsidies to its shipping industry to maintain its supremacy in the world markets. By the nineteenth century, maritime subsidies had become commonplace not only in the United Kingdom but also in other countries such as Japan and the United States. Today, we have a situation where there is not a maritime nation which does not offer some form of assistance to its national fleet (p. 1).

Since the start of the 1990s, with mounting pressure from their major trading partners, many Asia-Pacific governments have begun changing direction, moving more closely, albeit very slowly, towards the liberalisation of their shipping industries and the removal of barriers to their markets (OECD, 1994). Pressure has been applied in different ways. For instance, in the past decade, the US Federal Maritime Administration has conducted investigations into unfair trade practices of Asia-Pacific shipping, while the Korean shipping line, Hyundai, has been brought before the Commission of the European Directorate-Competition for unfair trade practices. OECD has ongoing discussions on harmonising shipping policies to bring the Asia-

Pacific more in line with their trading partners (OECD, 1994; Holste, 1993). There is growing impatience at the slowness with which the region has carried out its reforms. With the region in financial trouble at the turn of the century, and with a number of countries requiring huge financial assistance from international sources (e.g. the International Monetary Fund), there is strong likelihood that Europe and North America will use this as a leverage for greater trade liberalisation in the region.

*Maritime infrastructure*

A third contributory factor to the success of Asia-Pacific shipping has been its 'maritime infrastructure' (Lewarn and Hawkins, 1994). This includes a network of people, operations, and activities designed to support the seaborne transport of goods and people. There is a growing body of opinion and research that highlights the importance of a strong maritime infrastructure in maintaining the competitiveness of a national shipping industry.

The work of Lewarn and Hawkins (1994), Sletmo and Holste (1993), and Pelecanos (1992) all follow Svendsen's (1989) original argument that the long-term competitiveness of a national shipping industry requires a vigorous 'shipping milieu'. This is defined as 'the network of qualified men and women working in the cluster of shipping activities, private and government' (p.254). This network represents a dynamic pool of information, knowledge, and expertise. It includes a range of different users (importers, exporters), providers (port authorities, terminals, stevedores, agencies, customs, training bodies, brokers) and government services (safety, transport, customs, quarantine, research, search and rescue). Interaction and communication within and among these groups are needed to establish and maintain an environment within which national shipping can compete effectively.

Svendsen's view of a vigorous shipping milieu finds parallel outside the shipping industry in Porter's (1990) research on what he calls the 'home base' or the 'diamond of national advantage'. Porter argues that the home base is critical to long-term competitiveness because it provides the thrust for innovation, improvement, and change. It promotes the creation of domestic rivalry among suppliers which in turn fuels expansion into related industries. The home base also creates greater strategic flexibility. Porter's research was conducted over a four year period and involved ten of the world's most important trading nations. Of these, three were from the Asia-Pacific: Japan, South Korea, and Singapore. Focusing on the most successful industries of each nation, he found that the competitive advantage of a national industry depended on the strength of its national environment, i.e. the 'home base'.

In many Asia-Pacific countries, the development of the maritime infrastructure has been given prominent consideration in national maritime

44

policies and discussions. Largely as a result of this, the region is now a dominant player in world shipbuilding, ship repair, shipbroking, sale and purchase markets, and maritime training, research and development. It also provides the largest pool of low-cost seafarers. The forging of close working relationships between and among the various sectors of a country's maritime infrastructure has also led to many cost advantages. In South Korea, for example, the entire national fleet, which underwent massive expansion in recent years, was virtually built in Korean shipyards. When one large Korean operator got into trouble (KSC), it was simply absorbed by another (Hanjin). In Taiwan, a state-owned carrier (Yang Ming) acquired its new fleet from a state-owned shipbuilder (China Shipbuilders) on very favourable terms. These examples are repeated elsewhere across the region, both within shipping and outside it. Given this level of support, it is easy to see why the Asia-Pacific fleet has grown significantly both in size and commercial power within a relatively short period of time (Drewry, 1993; Holste, 1993; Pelecanos, 1992).

*Aggressive growth strategies*

The final element behind the success of Asia-Pacific's shipping are aggressive growth strategies. The Asia-Pacific fleet, particularly in liner shipping, grew faster than its own seaborne trade requirements, which led to more tonnage being offered in the already crowded markets of Europe and North America. Indeed, many analysts place the blame for the chronic over-tonnaging situation in liner trades to the excessive expansion strategies of Asia-Pacific shipowners, pursued with the tacit or express blessing of their national governments (Thanopoulou, 1995; Kim, 1992; Jon, 1986).

The new Asian carriers, particularly from Taiwan and South Korea, gained a foothold in Europe and North America through their aggressive push for growth and their unconventional approach of competing against the conference system, which caught the market by surprise. Commented Drewry (1993):

> The carrier establishment was used to running the world container trades in a completely different way to the strategy adopted by the new Asian lines, and the emergence of a new breed of competitor was an enormous culture shock. The spirit of compromise and conciliation which these lines had previously taken for granted in their liner operations was anathema to the new Far East carriers, who simply seemed to formulate a strategy and then put it into operation, with apparently unlimited financial resources (p. 104).

What also caught many by surprise was the global ambition of the Asia-Pacific carriers. Many came from large industrial conglomerates and had the support of their national governments, thus they had the resources to support global corporate strategies (Holste, 1993; Drewry, 1993; Kim, 1992). Drewry (1993) again encapsulates this view very well:

> With the Asia-Pacific region developing into a major generator of liner cargo, a simultaneous advance in liner shipping to service this rapid expansion could have been anticipated. What was less easy to anticipate—and certainly what the established carriers in Europe and elsewhere failed to appreciate fully— was the fact that the ambitions of the new Asian lines extended far beyond any national, or even regional, limitations. Almost without exception, these carriers had global horizons (p. 7).

A more recent trend is the move by Asia-Pacific shipowners away from independent operations to consortia and partnerships. With leading Asia-Pacific shipowners having successfully penetrated world shipping markets and with their governments coming under increasing international pressure to liberalise trade policies and practices, many Asia-Pacific shipowners are moving towards the conference system of consortia or partnership arrangements to maintain market share and profitability. This is not just happening at the regional level, but in the global markets as well. In the name of profitability and survival in the global market, shipowners from the Asia-Pacific, European and North American regions are all forming mega global alliances on a scale never seen before in container shipping (Containerisation International, 1997c; Lloyd's Shipping Economist, 1996a; Drewry 1995, 1996).

*A final word on Asia-Pacific competitiveness*

The influence of Asia-Pacific shipowners in world shipping cannot be ignored. It can only be expected to intensify, as the following quotes show:

> When this degree of control [of the world fleet] is combined with the competitively priced operations which so many of these owners/operators are able to offer, either because of their low cost native crews and/or the cost advantages of their open register status (low cost crews, low taxation, advanced depreciation of hull values etc), then the full extent of their challenge to world shipping becomes evident (Drewry, 1993, p. 112).

> With the help of such an expanded tonnage capacity and their competitive freight rates, the fleets of these nations will increasingly find themselves in an advantageous position over the advanced maritime nations' fleet. Hence, the international competition on the maritime transport market is expected to become more and more intensified (JAMRI, 1986, pp. 63-64).

Such pronouncements on the Asia-Pacific's influence are not without critics, however. With growing evidence that many Asia-Pacific shipowners are losing their competitive edge, nagging doubts have been raised about the region's staying power (Lee, 1996; Holste, 1993; Kim, 1992; Peters, 1986).

The implications of the recent financial turmoil gripping the region are also adding to this general feeling of unease and uncertainty. Would Asia-Pacific shipowners be able to maintain their success in world shipping? The answer it seems is that if Asia-Pacific shipowners are to maintain their new dominant position in shipping, then they have to learn better ways of competing. Holste (1993) best sums up the current mood:

> No market segment exists in which competitive advantages are permanent. If companies from the TMCs [traditional maritime countries] are to compete successfully, they will have to adapt frequently to changing market conditions and will have to form strategic alliances on a global level to best respond to the needs of an integrated world economy. Similar conditions for success apply to carriers from the NMCs [new maritime countries of the Asia-Pacific], which have to move beyond their cost advantage and use this temporary strength to build a lasting market advantage based on *innovative corporate strategies* and strategic alliances (p. 51).

Such calls for innovative corporate strategies are growing, but how ready are the Asia-Pacific shipowners to rise to this new challenge?

## Strategic management in Asia-Pacific shipping

Like Holste (1993), Peters (1986) makes a similar plea for more strategy research into Asia-Pacific ports and shipping. He argues that there is considerable potential for growth in the area, but much depends on shipowners' ability to pursue the right strategic approach and on their knowledge of the general shipping environment. Unfortunately, as he has found in his study, although a lot has been written about Asia-Pacific shipping, much of this is fragmented and dispersed, with no coherent base, which severely limits widespread use. Credibility is also suspect, with many studies often skewed to reflect vested interests or political viewpoints. Even conceptual contributions are based mostly on personal views, without any empirical backing. The rapidity and magnitude of change in shipping adds further complications because rapid change means that findings have a very short 'shelf-life'. Peters thus argues for a continuing need to carry out new investigations and update current knowledge. He cites, for instance, the need for a better understanding of how transport system planning, the efficient management of the transport system, and the financing of transport investments in ports and shipping are interrelated. According to him, these three areas are pivotal because they determine and are heavily influenced by the type of strategies selected by shipowners. Unfortunately, not much is known about how these three areas can be effectively integrated, and even less about the nature of strategies and strategic behaviour of shipowners.

Work by Wong (1991), Hawkins (1993), and Reker (1997) shows that the literature on shipping strategy is sparse and of very uneven quality, and specific reference to the new maritime nations of the Asia-Pacific is almost non-existent (Hawkins, 1993). Of the few available sources, attention has mainly focused on Europe and North America, with greater emphasis on the former (e.g. McKinsey, 1985; Hope and Boe, 1981; Lorange and Norman, 1972). This European orientation is perhaps to be expected given Europe's long tradition in world shipping. Even despite its gradual decline in fleet size since the 1970s, it still controls the largest share of the world's fleet (Lloyd's Maritime Information Services, 1997; Thanopoulou, 1995; Aspinwall, 1995; Ledger and Roe, 1992). However, there is some evidence that this geographical imbalance is slowly being addressed. Harvey's (1987) study on ship financing included both European and US shipowners, while Cullinane (1991) covered a broader geographical mix, including one prominent Asia-Pacific nation, Hong Kong, in his study of risk preferences in shipping. More recent studies (Wong, 1991; Hawkins, 1993; Barton, 1995; Reker, 1997) have shed more light on strategic management issues in the Asia-Pacific. Management texts on the area are also on the increase (e.g. Bartol *et al*, 1998; Chow *et al*, 1997). With the growing world interest in the region, the increasing globalisation of shipping markets, and the recent trends in liner shipping toward global alliances, it is likely that more studies will increasingly follow this pattern.

Geographical orientation aside, the lack of research into shipping strategy appears to be pervasive throughout the industry. In academic and trade journals, management books, scholarly publications, and graduate courses and training programmes, there appears to be a singular lack of attention to the theory and practice of shipping strategy. Shipping strategy has not received any prominent attention in leading journals in shipping and port management. *Maritime Policy and Management*, for instance, which is arguably the leading international academic journal on shipping and port research, has devoted little space to the subject: a few articles on strategic planning, and none on strategic management in general or corporate strategy in particular. While a number of articles have referred to corporate strategy, the treatment has been rather superficial, made only to support or clarify the main thrust of the authors' thesis (e.g. Aries, 1989, on business strategies; Hawkins, 1991b, on port strategy). Of the papers on strategic planning (Frankel, 1989; Arlt, 1987; Rich, 1978), all are concept papers in which the authors expound on their personal interpretations of the application of strategic planning to ports and shipping. Although no doubt these interpretations are drawn from the authors' extensive experience in the field, a major limitation is their lack of shipping-based research to provide empirical support. Even Frankel's (1989) highly influential work, which is the most frequently cited in shipping literature, shows no reference to shipping strategy research. Instead, support is drawn primarily from the general strategic management literature.

Other shipping publications and trade journals cover a wide range of subjects, but they too document very little research work. Some provide overviews of strategic management in shipping and ports, either in the form of historical reconstructions or general introductory descriptions (e.g. Fairplay, 1997; Hawkins 1993; Yui and Nakagawa, 1985; ESCAP 1985a). Others give a brief analysis of the strategies of individual companies such as MISC (Lloyd's Shipping Economist, 1996b), OOCL (Containerisation International, 1996b), K Line (Containerisation International, 1996d), COSCO (Containerisation International, 1996e), Korean Carriers (Containerisation International, 1997a), and Evergreen (Lloyd's Shipping Economist, 1997). Many others come in the form of conference papers, which, like the articles in shipping academic journals, are primarily concept papers with little or no supporting evidence from shipping research. Some examples of such papers include Soper (1980) who wrote on corporate planning in shipping, Carlson (1989) who focused on developing a business strategy for a port, and Hawkins who wrote about managing port investments (1991) and strategic management for Asia-Pacific shipowners (1996). Shipping management textbooks offer no better alternatives. Four widely used textbooks on the practices of shipping managers (Spruyt, 1994; Marcus, 1987; Yui and Nakagawa, 1985; Frankel, 1982) do not even have any meaningful discussions on strategic planning and shipping strategies.

Further evidence of this lack of research literature on shipping strategy can be found in the curricula of graduate degree courses on shipping. In western countries, many leading institutions offering graduate courses on shipping management normally include at least one subject on strategic management in shipping in their curricula. This subject usually comes under various titles, for instance, shipping policy (Master of Science in International Shipping, University of Plymouth), strategic management tools (Master of Transport and Maritime Management, University of Antwerp) strategic management (Master of Business in Maritime Management, Australian Maritime College), corporate strategy in marine industries (Master of Science in Maritime Management, Maine Maritime Academy), or shipping management strategy (Master of Science in Shipping Management, ,World Maritime University). While all these programs cite some general shipping literature on strategic planning for shipping and ports (notably Frankel, 1989) in their course material, they make no similar referencing for corporate strategies. Instead, they rely on the general strategic management literature, particularly on the work of Porter (1980, 1985) on competitive strategies at the business level.

In East Asia, the trend is the same. Course material in many maritime management and shipping programmes contains hardly any reference to shipping strategy research, while a significant part of the reading list is drawn from general strategic management literature (e.g. Kobe University of Mercantile Marine (Japan), Singapore Polytechnic, Korea Maritime University, Hong Kong Polytechnic University, Dalian Maritime University (China), Indonesian Merchant Marine Academy, Malaysian Maritime Academy, Vietnam Maritime University, Thailand Maritime College).

Theses and dissertations coming out of these graduate programs also reveal this lack in strategy research. Harvey's (1987) extensive review of the literature on corporate planning and strategy, for instance, draws almost exclusively on the general strategic management literature. In his review of the shipping literature on strategy, only two sources were cited, one by Rich (1982) and the other by the US Maritime Administration (1982), which had been prepared for them by Delta Steamship Lines and Temple, Barker and Sloane. Similar reviews by Wong (1991), Barton (1995), and Reker (1997) essentially take the same approach.


## The importance of strategy research in shipping

The lack of research work on strategic management in shipping is surprising for two reasons. First, there have been persistent calls for more strategic research in shipping since Lorange and Norman (1972) sounded the first call 25 years ago. And yet, although succeeding writers have echoed the same message in more recent years (Peters, 1986; Wong, 1991; Holste, 1993; Barton, 1995; Reker, 1997), the call has evidently not reached the wider shipping population. This continuing inattention to shipping strategy is even more surprising, given significant advances in our understanding of the role of strategy in competitive performance. Research evidence over more than two decades points to a conclusive link between strategic management and performance. Firms who practise strategic management have been found to be more profitable than those who do not (Miller and Cardinal, 1994). In spite of this substantial body of research, however, there is very little evidence of wide application in shipping, particularly in reference to the Asia-Pacific. Lasserre and Schutte (1995) strongly argue that to compete successfully with Asian companies, Western companies must gain a better understanding of the 'Asian' way of doing things. They assert that this involves not just learning how to do things differently, but also how to do different things. According to them, this process of adaptation and transformation is necessary to facilitate entry into the Asian markets and ensure long-term competitive success in the region:

> The [Asia-Pacific] region is changing and modernising rapidly, but it is a Western self-delusion to equate modernisation with Westernisation. As Japan's development over the last 100 years or so has shown, it is possible to modernise without losing one's own identity and culture. Managing this change in Asia is an enormous task and will bring setbacks and disasters...
> Implementing global strategies in the region will not always be easy and will create problems for those who believe in a simple, uniform world. Not many global consumers are at home in Asia Pacific. Only on a superficial level do we witness a convergence in beliefs and practices. Bearing in mind the successful development of Asia Pacific over the last few decades, it cannot be expected that the region will move towards Western societal, economic and management models soon, if ever. As Rudyard Kipling said at the turn of the last century, 'Asia is not going to be civilised after the methods of the West. There is too much Asia, and she is too old.' (p. 292).

These have important implications for shipping, especially given recent trends in liner shipping of global alliances and partnerships between European, North American and Asian shipping companies. The Western concepts and models of strategic management will need greater testing and adaptation before they can be assumed to work. Some may indeed not need any adaptation, while others may need a lot, but without adequate analysis and testing, we may be making bold and unsubstantiated assumptions.

*Toward a greater understanding of corporate strategies in shipping*

If work on shipping strategy at a general level is sparse, work *detailing* the nature of strategy is even rarer. A number of articles and books discuss the evolution of strategies in different shipping companies (Slack *et al*, 1996; Lim, 1996; Yui and Nakagawa 1985) and some maritime consultancy reports recommend specific strategies for container shipping (Drewry, 1991) and dry bulk shipping (Drewry, 1996b). However, none of these provide any detailed and comprehensive analysis of shipping strategies; neither do they offer insights into the strategic behaviour of Asia-Pacific shipowners.

Strategies can be classified in several ways, but of particular relevance to an organisation's long-term success are two types of strategies: business and corporate. Their names refer directly to the organisational level at which they are determined and pursued. Business strategies focus on the individual businesses or divisions of an organisation; corporate strategies focus on the entire organisation. In general strategic management literature, work on business strategies has predominated while that on corporate strategies, although not entirely neglected, is relatively lighter. In shipping strategy literature, however, both types have received minimal attention, with perhaps business strategies getting a little bit more exposure than corporate strategies.

A notable example of work on business strategies is Hansen's (1989) analysis of shipping strategies, which is based on his previous research into Norwegian shipping (McKinsey, 1985). He described this analysis as

... an effort to develop a better understanding of what it takes strategically to be successful in the highly dynamic shipping markets, how shipping companies can take advantage of opportunities that follow market changes, and how to understand and avoid being exposed to deadly risks (p. 13).

Drawing heavily on Porter's (1980, 1985) work on business strategies and Peters and Waterman's (1982) report on their 'search for excellence' among US companies, Hansen (1989) came up with four strategic types of shipping. They were contract (e.g. chemicals, container), industry (e.g. cruise), commodity (e.g. large bulk or oil), and special (e.g. LPG). Using these four types, he then proposed a number of business strategies for shipping, which essentially followed Porter's business strategy principles. In his analysis, Hansen concluded that superior analytical skills were one of the success factors common to all successful shipping companies; such skills enabled shipowners to assess market opportunities and threats and take advantage of company strengths. He also recommended the use of analytical frameworks to assist any such environmental analysis.

Following Hansen's lead, the Institute of Shipping Analysis conducted a similar analysis of shipping business strategies (Fairplay, 1997). The close resemblance in the approach used by the two studies could probably be attributed to the fact that the author of the Institute paper, Professor Tor Wergeland, was also part of the McKinsey study team who studied Norwegian shipping in 1985. Like Hansen, this latter study also drew heavily on Porter's work (1980, 1985), leading Fairplay (1997) to claim, rather mistakenly, a universal application of Porter's strategies to shipping.

Unlike business strategies, corporate strategies have not received similar attention in shipping. More recent studies on Asia-Pacific shipping (Barton, 1995; Reker, 1997) highlight this gap in the literature and urge for more research into the area, particularly in relation to Asia-Pacific shipping. In their surveys of East Asian shipowners, mainly in the liner trades, Barton (1995) and Reker (1997) found that the need for analytical tools and techniques to evaluate strategies was a major concern. Many shipowners complained of the lack of shipping-based analytical tools and criticised general tools, which many believed were inappropriate or untested in shipping, and hence were not used. Wong's (1991) analysis of the strategic planning tools used by North East Asian shipowners in the liner industry highlighted a similar problem of credibility and low level of use. Both users and non-users of analytical strategy selection techniques, such as those found in the general strategic management literature, voiced concerns over the relevance of such techniques to shipping. Although users were familiar with, and used to a limited degree, a number of mainstream analytical techniques and models, the general perception was that such techniques and models were not really that applicable to shipping. Non-users explained that because the language and layout used in the models was unfamiliar to them (presumably because they were drawn from manufacturing concepts and principles), they dismissed them as not relevant or applicable to their industry. Similar conclusions were reached by a study on information technology use by Hong Kong shipowners (Saxena and Joshi, 1992). According to them, although the conservatism of shipowners may be a factor, an even bigger factor is the poor design of such systems, which has created a 'credibility gap' in shipowners' minds and has made them more reluctant to use such systems (p. 61).

The studies by Wong (1991), Barton (1995) and Reker (1997) have shed some much needed light on the strategic behaviour of shipowners, particularly Asia-Pacific shipowners. Although the generalisability of their survey data is limited because of low response rates (less than 20 per cent), nonetheless their studies represent one of the initial steps toward developing a better understanding of strategy use by Asia-Pacific shipowners. They also highlight the need for more research into strategies and strategy selection techniques that can assist Asia-Pacific shipowners in competing more effectively among themselves and with other regions. If strategy is the answer to long-term competitiveness, what must Asia-Pacific shipowners do to achieve this objective?

# 3  Strategic management

## Strategic management

This and the following two chapters examine the strategic management literature. Three areas are covered: the historical development of strategic management as a field of inquiry, the types of strategies pursued by organisations to maintain their competitive edge in the markets in which they operate, and available tools for strategy selection and evaluation. In this chapter, the development of strategic management as a field of study is examined. The major theoretical perspectives that have shaped strategic management are discussed, and the development of the field over the last 30 years is analysed.

## Major influences on management thought

Anderson (1984) lists eight schools of thought that have been major contributors to the growth and development of our understanding of management. Classified into three main groups, they include:

- *Theories of management skills*
  The human relations school
  The organisation behaviour school
  The information and decision school

- *Theories of management functions*
  Scientific management
  The quantitative school (management science)
  The strategic management school

- *Theories of organisational systems*
  Administrative management
  The organisational theory school.

All these major schools of management thought have built on the contributions of other disciplines in the development of their theories. These disciplines have laid the foundation for and enriched m magement thought. However, their application, with their disparate theoretical orientations and methodological approaches within the same research area, has also produced confusion and disagreement. This disarray has been echoed within the strategic management field, particularly during its fledgling years.

## The development of strategic management as a field of inquiry

As an area of study within the field of management, strategy is of relatively recent origin, but the concept itself is not new, although up until about four decades ago, the term strategy had been associated mainly with military operations. Von Neumann and Morgenstern (1948), who developed the theory of games, provided the bridge from military to business usage, and once introduced, the concept of strategy found ready acceptance in the management field. As Ansoff (1965), one of the most influential voices in the field, noted:

> during the past ten years the idea of strategy has received increasing recognition in management literature ... This interest grew out of the realization that a firm needs a well-defined scope and growth direction, that objectives alone do not meet this need, and that additional decision rules are required if the firm is to have orderly and profitable growth. Such decision rules and guidelines have been broadly defined as strategy or, sometimes, as the concept of the firm's business (Ansoff, 1965, p. 103).

Since then, the practice and study of strategic management in general and of strategy in particular has developed steadily. It continues to be a dynamic, rapidly growing area, with research branching out into a widening array of organisations and industries covering different countries and geographical locations. The development of the strategic management field following the Second World War can be roughly organised into three stages, commencing in the 1960s and extending into the present. This section provides a brief overview of the three stages, and then discusses each stage in detail, highlighting the key issues, developments and thinkers in each.

*Overview*

The 1960s mark the formal emergence of strategic management as a separate field of inquiry. At this initial stage, the first attempts at theory building were published. The succeeding decade, the 1970s, which marked stage two, was characterised by a rapid growth in, and robust debate over, theoretical (and quasi-theoretical) perspectives and conceptual models. At this stage, much of the debate remained at the conceptual level; empirical evidence, although steadily growing, was not substantive enough to redefine the debate. Stage three began in the 1980s and extends into the present. This stage is characterised by a continuing refinement of concepts and models as more empirical evidence is gathered and the field matures. The debate now is not so much on the superiority of one paradigm or research method over another as on the suitability and appropriateness of combining different paradigms and methods to explain different situations. Empirical evidence to date points to the need for more eclectic, more integrated and inter-disciplinary approaches.

The first two stages in strategic management research, the 1960s and 1970s, were dominated by two competing schools of thought. One was the 'formal analysis' school, with its roots mainly in economics, scientific management, management science and administrative management. It was also known as the 'rational-analytical' or 'logical-positivistic' school. The second was the 'process' school (Morris, 1987a), with its roots in organisational behaviour, design of organisations, and human and organisational decision-making processes. These two schools have also come to be known as 'rationalist' and 'incremental' or 'emergent', respectively. The level of disagreement between these two schools was—and is—remarkably high. Proponents of the formal analysis school tend to discredit models based on the process school as non-rational, unstructured, and reactive; proponents of the process school, on the other hand, argue that models based on the formal analysis school were too mechanistic and formalistic.

In recent years, a third school of thought has emerged. Although there is no widely accepted name for it, it can be aptly called the 'holistic' or 'synthesis' school, because it advocates a more holistic and interdisciplinary approach to the study of management. The word 'synthesis' is borrowed from Miller and Mintzberg (1983) who argue that management research can be best served by an approach that seeks to integrate various attributes of management into composite frameworks or configurations.

*Stage 1: Theory building (1960s)*

The study of strategy and strategic management became an identifiable field of inquiry in the business literature in the 1960s with the simultaneous publication of three seminal pieces of work. They were Alfred Chandler's *Strategy and Structure: Chapters in the History of American Industrial Enterprise*, published in 1962; Igor Ansoff's *Corporate Strategy: An Analytic Approach to Business Policy for Growth and Expansion*, published in 1965; and the Harvard Business School's (Edmund Learned, C Roland Christensen, Kenneth Andrews and William Guth) *Business Policy: Texts and Cases*, published in 1965.

The formal analysis school dominated this initial stage. Among its leading proponents were Kenneth Andrews and Igor Ansoff. Both men are typically credited for first articulating the concept of corporate strategy. They were the first to focus specifically on the concept of strategy and to develop analytical frameworks within which the concept can be defined. However, although both built on Chandler's (1962) dictum, 'structure follows strategy', their interpretation of the scope of strategy differed. To Andrews (1965, 1971), strategy included both an organisation's goals and the means to achieve these goals; to Ansoff (1965), it was limited to the means of achieving organisational goals. As we shall see in the succeeding discussion, later writers would carry on this basic difference.

It should also be mentioned here that another work actually predated these three publications: Peter Drucker's *The Practice of Management*, published in 1954. According to Hofer and Schendel (1978), Drucker was actually the first to address the issue of strategy in business management, but he did so only implicitly, framing it instead in terms of two questions: 'What is our business? And what should it be?' As a result, it was not until the latter half of the 1960s, when interest in strategy had become more widespread, that Drucker's seminal work was 'rediscovered'.

*Stage 2: The debate between competing schools (1970s)*

The energetic inquiry into the concept of corporate strategy that followed the work of Andrews and Ansoff, and the emergence of a contrary viewpoint in reaction to the dominant formal analysis theme, characterised stage two in the development of the field.

Much of the work produced during this period built upon the work of Andrews and Ansoff and reflected the same formal analytical perspective. Major contributors included, according to year of publication, Katz (1970) Argenti (1974), Drucker, (1974), Rumelt (1974), Vancil and Lorange (1975), Hofer (1975), Hedley (1976, 1977), and Steiner and Miner (1977). Within the formal analysis school, there was a distinct pattern of growth: from an early emphasis on long-range planning to strategic planning and finally to strategic management. The move away from formal long-range planning was easy to understand. Plans became too elaborate and too unwieldy; often they did not match the realities existing within the organisation; and they were limited to financial forecasts based on the organisation's previous performance (Ansoff, 1987).

The shift to strategic or corporate planning partially silenced some of the major criticisms levelled against long-range planning, but not for long. Although there was overwhelming evidence suggesting that firms that planned performed better than those that did not (Rumelt, 1974), research also showed that almost every organisation followed different 'planning' models.

Some of them were not always formally conceived, *a priori*, as the word 'plan' would normally suggest, or were limited to financial considerations. Indeed, research showed that the strategy process was much more complex, more encompassing, than that suggested by the concept 'strategic planning'. Thus was born the concept of strategic management (Ansoff, 1965; Ansoff *et al*, 1976).

It was also during the 1970s that the formal analysis approach to the study of management came under criticism for ignoring the behavioural aspects of management. Criticism centred on the approach's exclusive reliance on measurable quantitative factors and its lack of attention to vital qualitative, organisational and power-behavioural factors that so often determined strategic success in any one situation. Critics contended that in practice, planning was 'just one building block in a continuous stream of events that really determine corporate strategy' (Quinn, 1978, p.7). The process school also extended its criticisms to previous behavioural studies.

The most prominent members of the process school were Bower (1970), Child (1972, 1974, 1975), Mintzberg (1972, 1973, 1976, 1978), Miller and Friesen (1977), Quinn (1978), and Miles and Snow (1978). Proponents of the process school drew on studies on the dynamics of human behaviour in business settings and on earlier studies done in other fields, notably public administration, sociology and politics (e.g. Cyert and March, 1954, 1964; March and Simon, 1958; Lindblom, 1959). They argued that strategies were not always formally made or formulated and that strategic decision making was not the exclusive domain of top management. The main thesis of the process school was that strategies were formed as part of the decision-making processes occurring at various levels of an organisation, emerging as recognisable patterns only afterwards.

*Stage 3: Redefining the debate (1980s to the present)*

This last stage is characterised by two trends: the move toward a holistic approach to the study and practice of management, and further refinements within the formal analysis and process schools.

The need for a more holistic approach to management was first articulated by Bowman (1974) who recommended the use of different approaches to understand corporate strategy more easily. However, his call was largely ignored until the more prominent writers in the field took up the same cause.

By the end of the 1970s, the mood of the debate had started to change. Summing up the research findings of the period, Hofer and Schendel (1978) noted:

> Recent policy research has shown ... that while strategies do differ among different types of businesses, there are also patterns of strategies that are appropriate to broad sets of

environmental conditions ... Research in the areas of organisational theory, organisational behaviour, and accounting have indicated that different methods of organising, staffing, directing, and controlling are appropriate for different situations... (p. 196).

Hofer and Schendel (1978) also cited the work of Mintzberg (1973) and others, which clearly showed that all levels of management performed similar management functions, but that the nature of the work performed at each management level differed. They also noted that 'these ideas [had] not yet been extensively integrated in management practice' (p. 196) nor were they 'yet reflected in most writings in the policy, organisational theory, and organisational behaviour fields' (p. 197). However, they closed with a clear statement about what needed to be done:

What is clear ... is that a firm's strategic management process must be treated as an integrated total system. Thus, it would be counter productive to try to implement some of the strategy formulation tools and techniques described in this text without concurrently altering all the implementation processes and systems of the firm, including its staffing and promotion practices, measurement and evaluation systems, compensation systems, and management control systems (p. 198).

Since then, research in the area has increasingly focused on a more holistic, interdisciplinary, eclectic approach to strategic management. Today, the focus of the debate is not so much on which school provides the better theory and research methodology. Rather, it is on deciphering the appropriate strategic configurations for different situations and on choosing the appropriate research methodology for examining or validating different theoretical, conceptual or practical issues (see, for instance, Snow and Thomas, 1994; Lyles, 1990). While debate continues between the rationalistic and process schools, which one writer describes as at heart a conflict between proactive purposefulness versus reactive powerlessness (Gaddis, 1997), the general trend is toward more integrated, systemic and interdisciplinary approaches to the study of management (Taylor, 1997). Greater emphasis is placed on the need to acknowledge, in both theory and practice, the equal importance of intuition and analysis in strategic management, and of the existence of various configurations in which strategies are managed. This new way of thinking is increasingly reflected in more recent editions of many management textbooks (e.g. Collis and Montgomery, 1997; Johnson and Scholes, 1997, Pearce and Robinson, 1997; Thompson and Strickland, 1996).

The advent of the holistic or synthesis school has not necessarily meant the demise of either the process or formal analysis school. Although criticisms of both schools are expected to continue, nonetheless, each school has made some significant advances and helped clarify our understanding of strategy. Within the formal analysis school, work by Glueck (1980), Porter (1980, 1985, 1990), Hamermesh (1983, 1986), Rumelt (1991), Hamel and Pralahad

(1989, 1990, 1993), Goold et al (1994), and Collis and Montgomery (1995, 1997) has substantially advanced our knowledge of strategy.

Model testing and validation has continued, with a stronger emphasis shown on the applicability of models across industries and geographical regions. In his review of the literature, Morris (1987a) cited several such recent attempts: Galbraith and Schendel (1983) and Dess and Davis (1982) tested Porter's models; Hammermesh (1983, 1984) tested portfolio planning; and Herbert and Deresky (1987) tested typologies of business strategies.

There has also been a clear trend towards greater research on the content of strategy, focusing specifically on particular strategies and their impact on economic performance (Morris, 1988). This is borne out by more recent syntheses (David, 1997; Hussey, 1994). They show that more recent research on strategy and performance (e.g. Rumelt, 1991; Ramanujam and Venkatraman, 1987; Cook and Ferris, 1986; Rhyne, 1986; Allen, 1985) further strengthens the evidence that high-performing organisations tend to be more strategic in both orientation and practice. With the reality of global trading and the rapid multiplication of multinational companies, greater attention is also being placed on the role of corporate bodies in managing their portfolio of businesses for greater profitability. Leading the way in this area are Goold and Campbell (1987, 1994).

A revolutionary new idea on viewing strategy has also taken hold. From merely attempting to find a fit between what an organisation has and what the market offers, there is a new view that defines the organisation in terms of its core competences (Hamel and Pralahad, 1990). It examines the various ways the organisation can take advantage of these competences to make itself competitively strong. This view has come to be known as the resource-based view of the firm (Wernerfelt, 1984; Collis and Montgomery, 1995). As Collis and Montgomery (1997) assert, it 'more broadly and accurately defines the assets that can function as core competences and lays out the conditions under which they can be sources of value in multiple businesses' (p.22).

Within the process school, similar model building and verification is occurring. Research focuses on such key areas as the politics of strategic decision making, the link between structure and the strategy process, the role of informal decision making and managing in strategy implementation and the fit between managerial skills, styles, and responsibilities. Some of the more noteworthy work on these areas includes Fredrickson (1984), Fredrickson and Mitchell (1984), Warner and Arnold (1986), MacMillan (1986), and Miles and Snow (1986).

Further work on the nature of strategy as a process has also been undertaken, notably by Mintzberg and Waters (1985) and Mintzberg (1987). Mintzberg's main thesis is that strategy formation has less to do with formal planning than with the intuitive knowledge and experience of decision makers whom he likens to highly skilled craftsmen who 'craft' rather than deliberately plan strategies (Mintzberg, 1987). Strategy itself is not always deliberate; it can emerge from the various political processes and decisions made within the organisation (Mintzberg and Waters, 1985).

Since the 1990s, both schools have also moved towards a stronger international orientation, which is largely a reflection of recent developments in world trade. As the world's markets continue to be reorganised into regional trading blocs, and as companies increasingly seek entry into national markets around the world, the need for appropriate strategies to deal with competition at this global scale has become a primary focus in the field. This is evident in the work of Porter (1990) on the competitive advantage of nations, and Yip (1995) on global strategy, and as reflected in recent reviews of the strategic management research agenda (Gopinath and Hoffman, 1995; Lyles, 1990). There has also been a geographical broadening of the research base, with attention increasingly drawn to the Asia-Pacific region (e.g. Bartol, *et al*, 1998; Lasserre and Schutte, 1995). The region's dynamic growth in the last three decades has attracted large-scale commercial and academic interest, and as more western organisations venture into the relatively 'unknown world of the Asian', this interest is likely to continue into the next century.

In summary, it can be seen from the literature over the last three decades that there has been a steady maturation of the field, which has considerably expanded our knowledge of the subject, both in breadth and depth, across different businesses, industries, and geographical regions. A sign of this maturity has been the move away from espousing the superiority of one particular school of thought, paradigm or research method over another. Instead, the need for greater integration between intuition and analysis or between formal and informal strategy processes has been identified, and thus a growing adoption and advocacy of more eclectic, interdisciplinary approaches. However, there still remain some conceptual and methodological problems that prevent a broader application of strategy, and the meaning and use of key terminology still remain unresolved. More importantly, empirical evidence to demonstrate the practical application and validity of conceptual models across business, industrial and geographical settings is still wanting (Lasserre and Schutte, 1995; Miller and Cardinal, 1994; Snow and Thomas, 1994; Lyles, 1990).

What then does the future hold? Clearly, the debate will continue as empirical evidence builds up and theory building and refinement is pursued. From the major trends emerging in the literature, which have been summarised in the preceding sections, greater emphasis on the following areas can be expected:

- the content of strategy, specifically, of generic strategies and their applicability to a variety of business, industry, and geographical settings;

- the link between content and process, specifically in relation to behavioural variables (values, motivations, power, etc.) and organisational processes; and
- a more eclectic, interdisciplinary approach to theory building and research.

Of these issues, the study of corporate strategic choices by Asia-Pacific shipowners falls within the first domain, the content of strategy. In the next two chapters, therefore, discussion will focus on the types of strategies needed for competitive survival (chapter four) and the analytical tools that can facilitate strategy selection and evaluation (chapter five).

# 4  The content of strategy

## Introduction

The literature on strategy can usually be organised into two areas, one focusing on the content of strategy and the other focusing on the process. Of these two areas, work on content is far more extensive (Bailey and Johnson, 1995). Much of what is written about the content of strategy, both in terms of conceptual frameworks and empirical evidence, has been drawn from the manufacturing industries, rather than service industries such as shipping. While there continues to be disagreement about the definition of concepts such as 'strategy', there is a remarkable high degree of agreement on everything else. In particular, there is agreement on such key areas as the purpose of strategy, the major strategy types an organisation can pursue to maintain a competitive edge, and the organisational levels at which these strategies should be pursued. This chapter examines these aspects of strategy, and by way of conclusion, pulls together what is currently known about strategy types into a comprehensive typology of strategies. This typology is then used as part of the conceptual framework for examining the Asia-Pacific shipping industry.

## The nature of strategy

It has been stated earlier that the literature on strategic management suffers from semantic problems, the most serious of which is the lack of consistency in the use of fundamental concepts like strategy and business strategy. In some instances, strategy is defined as the means to achieve a goal; in others, the definition is broadened to include both the goal and the means to achieve this goal. When stripped of the surrounding polemics, however, it is easy to see that any differences in definitions lie mainly in scope: some authors bring goals into the definition; others do not. What is never in question is the key attribute of strategy: the *means* of achieving a strategic goal. In this regard, there is clear unanimity in the field. Basic tenets about strategy—for instance, importance to a firm's competitive survival, the components of effective strategy, levels of strategy—receive almost universal acceptance.

*The power of strategy*

Strategy has long been held to be one of the most important areas of management (Howe, 1986). Harvey (1988, p. 9) attributes this to strategic management's ability to give a business and its top management a distinct advantage in 'providing long-term direction, adapting to an increasing rate of change, gaining a competitive advantage in a high-risk environment, and achieving a more effective organisation'. David's (1997) synthesis of the research over the last several decades amply shows a strong link between strategy and performance. Those who use strategic management concepts are more profitable and successful, are more likely to engage in systematic planning, are better at understanding their environment and anticipating future changes, take a more long-term perspective, and empower both managers and employees by involving them in the strategy decision-making processes. Research also shows that 'the process, rather than the decision or document, is the more important contribution of strategic management' (p. 15).

*Elements of an effective strategy*

In their review of strategy research, Hofer and Schendel (1978) identified four key elements of an effective strategy: scope, resource deployments, competitive advantage and synergy. Briefly, these can be defined as follows:

- Scope (or domain) is the range of a firm's present and planned inter-actions with the environment. It includes such factors as product and market segments, geography, technology, distribution channels, etc.
- Resource deployments (distinctive competencies) refer to the availability of certain skills and resources that a firm requires to achieve its goals and objectives (Porter, 1980, 1985).
- Competitive advantage is the relative position of a firm vis-à-vis its competitors, which results from the firm's product positioning, market positioning and/or resource deployments.
- Synergy. This is similar to Ansoff's 2+2=5 concept, which is premised on a holistic view of the firm. Hofer and Schendel (1978, p. 26) define it as 'the degree to which the various resource deployments and interactions of the organisation with its environment reinforce or negate one another'.

These four components are widely regarded as equal contributors to a firm's overall success, although in some cases, one component may assume a greater role than another. Taken together, an organisation's scope, resource deployments, and competitive advantages determine its effectiveness. The prime determinants of its efficiency, however, are the synergies it develops among its various distinctive competencies and product/market entries.

## The levels of strategy

Another area where there is strong agreement is in strategy levels. There are three acknowledged levels—corporate, business and functional—which correspond to the organisational levels of a complex firm: top management, single-business units and functional departments, respectively.

*Corporate strategy* is the domain of top management. It encompasses both the business and functional levels and provides the general parameters within which strategic choices at each level should be made. Corporate strategy is used to define the mix and match of businesses in which a firm should compete, and to ensure a proper alignment between these choices and the requisite resources and organisational structures (Hofer and Schendel, 1978). Corporate strategy typically implies usage within a national market. However, with the rapidly increasing globalisation of markets, its meaning has now been extended to include multinational strategy, or strategy aimed at dealing effectively with competitors on a world-wide basis.

Where corporate strategy involves the whole firm and is primarily concerned with where the firm must compete, *business strategy* focuses on the individual business units that make up the firm and how the firm must compete in each of these businesses. Also known as *competitive strategy*, business strategy is designed to improve the competitive position of a specific business or product in the markets in which the firm competes. Porter (1985), the leading expert in business strategy, explains:

> Competition is at the core of the success or failure of firms. Competition determines the appropriateness of an organisation's activities that can contribute to its performance, such as innovations, a cohesive culture, for good implementation. Competitive strategy is the search for a favourable competitive position in an industry, the fundamental arena in which competition occurs. Competitive strategy aims to establish a profitable and sustainable position against the forces that determine industry competition (p. 1).

At the third and lowest level is the *functional* or *operational strategy*. Its main area of responsibility is determining how the different functions of a firm can contribute to the business and corporate levels.

> The functional level is concerned with managing product, geographic, or functional areas and the actual production and marketing of goods and services. The principal focus of functional strategy is on maximising target objectives as an element of a business strategy, such as becoming the lowest-cost producer of a product. There is a functional strategy for each major segment of the business, including marketing,

manufacturing, finance, human resources, research and development, and indeed for each functional unit that makes up a total business strategy (Harvey, 1988, pp. 14-15).

In more recent years, a fourth level has been identified in the literature. Called *enterprise strategy* or *societal strategy*, its scope is broader than corporate strategy. In brief, the main difference between the two lies in their interaction with their external environment. Corporate strategy focuses on giving the firm a winning edge in market competition; enterprise or societal strategy deals with an organisation's interactions with various sectors of the public with which it conducts its business. A sub-group of enterprise or societal strategy is collective strategy (Quinn *et al*, 1988; Astley and Fombrun, 1983; Pfeffer, 1976), where the aim is to band with other firms to promote a common cause.

Figure 4.1 illustrates the hierarchical relationship of the four strategy levels. Business strategy and corporate strategy have received by far the most attention in the literature, as these are the strategies primarily required to sustain an organisation's competitive edge in the market. By comparison, the conceptual work that has gone into delineating the other strategy levels, functional and societal, is relatively light, as is the empirical evidence available on them.

## Types of strategies

Over the last 30 years, a considerable body of work has accumulated on specific strategies that firms use to remain competitive in the markets in which they operate. Particularly during the initial years, much of the work involved individual research attempts on a specific level, a specific organisation or spread of organisations, and a specific industry. However, no attempt was made to pull this growing body of knowledge together, examine it, and draw a more comprehensive picture of what was known about strategy. Without this synthesis, it was probably inevitable that confusion over terminology arose as a seemingly wide array of strategies entered the strategic management literature.

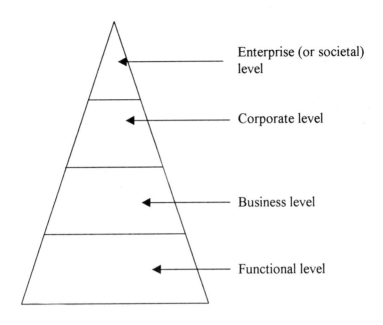

**Figure 4.1 Hierarchy of strategy levels**

Efforts to put more order into the research on strategies commenced in the early 1970s, when typologies of strategies began to appear. Since then, numerous attempts at classifying strategies have continued to appear, leading one critic to call 'the construction of lists' as 'the dominant methodology of strategy'. Although widely used, this approach is erroneous because most of these lists are not subjected to empirical testing to establish their practical application (Kay, 1995, p. 360).

Today the typologies on offer are just as numerous, and at first glance just as confusing. However, careful examination will show that in spite of differences in terminology and scope, all currently available typologies are based on one or a combination of the following classification criteria:

- Product/market/corporate life cycle (e.g. Herbert and Deresky, 1987; Glueck, 1980; Hofer and Schendel, 1978; BCG, 1976; Buzzell, *et al*, 1975; James, 1974)
- Market positioning (e.g. Porter, 1985; Hofer and Schendel, 1978)
- Geographical scope (e.g. Leontiades, 1985; Shanks, 1985; Doz, 1980)

- Organisational structure (e.g. Galbraith and Schendel, 1983; Miles and Snow, 1978; Rumelt, 1974; Wrigley, 1970)
- The organisational level at which the strategy is used (e.g. Melcher and Kezner, 1988; Hofer and Schendel, 1978; Pfeffer, 1976)
- The strategic management process (e.g. Mintzberg, 1988, 1996)
- Management styles (e.g. Mintzberg, 1980).

Of these seven classification criteria, the fifth, organisational level, is used as the main basis for classifying strategies in this book. This criterion has been chosen to provide a clearer link between strategies and organisational structure and because it allows an easy incorporation of the first four classification criteria. The last two classification criteria, strategic management process and management styles, are excluded from consideration because they deal more with the process rather than the content of strategy.

The discussion that follows covers the three main strategy levels: corporate, business and functional. Of these three levels, the study's primary concern is with corporate strategy; to better understand its role and place in an organisation. However, it is necessary also to bring into focus business and functional strategies. The fourth level, enterprise or societal, is not included in the discussion largely because of the paucity of information about it, both conceptually and empirically.

## Corporate-level strategies

Corporate strategies, as defined earlier in this chapter, are the domain of top management. They define the general parameters within which an organisation makes its strategic choices. Originally used to imply usage within national markets, today corporate strategies also encompass multinational or global strategies. Both types of corporate strategy will be discussed in this section. What is currently known about corporate strategies? To answer this question, a comprehensive comparison of corporate strategies identified in the literature was made (Hawkins, 1989), and the results are summarised in Tables 4.1 to 4.3.

*A generic typology of corporate strategies*

Since the early 1970s, a number of typologies have been developed to aid strategy identification and selection. They include James (1974), Hofer and Schendel (1978), Wissema *et al* (1980), Glueck (1980), Galbraith and Schendel (for consumer products, 1983), Galbraith and Schendel (for industrial products, 1983), Buzzell, Gale and Sultan (1983), Day (1984), Allaire and Firsirotu (1985), Smith, Arnold and Buzzell (1985), Howe

(1986), Herbert and Deresky (1987), and Harvey (1988). At first glance, the typologies offer a seemingly wide variety of corporate strategies. However, when the strategies were compared in terms of objectives and general 'plan of attack', a high degree of similarity across typologies surfaced. Although the terminology used in the various typologies varied, there was enough commonality among them to warrant grouping them into five generic types: develop, grow, stabilise, turnaround, and harvest (Herbert and Deresky, 1987).

*Develop/grow strategies* Strategies designed for development and growth are often bracketed together for two reasons: both are characterised by an aggressive push to dominate, and both are preferred by young firms. They differ only in that 'develop' strategies are more applicable to businesses at the very embryonic stage of their life, while 'grow' strategies are more applicable to those that have achieved a foothold in the market and now have the ability to go ahead. Both strategy types are aggressive by nature. The objective is to intimidate the competition and dominate the market. The level of aggressiveness depends on the nature of the industry in which a firm competes: the more competitive and technology-driven an industry is, the more aggressive a firm needs to be. There is strong evidence that companies that pursue develop/grow strategies are strong market leaders, both within and across national boundaries. They are most likely to operate in, or seek entry into, high growth markets and segments within these markets (Gutman, 1964; Chevalier and Catry, 1974). Research indicates that companies that do not compete aggressively in this type of industry will have serious problems staying healthy (Howe, 1986; Glueck, 1980; Henderson, 1979).

*Stabilise strategies* Strategies designed for stabilisation aim to maintain the status quo either by keeping to a tried and tested course of action, changing incrementally in response to environmental changes (Quinn, 1978), or both. Those who pursue this strategy type are typically mature companies whose main objective is to maintain their dominance in the market(s) in which they are competing by penetrating new products and markets in an incremental fashion. Even companies with low market shares use this strategy with a high degree of success. Research shows that those who concentrate on maintaining their niche in a particular market, operate efficiently, and aim for profitability are likely to achieve excellent returns on investments (Hamermesh *et al*, 1983). However, stabilisation strategies are not meant to be long-term alternatives. Citing the work of Thomas (1977), Howe (1986) argues that they are appropriate for limited periods of time only, for instance, when the level of change in the industry is low. Howe points to the 'crop of business failures in recent years [as the result of a] complacent adherence to untenable positions' (p. 61).

*Turnaround strategies* 'Turnaround' strategies are short-term survival measures aimed at reducing or eliminating those activities that inhibit a firm's growth and hurt its performance (Herbert and Deresky, 1987). The objective is simultaneously to cut down costs, increase revenue and reshape the organisational structure into a more suitable form. Companies that pursue this strategy type are usually more mature and in financial trouble, due, for instance, to such external conditions as economic recessions, market decline and innovative breakthroughs by competitors, and/or to internal haemorrhages caused by mismanagement, production inefficiencies and shortage of resources.

*Harvest strategies* Like turnaround strategies, harvest strategies are short-term measures designed to reduce or eliminate poorly performing businesses. These strategies may either be deliberate or emergent (Herbert and Deresky, 1987). They are deliberate if they form part of a long term disinvestment plan; emergent, if they result from either unsuccessful turnaround attempts, unanticipated forces from the environment or new and better opportunities in other businesses. The basic strategy in both cases is the same. Once a firm holds a stable and dominant position in a given market (or fails in its attempt to turn around a business), the next phase is to scale down operations by selectively tapering off unprofitable segments, milk the remaining investment for cashflow and divest at the most opportune time. Kotler (1978) suggests that harvest strategies are likely to succeed if a particular business is in a stable or declining market, does not provide sales stability or prestige to the firm, has a small market share which would be too costly to increase, and does not contribute a large percentage to total sales.

The major features of the five strategy types are summarised in Table 4.1. As the table shows, develop and grow strategies, as well as turnaround and harvest, are so closely related that they are often treated together.

*Specific strategies in support of the five generic types*

Depending on its internal and external environmental conditions, a firm can choose from eleven specific strategies in support of the five generic types (develop, grow, stabilise, turnaround, harvest). The first nine can be regarded as *internal* strategies because they rely solely on a firm's own resources and capabilities, while the last three are *external* because they use resources and capabilities of other firms as well.

**Table 4.1**
**Major features of generic types of corporate strategies**
(Adapted from Harvey, 1988, p. 112)

| Strategy Type | Purpose | Type of Business Environment | Frequency of Usage |
|---|---|---|---|
| Develop/grow | To increase sales/earnings | High market growth, economic prosperity | 54.4% |
| Stabilise | To increase profitability | In a mature industry, stable environment | 9.2% |
| Turnaround/ harvest | Survival, to cut costs, to eliminate losses | In crisis, when facing severe losses | 7.5% |
| Combination of the above | To increase earnings, to cut costs | In economic transition, multi-division companies | 28.7% |

The strategies are briefly defined below, but full treatment is not provided here because they lie outside the scope of the study.

*Internal strategies*

- Concentration: to do one thing only but to do it well
- Integration: to control a number of similar economic processes previously carried out independently
- Diversification: to increase the variety of products/services that a firm offers ( which ... )
- Divestiture: to sell off a business or a major part of it as a going concern
- Liquidation: to sell off a business or a major part of it as a tangible asset due primarily to bankruptcy
- Timing: to introduce a real-time rapid-response system into a business
- Samegame: to imitate industry success factors and use them to create a market niche
- Newgame: to redefine industry success factors and use them to create a market niche.

*External strategies*

- Merger: to combine two or more firms into one
- Acquisition: to purchase the assets of another firm and absorb these assets into the firm's own operations

72

• Joint venture: to join forces with another firm to achieve a common purpose.

Table 4.2 classifies these eleven strategies according to the generic types for which they are most suited.

**Table 4.2**
**Matching specific strategies with generic strategy types**

| Specific Strategy | Generic Strategy Type | | | |
|---|---|---|---|---|
| | Develop/ Grow | Stabilise | Turn-around | Harvest |
| *Internal* | | | | |
| Concentration | ● | | | |
| Diversification | ● | ● | ● | ● |
| Divestiture | ● | | ● | ● |
| Integration | ● | ● | | |
| Liquidation | ● | | ● | ● |
| Newgame | ● | | ● | |
| Samegame | ● | ● | | |
| Timing | ● | ● | | ● |
| *External* | | | | |
| Merger | ● | | ● | |
| Acquisition | ● | | | |
| Joint venture | ● | ● | | |

*A generic typology of multinational corporate strategies*

As discussed earlier in this chapter, multinational strategy is part of corporate strategy, but differs from other corporate strategies in its geographical scope. It requires separate treatment because of the complexities associated with operating across national boundaries and markets. Very little has been written about specific types of multinational strategies. Major contributors include

Porter (1986), Leontiades (1985), Shanks (1985), and Doz (1980), all of whom have developed typologies to classify multinational strategies. In spite of their differences in terminology, a comparative analysis of the four typologies conducted as part of this study has revealed enough commonalities to warrant their classification into five basic types: global cost leader, global niche, protected national market, national niche, and follower. Table 4.3 compares the four typologies according to these five types.

## Table 4.3
## Comparison of global strategies

| Generic Multinational Strategy | Porter 1986 | Leontiades 1985 | Shanks 1985 | Doz 1980 |
|---|---|---|---|---|
| Global cost leader | Global cost | Global high share | Global leader | Worldwide integration |
| Global niche | Global segment | Global niche | | |
| Protected national market | Protected market | National high share | Domestic defender | National responsiveness |
| National niche | National responsiveness | National niche | | |
| Intelligent follower | | | Follower | Administrative co-ordination |

### Global cost leader

Firms that pursue a strategy sell a standard product or service to many different mass markets. The product or service may not be at the cutting edge of technology, but it is at least at the forefront. With high market shares and economies of scale, firms of this type are able to keep their costs down, effectively undercutting competitors. This also enables them to maintain a high level of research and development at relatively low costs. Operations are co-ordinated across a range of national boundaries in order to secure a major share of the global market. Companies pursuing this strategy require a huge amount of resources to support their activities. This is why most companies that use this strategy are the giants of the industry, e.g. Toyota, IBM, Shell and General Motors. In addition, they prefer to act alone.

### Global niche

Firms pursuing this strategy seek to avoid direct competition with global cost leaders by focusing on a particular market segment. Their specialist area may be technology, unique products, special geographical characteristics, or some stage of the production cycle (finished or semi-processed products). The scale of operations, as the strategy name implies, is world-wide, which gives a firm the opportunity to increase in size within its specialist area. There are also opportunities to achieve a certain amount of cost advantages through joint ventures with other firms. Fewer resources are required for this type of strategy, which is why it is often the first strategy used by national competitors seeking entry into the global market.

## Protected national market

Firms using this strategy seek out countries in which market positions are protected by host governments. Many firms that do not have the resources or the skills required to go global, or that seek a tax shelter to offset the profits of other business units, often find this strategy attractive. Typically, firms seek a competitive advantage in the national market by taking full advantage of government measures designed to protect this market. They include national entry barriers (high tariffs, stringent import quotas, high entry costs); national government support or preference (subsidies, local purchasing requirements, excessive regulations); and local economic advantages (greater knowledge of national conditions and customer needs, closer and shorter communication with the customer, national preference for dealing with local partners, flexibility to tailor operations more to customer needs and only one set of national conditions). However, this is a high-risk strategy for firms. Stronger global competitors may enter the market and edge them out, or government protection may be discontinued.

## National niche

Firms using this strategy specialise on a particular product or service within any number of national markets. These firms capitalise on local or national differences. Provided there is sufficient size involved and a cost advantage to be attained, they will seek out national customers with special or unusual needs (e.g. a chemical production business, which requires special products at short notice in various amounts and where the product to be supplied cannot be stored). As with the protected national market strategy, this strategy is appropriate for firms who do not have the resources or skills to compete globally. It is sustainable only to the extent that local or national differences remain strong and the firm is able to offer lower prices than its competitors, both national and global. National niche and protected national market strategies can be pursued simultaneously whenever governments provide protection to a market segment that is highly specialised and has unusual market needs.

Firms that pursue this type of strategy have one common characteristic: they follow tried and tested formulas, preferring the security of established products or services to high-risk entrepreneurial ventures. They are classic 'middle-of-the-road', taking advantage of opportunities as they come, and always making sure a high level of profitability is maintained. Table 4.4 summarises the main features of these five generic types of multinational corporate strategies.

## Business-level strategies

Of all strategy levels, business strategies have been the most discussed and examined in the literature. It has been noted earlier in the chapter that business strategy focuses on how to compete in one particular business. In a diversified company, business strategies are based on higher-level corporate strategies. In a firm involved in a single business, however, business strategies assume the role of corporate strategies. To a great extent, this dual interpretation of 'business strategy' has contributed significantly to the enduring confusion over terminology within the strategic management field. Any analysis of empirical data on business strategies, therefore, must carefully establish whether 'business' is used in the first sense, or whether it is used at the same level as 'corporate'.

The acknowledged leader in the field of business strategy is Porter (1985). Much of what is written on the subject draws upon Porter's extensive work and builds on his conceptual frameworks. Porter (1985) argues that a firm can gain a competitive advantage either through low cost or differentiation. When these are combined with a firm's scope of activities, three types of business strategies can be pursued: cost leadership, differentiation and focus. These strategy types are presented in Table 4.5. They will be discussed in more detail in the following chapter, when analytical models for strategy selection and analysis are examined.

**Table 4.4**
**Five generic types of multinational corporate strategies**

| Generic Multinational Strategy | Key Features |
|---|---|
| Global cost leader | • Sell a well-known product or service to different mass markets<br>• Pursued by firms with high market shares and economies of scale (i.e. industry giants)<br>• Requires substantial resources |
| Global niche | • Focus on a particular specialism and market segment, and avoid competing with global cost leaders<br>• Pursued by national competitors seeking entry into the global market<br>• Requires fewer resources than global cost leader, and cost advantages are possible through joint ventures |
| Protected national market | • Seek entry into countries which offer protection to national markets, and take advantage of protective measures to gain a competitive edge<br>• Pursued by firms with neither the resources nor the expertise to establish global operations, or seek tax shelters to offset profits<br>• High risks involved |
| National niche | • Similar to protected national market except here the strategy is to specialise on a particular and unusual product or service within a number of national markets<br>• Pursued by firms with neither the resources nor the expertise to establish global operations |
| Intelligent follower | • Stick to established products or services which provide a high level of profitability |

There are other typologies of business strategies, but though names may vary, the underlying concepts differ little from those of Porter. A comparison of Porter's typology (1980, 1985) with another well known typology, for instance, which has been developed by the Strategic Planning Associates (1981), shows that both typologies are based on the fundamental premise of competitive advantage. Each pair of strategy types (i.e. cost leadership versus commodity, differentiation versus specialty, cost focus versus hybrid, cost differentiation versus transitional) are highly similar in approach and orientation. They differ only in the wording of their variables, which could be attributed to the authors' individual orientations. Porter's approach is more oriented towards economics; the Strategic Planning Associates towards marketing.

### Table 4.5
### Porter's typology of business strategies

| Business Strategy | Objective |
| --- | --- |
| Cost leadership | To gain a cost advantage by providing a highly standardised product or service and under-pricing the competition |
| Differentiation | To seek a position that enhances the special qualities of a product or service that is widely valued by customers and that will allow the firm to charge higher than average prices |
| Focus | To concentrate on achieving a cost advantage (cost focus) or providing a specialised product/service (differentiation focus) within a narrow segment of the market |

### Functional-level strategies

Strategies at the functional level are the domain of the specific operational units within a business. They specify the means by which the different functional areas of the business must contribute to the business and corporate levels of strategy. According to Pearce and Robinson (1988), three characteristics differentiate functional strategies from business and corporate strategies: time horizons, specificity and participants.

*Time horizons* Functional strategies are designed to identify and co-ordinate short-term action programs, usually for no longer than one year. These short time horizons force functional managers to be more proactive and vigilant. They are expected to act on what currently needs to be done to implement higher level strategies, constantly scan the environment for opportunities and threats, and be ready to make the appropriate adjustments when necessary.

*Specificity* Functional strategies must be specific, ready to be put into operation by lower-level managers. They should therefore come in the form of detailed project plans or outlines, specifying all key aspects of strategy implementation (resources, control, time, etc.).

*Participants* The responsibility for the development of functional strategies is typically delegated by the business-level manager to the principle subordinates responsible for the operating areas of the business (e.g. marketing, production, finance). Furthermore, it is up to the business-level manager to ensure such functional strategies meet the requirements of the business-level strategy. The active involvement by operating managers helps in the implementation of the functional strategy because they end up gaining a thorough knowledge of exactly what needs to be achieved. It also tends to increase their commitment to the business.

Efforts to classify functional strategies into typologies are far less substantial that those devoted to corporate and business strategies. Of the few attempts made over the last three decades, the most well known include Melcher and Kerzner (1988), Pearce and Robinson (1988) and Argenti (1974). Table 4.6 compares the work of these three sets of authors on functional strategies. The number of functional strategies depends largely on the organisational design of the business. The basic rule is that each operating department (production, finance, personnel etc) in a single business unit must have its own set of functional strategies, and that these strategies should be based on, and support, the business strategies of the organisation.

Overall, the literature on strategy does not devote as much attention to functional strategies as it does to strategies at the higher levels. This is understandable, as the literature on strategy focuses primarily on those areas within the domain of top management, and functional strategies do not fit this category. In essence, corporate and business strategies are considered the domain of the generals and strategists; functional strategies, that of the soldiers on the battlefield.

## Table 4.6
### Three views of functional strategies

| Argenti 1974 | Pearce and Robinson 1988 | Melcher and Kerzner 1988 |
|---|---|---|
| Market | Marketing | Marketing |
| Financial | Finance/accounting | Finance |
| Product | | |
| Supplies | Production/operations | Manufacturing |
| Facilities | | |
| Research | Research and development | Research and development |
| Organisational | Personnel | |

## A comprehensive typology of strategies

The relationships between the various types and levels of strategies examined in this chapter can be more clearly understood if synthesised into a comprehensive typology of strategies. This typology is presented in Table 4.7. This typology of strategies will be used as part of the shipping strategy conceptual framework, which will be discussed in chapter six.

**Table 4.7**
**A comprehensive typology of strategies**

| Strategy Level | Generic Strategy Type | Specific Strategy | | | |
|---|---|---|---|---|---|
| | | Primary | | Secondary | |
| | | Internal | External | Internal | External |
| Corporate (General) | Grow Develop Stabilise Turnaround Harvest | A common pool of specific strategies can be used to support generic strategy types at the corporate or business levels. This pool is also the source of functional strategies. Among the more well known specific strategies are: | | | |
| Corporate (Multi-national) | Global cost leader Global niche Protected national market National niche Intelligent follower | *Internal:* Concentration Diversification Divestiture Integration Liquidation Newgame Samegame Timing | *External:* Merger Acquisition Joint venture | | |
| Business | Cost leadership Differentiation Cost focus Differentiation focus | Strategies are internal when they require a company's own resources; external when they require external resources. | | | |
| Functional | | If they are first choice, they are called primary; if they are alternative choices, they are called secondary (or ancillary or contingency). | | | |

# 5   Strategy selection models

Corporate strategy, as discussed in the previous chapter, is primarily concerned with deciding which businesses a firm should be in and what the firm must do to ensure these businesses contribute to its overall profitability. Decision making on strategic issues as identified by Bowman and Asch (1996)—mix of businesses and industries, deployment of resources, organisational structure, long-term goals and strategies for growth— obviously has to be done within an integrating framework. Otherwise the relationships between and among businesses, and their implications to the firm's overall profitability and competitiveness, cannot be adequately assessed. Fortunately, a wide range of alternative frameworks to facilitate strategy selection and analysis is available. While they may vary in focus and scope, as well as in conceptual and methodological rigour, these frameworks or models provide firms with the tools to evaluate strategic decisions at the corporate level. They are what Porter calls 'consistency checks' (1980, p.388) that firms can use to assess their market positions and on this basis select appropriate strategies to maintain a strong competitive presence in the marketplace. The literature offers a wide range of models for strategy selection and analysis, but only the most widely used models have been included in this book.

## Approaches to strategy selection and analysis

Out of an array of possible choices, how can the manager know which strategy, or set of strategies, will promote the firm's continuing competitiveness and profitability?

Traditionally, the answer has been to use a technique that is popularly known as *portfolio analysis*. This refers to the evaluation of the various businesses that a firm has in its portfolio to determine how well they contribute to the firm's overall goals and objectives and what the firm must do to maintain a competitive edge in the markets where it operates. Portfolio analysis typically involves the use of a portfolio model, usually presented in matrix form, where the relative positions of businesses in a firm's portfolio are plotted in terms of profitability and market share.

While it is widely acknowledged that the various models used for portfolio analysis are equally applicable to corporate and business strategies, portfolio analysis is predominantly associated with firms with multiple businesses (i.e. diversified companies). This is how it was introduced in the 1960s by the Boston Consulting Group (BCG), the authors of the portfolio concept, and how it has been subsequently embraced by the management field. However, there is now a growing trend away from the use of the term 'portfolio models' in favour of more encompassing terminology such as 'strategy selection models' or some similar derivation, as this does away with the arbitrary demarcation line drawn between corporate and business strategy selection. Behind this shift in thinking is the argument that, if portfolio models are equally applicable to multiple-business firms and single-business or less diversified firms, then the terminology should be changed to reflect this broader use of the models. The shift also moves the field away from the continuing debate surrounding the usefulness of portfolio analysis and its different models, and pushes the field on to the next level of theory building and testing.

Of the many models available for corporate and business strategy selection, there are about eleven which are the most widely used in the field. These models can be broadly categorised into three groups:

*Group 1: Early models*
- BCG business portfolio model
- GE's business screen

*Group 2: Derivations of Group 1 models*
- Royal Dutch Shell's directional policy matrix
- Thompson-Strickland matrix
- Arthur D. Little life cycle model
- Porter's product/market life cycle model
- Hofer and Schendel's product/market life cycle
- Porter's model of generic competitive strategies

*Group 3: More holistic approaches*
- SWOT analysis matrix
- Grand strategy selection matrix
- International competitiveness matrix.

The groupings are based mainly on chronology to signify the changing shifts in strategic management thought. The earliest and most well known model is the BCG matrix, developed by the Boston Consulting Group to help their clients manage their business portfolios. After this initial attempt came other models, each designed to address some identified weakness in the BCG model and each following essentially the same matrix format. As the three groupings suggest, over the years there has been steady progression in model building, from the more simple models of BCG and GE to broader, more holistic approaches like the SWOT, grand strategy selection, and international competitiveness matrices. All models are still current, with the BCG model still leading the way.

## BCG business portfolio model

The BCG model, considered the progenitor of strategic planning matrices, uses two variables, market share and market growth, as bases for classifying single business units. For this reason, it is also widely known as the growth/ market share matrix. The BCG model measures market share and market growth in terms of what might be called the experience curve principle. This states that 'each time the accumulated production of a product is doubled, unit costs in real terms shall decline by a percentage, characteristically in the vicinity of 20 to 30 per cent' (Smith, 1985, p. 89; see also Day, 1986; Hax and Majluf, 1983a; Hedley, 1977).

Based on this principle, we can say that if a firm doubles its market share as it becomes more experienced with its product or market, it is likely to enjoy a 20 to 30 per cent cost advantage over its competitor. Simply, this means more cash for the firm, and the more experienced it becomes, the more cash it can generate. However, since the firm's market share is dependent on how fast the market grows, then the faster the market grows, the more cash the firm will need in order to compete. The relationship between market share and market growth is illustrated in Figure 5.1. On the horizontal axis is the market share of each business relative to the industry leader; on the vertical axis is the annual market growth rate for each business' particular industry. Within the cells are four types of businesses: Stars, Cash Cows, Question Marks (also known as Problem Children and Wild Cats) and Dogs.

*Stars* are business units that are characterised by high market growth and high market share. They usually generate considerable cashflow but also absorb it in the form of investment to maintain market share. Stars usually show positive profits whether the cashflow is positive or not. A star eventually evolves into a cash cow when growth and reinvestment requirements slow down.

*Cash cows* are business units that are characterised by a high market share and low market growth. They frequently generate a large amount of cash, but not all of this is ploughed back to them. They get back only what they need to maintain their position, and any excess cash goes to other businesses.

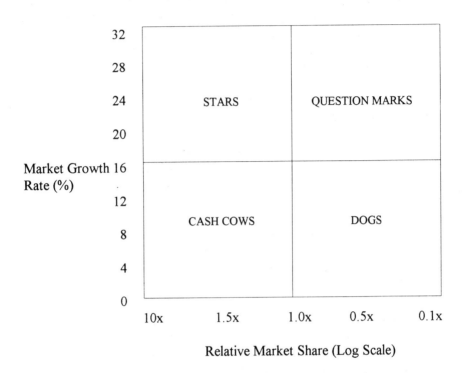

**Figure 5.1 The BCG market growth/share matrix**
Source: Naylor (1982, p. 7)

*Question marks* are business units that are characterised by high market growth and low market share. They are typically at the very earliest stage of their life cycles. Question marks generate very little cash but they require considerable investment in order to survive. As their name suggests, their future is questionable: if all works well, they turn into Stars; if not, they become Dogs.

*Dogs* are business units that are characterised by low market share and low growth. They are often cash traps: although they may be able to show positive profits, the profit must consistently be reinvested to maintain market share.

Viewing business units from this perspective certainly helps a firm maintain a balanced business portfolio. The basic strategy is simple: The first goal is to maintain the Cash Cows without investing too much in them. The cash generated by the Cows should be used to consolidate the position of the Stars, and any surplus could be devoted to developing *some* of the Question Marks. The Dogs must be recognised as the weak link for the company and handled ruthlessly; they should be managed for cash, with minimal or no investment (Smith, 1985). Figure 5.2 presents the corporate strategy types appropriate for each business category.

Since its introduction, the BCG model has come under criticism. It has been described as too simplistic, with no allowance made for businesses that fall right in the middle of the matrix. It reflects no temporal qualities so that, although it is based on long-term relationships, it is mistakenly used as a short-term adjustment technique. Market share, which is used in the model to measure the competitiveness of a business, is not necessarily directly correlated to profitability or business strength. Finally, it does not address the issue of new business development, especially in determining growth rates (Harvey, 1988; Smith, 1985; Smith *et al*, 1985; Porter, 1980; Hofer and Schendel, 1978; Rumelt, 1974).

In spite of these criticisms, the BCG model continues to be widely used today. Although empirical support for the model is sparse (Hambrick *et al*, 1982, cited in Harvey, 1988), to many in the management field, the enduring power and popularity of the BCG model is proof enough of the robustness of its precepts. Unlike other models that have come and gone after it, without leaving too much of an impact on the field, the BCG model continues to serve as a popular tool in strategy selection and analysis.

There have been a number of elaborations made on the BCG matrix since the Boston Consulting Group in the mid-1960s first articulated it. Michael Gould of the BCG has offered a revised matrix in which market share is replaced by competitive position as a measure of market leadership and products are regrouped in terms of the manufacturing process so as to reflect economies of scale in manufacturing (Smith, 1985). Others have substituted market share for an investment threshold cut-off rate, which should indicate to management when to withhold investment because present cash generation is more valuable than the future equivalent (MacMillan, 1986). Companies like Arthur D. Little and Mckinsey and Company also offer planning models that are highly similar to BCG models (Naylor, 1982).

The rest of the models discussed in this chapter are all derivations of the BCG model. The main difference between these latter models and the BCG matrix is the move away from single measures of business strength (market share) and market conditions (market growth). Market share is broadened in these latter models to include a wide array of factors affecting a firm's business strength (or competitive position, as it is more commonly called in the literature), and market growth is replaced by the product/market life cycle as a measure of industry maturity or attractiveness.

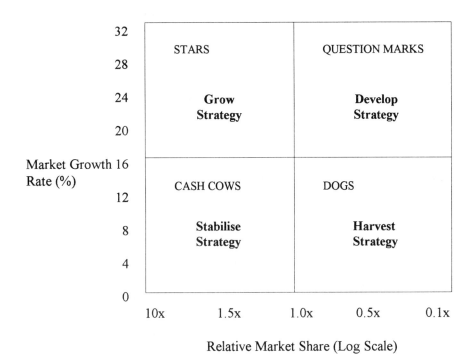

Figure 5.2  Generic strategies for the BCG model


**General Electric's business screen**

One popular elaboration of the BCG matrix is the General Electric business screen. Also called the GE planning grid or the Industry Attractiveness-Business Strength Matrix; the GE model is broader in approach and more qualitative in nature. Instead of relying on market share alone, it uses a wide range of factors (size, growth, share, position, profitability, margins, technological position, strengths and weaknesses, image, pollution, people) as criteria for assessing a firm's position in the market. Its criteria for assessing industry attractiveness are similarly wide-ranging, including size, market growth, pricing, market diversity, competitive structure, industry profitability, and an array of technical, social, environmental, legal, and human issues (Porter, 1980).

The general approach to assessment is relatively straightforward. First, relevant factors are selected, then a weight is assigned to each factor to signify its relative importance. Using a rating scale, future conditions for each factor are forecast. The weight and rating assigned to each factor are then multiplied to produce a total score for that factor. While the combinations of factors on both scales do have a weighted multivariate approach, there are no definitive weights per se. Ultimately, choices are made on the basis of judgement and consensus. Hax and Majluf (1983b), Rothschild (1976, 1979) and Businessweek (1975) provide methodological frameworks for the use of the GE grid.

On the GE grid, the outcome of the assessment is portrayed in the form of circles. Each circle represents the size of the industry in which a firm competes; thus, the bigger the circle, the bigger the industry. The pie slices within each circle reflects the firm's market share within the industry; thus, the bigger the slice, the bigger the share. The complete grid is presented in Figure 5.3, together with the generic strategies appropriate for each cell in the matrix. The other names by which each generic strategy is known are also presented (Porter, 1980; Hofer and Davoust, 1977).

Business Strength

|  |  | Strong | Average | Weak |
|---|---|---|---|---|
| Industry Attractiveness | High | Grow (invest, build) | Grow (invest, build) | Stabilise (improve, defend, hold) |
|  | Medium | Grow (invest, build) | Stabilise (improve, defend, hold) | Harvest (divest) |
|  | Low | Stabilise (improve, defend, hold) | Harvest (divest) | Harvest (divest) |

**Figure 5.3  The GE business screen**
Source: Adapted from Pearce and Robinson, 1988, p.287

As Figure 5.3 shows, when both industry attractiveness and business strength are high, a firm should pursue a *grow* strategy, but when attractiveness and business strength are both low, the firm should *harvest* or *divest*. In intermediate positions, the firm would need to be selective in the way it allocates resources, giving priority to most attractive segments or in segments where the firm has a unique competence. The strategy is to *stabilise*, either by improving the business, or defending its market position and maintaining the status quo.

Like the BCG matrix, the GE planning grid has received its fair share of criticism. Mainly, it is criticised for its failure adequately to represent new businesses in industries that are at an embryonic stage of evolution, a weakness it shares with the BCG model (Hofer, 1977). Hax and Majluf (1983b) also criticise the pseudo-scientific nature of the model's weighted-score approach, which assigns quantitative values to highly judgmental assessments. They offer no alternative approach, however, as they also admit that 'when dealing with multi-attributes, a weighting process is unavoidable, whether done explicitly or implicitly' (Hax and Majluf, in Dyson, 1993, p. 91).

**Directional policy matrix**

Like the GE grid, the directional policy matrix, which was developed by Royal Dutch Shell specifically for the petroleum-based sector of the chemical industry, uses a weighted multivariate approach to determine a business' position in the market. It is designed to assist in the selection of appropriate criteria for defining and assessing the two dimensions of the matrix, business sector prospects and a company's competitive capabilities. The same analytical procedures as those applied to the GE grid are used. In addition, competitors' ratings can be represented alongside those of the firm. The directional policy matrix is illustrated in Figure 5.4, along with appropriate strategy options for each cell in the matrix. The corresponding generic corporate strategies are also identified.

There are eight likely strategies a firm can choose from depending on the position of a business on the matrix: disinvest, phased withdrawal, custodial, cash generation, double or quit, try harder, growth, and leader.

In low-growth areas, where the firm is not likely to make substantial earnings, the strategy is to *disinvest* right away or *withdraw* gradually. The difference between these two strategies is mainly one of time; like the generic harvest strategy, the ultimate objective is to cut losses and redeploy resources into more profitable areas. However, if the firm has strong competitive capabilities in such areas, so that the business is able to generate respectable profits for the firm, then the business should be nurtured with commensurate resources to enable it to continue being a cash generator. A similar approach should also be pursued in fairly stable areas where the firm has average to weak competitive capabilities. Here the firm should take on a custodial role to ensure the business remains in stable condition and to shift to other strategies should conditions change.

Business Sector Prospects

| | | Unattractive | Average | Attractive |
|---|---|---|---|---|
| | Weak | Disinvest (harvest) | Phased withdrawal (turnaround, harvest) | Double or quit (develop/grow) |
| Company Competitive Capabilities | Average | Phased withdrawal (turnaround, harvest) | Custodial (stabilise)  Growth | Try harder (develop/grow) |
| | Strong | Cash generation (stabilise) | Growth (develop/grow)  Leader (stabilise) | Leader (stabilise) |

**Figure 5.4 Directional policy matrix**
Source: Adapted from Harvey (1988, p. 158)

Where business prospects are average to attractive, the firm has several choices depending on its competitive strength. In highly profitable areas where the firm is a weak competitor, there are two choices available. If it wants to stay it should significantly improve its competitive capabilities; otherwise, it should quit the sector altogether. In fairly stable areas where the firm's competitiveness is average to strong, the strategy is to grow through commensurate allocation of resources. The same is true in highly profitable areas where the firm is not as strong as its competitors; it can try harder by allocating the necessary resources to gain competitive equality. Finally in highly profitable areas where the firm is the undisputed leader, the strategy is to give businesses in these areas top priority to ensure they maintain market leadership.

## The Thompson-Strickland matrix

Another derivation of the BCG matrix is provided by Thompson and Strickland (1983). Their matrix retains market growth as a dimension of analysis, but like other post-BCG models, it uses the broader concept of competitive position in place of market share. The Thompson-Strickland matrix is presented in Figure 5.5. Using this matrix, businesses can be positioned in any one of four quadrants, and strategies appropriate for each quadrant identified.

*Quadrant I* Businesses with a dominant market position. They should pursue strategies for growth or maintenance to ensure they remain in this position.

*Quadrant II* Businesses with an uncertain outlook. There is scope for growth, as in the case of new businesses, but there is also a lot of risk involved. The appropriate strategy should be to focus on gaining a stronger competitive position while continuing to achieve rapid market growth. However, for businesses which are unable to achieve this, divestiture and liquidation are the appropriate strategies.

*Quadrant III* The worst position in the matrix. Typically, businesses within a stagnant industry are found here. The strategy is to tightly manage the business for profitability and when appropriate, to divest and liquidate.

*Quadrant IV* Businesses with a promising future. They have slow market growth but strong cash flow. The most appropriate strategy is for a firm to pursue a hold/maintain strategy for existing businesses and free up some of its cashflow for new ventures.

## Life cycle models

Other authors attempting to overcome the shortcomings of the BCG and GE matrices have not only replaced market share with competitive position, they have also replaced market growth with the product/market life cycle concept. The most well known include the consulting firm Arthur D. Little (Harvey, 1988), Porter (1985), and Hofer and Schendel (1978).

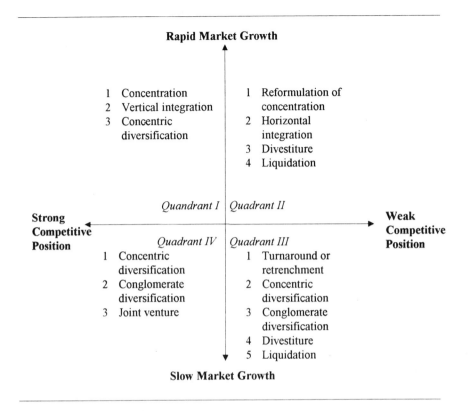

**Rapid Market Growth**

| *Quadrant I* | *Quadrant II* |
|---|---|
| 1 Concentration<br>2 Vertical integration<br>3 Concentric diversification | 1 Reformulation of concentration<br>2 Horizontal integration<br>3 Divestiture<br>4 Liquidation |

**Strong Competitive Position** ← → **Weak Competitive Position**

| *Quadrant IV* | *Quadrant III* |
|---|---|
| 1 Concentric diversification<br>2 Conglomerate diversification<br>3 Joint venture | 1 Turnaround or retrenchment<br>2 Concentric diversification<br>3 Conglomerate diversification<br>4 Divestiture<br>5 Liquidation |

**Slow Market Growth**

**Figure 5.5 Thompson-Strickland matrix**
Source: Adapted from Thompson and Strickland (1983, p. 154)

Arthur D. Little developed a nine-cell matrix to analyse the relationships between a business' competitive position and the stage of the industry life cycle at which it is found. According to this model, a business' competitive position is assessed in terms of a five-point rating scale (dominant, strong, favourable, tenable and weak) while its attractiveness to the industry is assessed in terms of its position in the product/market life cycle (embryonic, growing, mature, ageing). Using this matrix, the typical strategy is to maintain a balanced mix of businesses, avoiding such pitfalls as having too many embryonic or ageing businesses. Although businesses in their embryonic stages may have a bright future outlook, they can give the firm cash flow problems in the short term; those in the ageing sector may offer short term profits but they may in fact have a very poor future outlook. The Arthur D. Little model is presented in a slightly adapted form in Figure 5.6, together with some specific strategies that are appropriate for each cell in the matrix.

91

|  |  | Embryonic | Growing | Mature | Ageing |
|---|---|---|---|---|---|
| Competitive Position | Dominant | Invest | CONSOLIDATE | | Hold |
|  | Strong |  | Improve | MAINTAIN | |
|  | Favourable | Selective |  |  | Harvest |
|  | Tenable |  |  | Niche | |
|  |  |  |  | LIQUIDATE | |
|  | Weak |  |  |  | Divest |

**Figure 5.6  Arthur D. Little's life cycle model (slightly adapted by authors)**
Source: Harvey (1988, p. 160)

Porter (1985) provides an alternative perspective. In contrast to the Arthur D. Little model, Porter limits the product/market life cycle to three stages (growth, maturity, decline) and classifies a business either as leader or follower. His model also focuses more on a single business rather than on a complex firm. It is illustrated in Figure 5.7 and shows the range of strategies that are applicable for each cell in the matrix.

# Product/Market Life Cycle

| | | Growth | Maturity | Decline |
|---|---|---|---|---|
| **Strategic Position of the Organis- ation** | Leader | Keeping ahead of the field | Cost leadership<br><br>Raise barriers<br><br>Deter competitors | Redefine scope<br><br>Divest peripherals<br><br>Encourage departures |
| | Follower | Imitation at lower cost<br><br>Joint ventures | Differentiation<br><br>Focus | Differentiation<br><br>New opportunities |

**Figure 5.7  Porter's life cycle model**
Source: Johnson and Scholes (1988, p. 182)

A third life cycle model is provided by Hofer and Schendel (1978). Like Arthur D. Little and Porter, they also use product/market life cycle and competitive position in their matrix, but the life cycle is assumed to have five stages (development, shake-out, growth, maturity, decline) and competitive position is assessed on a four-point rating scale (strong, average, weak, drop-out). Like Porter's life cycle model, the focus is on a single business. In both cases, however, the models can be applied equally well to multiple-business firms. Conceptually, all three life cycle models vary little; hence, there should be no problem in using any of them as alternative models for corporate strategy selection and analysis.

The Hofer and Schendel model is presented in Figure 5.8, together with suitable strategies for each cell in the matrix. Of the five stages of market evolution, changes in competitive position can occur most easily during the development, shakeout and decline stages.

| Stage of Market Evolution | Relative Competitive Position | | | |
|---|---|---|---|---|
| | Strong | Average | Weak | Drop-out |
| Development | Share increase | | | Turnaround |
| Shakeout | Share increase | | | |
| Growth | Growth | | | Liquidation |
| Maturation | Profit | | Market Concentration | Divestiture |
| Decline | Asset reduction | | | |

**Figure 5.8 Hofer and Schendel's life cycle model**
Source: Adapted from Hofer and Schendel (1978, p. 104)


**Porter's model of generic competitive strategies**

Other models for strategic analysis offer slightly different variations. Porter, for instance, uses a two-dimensional grid to determine a firm's competitive advantage and its competitive scope. The grid is shown in Figure 5.9, together with the appropriate strategies for each quadrant. According to Porter, a firm must decide whether to aim for a broad or narrow target (competitive scope) and what it wants to be (competitive advantage); trying to be everything is simply a recipe for failure (what he calls 'being stuck in the middle'). He identifies three appropriate generic strategies: cost leadership, differentiation, and focus. These strategies were introduced in chapter four. According to this matrix, a firm has four options:

- To produce a highly standardised product or service and under-price the competition, that is, to be a *cost leader*.
- To specialise on a particular product or service that is considered unique throughout the market and, thus, be able to charge higher than average prices (*differentiation*).
- To concentrate on a particular product or service or a particular segment of the market, and be known for:

- providing a better product or service than others, and, as in the second option, be able to charge higher than average prices (*differentiation focus*), and/or
- servicing this target at lower costs than most (*cost focus*).


**Competitive Advantage**

| | Lower Cost | Differentiation |
|---|---|---|
| **Broad target** | Cost leadership | Differentiation |
| **Narrow target** | Cost focus | Differentiation focus |

**Competitive Scope**

**Figure 5.9 Porter's generic competitive strategies model**
Source: Porter (1980, 1985, p. 12)


Porter's model is one of the most popular in the field today. It has undergone a series of testing (Miller and Dess, 1993; Wright, 1987; Miller and Friesen, 1986; Galbraith and Schendel, 1983; Dess and Davis, 1982), and as would be expected in a healthy research environment, this has revealed a number of weaknesses. The model's reliance on qualitative analysis has attracted the inevitable complaint that it lacks quantitative rigour (see, for instance, Asseldonk, 1988). However, the more serious criticism comes from Quinn (1988) and Grimm *et al* (1988) whose research disputes Porter's assertion that companies 'stuck in the middle' have inferior strategies. Grimm and his associates argue in particular that firm size plays an important role in determining the appropriate strategy: for example, they found out that larger companies did quite well when stuck in the middle while smaller firms did not.

**Swot analysis matrix**

This section marks the first of the third and last group of strategy selection models covered in this chapter. In contrast to the preceding models, the models in this last group are more holistic in their approach to strategy selection and analysis.

SWOT is an acronym for Strengths, Weaknesses, Opportunities and Threats. Strengths and weaknesses refer to the internal environment of a business, and opportunities and threats, to its external environment. In this regard, therefore, the SWOT matrix can be used as a comprehensive tool for strategic environmental analysis. The main value of the SWOT framework is its emphasis on a holistic approach to environmental analysis. Its four cornerstone concepts—internal strengths and weaknesses, external opportunities and threats—are broad enough to encompass a full range of environmental factors (organisational, economic, psychological, social, technological, political, etc). Yet, they are also flexible enough to be tailored according to company specifications. A company interested only in economic variables, for instance, can tailor its SWOT analysis along this particular line.

Because a SWOT analysis is aimed at maximising a business' internal strengths and opportunities and at the same time minimising its weaknesses and threats, it is a particularly useful tool in strategy selection. Figure 5.10 is an example of a SWOT analysis matrix where appropriate strategies are selected for each cell in the matrix. As this figure indicates, it is possible for a business to find itself in any of four quadrants.

*Quadrant I* This is clearly the most favourable position for a business to be in, and strategies should be directed at increasing and maintaining this dominant position.

*Quadrant II* Businesses in this quadrant have an uncertain future. While there are many opportunities for growth, internal weaknesses prevent them from taking advantage of these opportunities. Their main goal should be to select those strategies that can turn them around, that is, that can increase their internal strengths and help them compete more effectively in the market.

*Quadrant III* Businesses in this quadrant are typically good performers but they also face serious external threats. They should seek strategies capable of building long-term opportunities in other environments where they can use their internal strengths to the fullest.

*Quadrant IV* This is the worst position for a business to be in. The appropriate strategy is to manage the business for cashflow or profitability and when appropriate to divest.

|  | | **Internal (Organisational)** | |
|  | | Strengths | Weaknesses |
| External (Environ-mental) | Opport-unities | I Aggressive strategy | II Turnaround strategy |
|  | Threats | III Diversification strategy | IV Defensive strategy |

**Figure 5.10 Sample SWOT analysis matrix**
Source: Pearce and Robinson (1988, p. 294)

**Grand strategy selection matrix**

The Grand Strategy Selection Matrix is an alternative to the SWOT matrix. Unlike the latter, which focuses on internal and external environmental factors, the Grand Strategy Selection Matrix is more specific. It targets two key variables in the strategy selection process: the purpose of the strategy (overcome weaknesses, maximise strengths) and the area of emphasis (internal, external). When the emphasis is internal, resources are redirected within the firm; if it is external, the firm may choose to acquire new assets or enter into a merger to improve resource capability. The Grand Strategy Selection Matrix is shown in Figure 5.11.

The term 'grand strategy' in this case refers to both corporate strategies of multi-business firms and business-cum-corporate strategies of single-business firms. Like the other models discussed earlier, the Grand Strategy Selection Matrix leaves the selection of relevant factors to the company itself. The matrix allows four strategic choices:

**Areas of Emphasis**

|  | Internal | External |
|---|---|---|
| **Overcome weakness** | **I**<br>• Vertical integration<br>• Conglomerate diversification | **II**<br>• Turnaround or retrenchment<br>• Divestiture<br>• Liquidation |
| **Maximise strength** | **III**<br>• Concentration<br>• Market development<br>• Innovation | **IV**<br>• Horizontal integration<br>• Concentric diversification<br>• Joint venture |

(left axis label: **Purpose of the Grand Strategy**)

**Figure 5.11  Grand strategy selection matrix**
Source: Adapted from Pearce and Robinson, 1988, p. 296

*Quadrant I*  A firm in this quadrant has limited growth opportunities in its existing business; therefore, the approach is to expand its external scope of operations. However, there are inherent risks with this approach, e.g. costs of expansion, learning to cope with significantly new and/or larger businesses, and gaining a position of strength. Care must be taken not to trade one weakness for another, otherwise, the firm may find itself in a worse position.

*Quadrant II*  Businesses in this quadrant elect a more conservative approach; the basic strategy is to slim down the business and become more efficient as a result. Resources will tend to be redirected only towards more efficient or pressing activities. Many activities may also need to be consolidated, thus resulting in a much leaner business.

*Quadrant III*  This quadrant includes businesses who pursue an aggressive build/maintain strategy to support internal development.

*Quadrant IV*  Businesses in this quadrant have similar options as in quadrant III, except the focus is on strategies that will support external development. The aim is to take advantage of market opportunities and strengthen one's position in the industry.

## International competitiveness matrix

The international competitiveness matrix, the final one in this series, was developed by Leontiades (1985). The focus is international, and strategy selection is based on two factors, market share objectives and geographical scope. The matrix is presented in Figure 5.12.

**Market Share Objectives**

|  | High | Low |
|---|---|---|
| **Global** | Global high share | Global niche |
| **National** | National high share | National niche |

**Figure 5.12 International competitiveness matrix**
Source: Leontiades (1985, p. 53)

From Figure 5.12, it is readily evident that companies that desire high market share on a global level should pursue a high share strategy. However, this option is only really available to companies with substantial resources. Those with fewer resources are better off building a particular strength or niche in the market and then competing on this basis in the global market.

Companies seeking to establish or maintain a high market share within a national market should limit the entry of global competitors into this market through such protective measures as entry barriers, providing costs advantages in local production or services, creating strong customer loyalty, etc. Those companies that have carved special niches for themselves within a national market should do the same to limit the entry of both national and global competitors into their particular segments of the market.

# A critique of strategy selection models

The strategy selection models presented in this chapter are among the most widely used in the management field today. Although there are obvious differences, the similarities among the models far outweigh the differences. Indeed, what differences there are lie mostly in four areas:

- the terminology used to describe *a company's position in the industry* (e.g. competitive position v. business strength v. internal strength);
- the terminology used to describe *generic strategies* (e.g. stars v. cost leadership v. growth strategy v. aggressive strategy v. invest strategy);
- the number of *stages in the product-market life cycle* (e.g. Porter has three; Arthur D. Little, four; Hofer and Schendel, five); and
- *scope* (except for one, all the models focus on competition within domestic markets; while some limit their analysis of the industry to include economic variables only, others look at a wider range of environmental factors).

There is one key difference that should be highlighted, however: the models do differ in terms of the organisational level at which strategies are examined. Some models specifically focus on strategy selection at the corporate level; others, at the business level, and a few on a world-wide basis. However, it has been noted earlier in this chapter that this need not be a major concern, since it is widely acknowledged that strategy selection models, particularly those examined in this chapter, are equally applicable to single-business or multi-business organisations. In chapter four, it has also been stressed that the division between corporate and business levels is more likely to be found in complex multi-business firms, whereas single-business firms are more likely to collapse these two levels into one. Thus, where a multi-business firm would use the models to decide on which businesses and industries it should be in, the single-business firm would use the same models to decide which products, services or markets it should be in.

In terms of the more important underlying concepts, all models exhibit highly similar characteristics. The one exception is the original BCG model whose basis of analysis remains firmly anchored on two simple measures, market growth and market share. Unlike the BCG model, the other models share two main assumptions. First, a company's position in the marketplace is not a function of market share alone, but is dependent on a host of interrelated factors (economic, social, technological, organisational, etc.). In addition, situations and conditions change, much faster in some industries than in others, and a firm must be able to act accordingly in the face of these changes. Consequently, strategy choices are seen as contingent on the set of circumstances and conditions under which a firm is operating at any one time.

The strategy selection models, again with the exception of the BCG model, also follow similar analytical procedures. They use a multivariate approach to assess the position of a company vis-à-vis its competitors. They leave the selection, definition, weighting, and ranking of specific variables to individual companies, and rely heavily on qualitative analysis and judgement calls, while at the same time acknowledging the usefulness of reasoned and statistical arguments.

The critical examination, to which the strategy selection models have been subjected over the years, has allowed the field to further its knowledge of the use of such models, and the vastly different ways that individual businesses and industries are likely to behave under different organisational and market conditions. As the literature suggests, these models are not stale, static, pseudo-scientific approaches to strategic decision making. Rather, they are tools for 'asking questions' (Lewis *et al*, 1993, p. 224) and they provide decision makers with a disciplined method of evaluating strategic decisions at the corporate, business and functional levels of the organisation. Most likely because of this, strategy selection models (or portfolio models, as they are still widely known in the field) continue to be very popular, even when empirical evidence on whether their use does lead to better performance hangs in the balance (Mintzberg, 1994). Haspeslagh (1982) provides a clue to the models' enduring success. In his research, he found a fairly high level of use of portfolio analysis among leading companies (36% of Fortune 1000 companies and 45% of Fortune 500 companies). Most importantly, he also found the use of portfolio analysis had profoundly affected the way executives thought about the way they managed their businesses. Today, two decades later, executives apparently still think so.

**A composite strategic choice model**

In addition to the similarities highlighted in the preceding section, a closer examination of all eleven models reveals that, regardless of the seemingly varied approaches advocated, they all recommend the same basic strategies. These strategic choices are listed in Figure 5.13, which shows a composite model for strategy selection and analysis.

The composite model assesses a firm's profitability and competitiveness on two dimensions: organisational competitive factors (high/strengths, low/weaknesses) and market factors (high/opportunities, low/threats). These two factors are designed to serve as umbrella concepts under which the various terms used by the models covered in this chapter can be categorised.

The first would include competitive position, business strength, etc; the second would include market growth, product-market life cycle, etc. As the figure also indicates, the composite model is very similar to the SWOT framework.

**Organisational Competitive Factors**

|  | High (Strengths) | Low (Weaknesses) |
|---|---|---|
| High (Opportunities) | *Quadrant 1*<br><br>Grow | *Quadrant 2*<br><br>Develop or Turnaround |
| (Threats) Low | *Quadrant 3*<br><br>Stabilise | *Quadrant 4*<br><br>Harvest |

**Market Factors**

**Figure 5.13   A composite model for strategy selection and analysis**

At a general level, the matrix provides five basic corporate strategies: grow, develop, turnaround, stabilise, and harvest.

*Grow strategies* are for firms with high quality business factors and high quality industry factors. These are the high fliers, the leaders.

*Develop and turnaround strategies* are for firms with low quality business factors and high quality industry factors. Typically, the *develop* strategy applies more to new or emerging businesses while the *turnaround* strategy is more applicable to mature industries.

*Stabilise strategies* are for firms with high quality business factors and low quality industry factors.

*Harvest strategies* are for firms with low quality business factors and low quality industry factors.

# 6   A strategy model for Asia-Pacific shipping

**The strategic choice model**

There are no set organisational or market factors to consider when analysing an organisation's strategic position. Shipping research suggests that the number and nature of organisational and market factors differ according to shipowner and market segment. They also change over time as markets and the competition change (Anderson *et al*, 1993; Brooks, 1995). The same is true in general management where, as Wind and Mahajan (1981, p. 160) found out, 'the factors defining the composite dimensions naturally vary among companies and even (though not often) among different businesses of the same company'. Therefore, an important assumption in the use of the strategic choice model is that the user must be able to define, or be cognisant of, the key success factors that are applicable to the time period under analysis.

To ensure that the analysis of organisational and market factors is thorough, the literature on shipping and ports (Rich, 1978; Arlt, 1987; Frankel, 1989; Hawkins, 1991a, 1991b, 1993) and on general strategic management (Johnson and Scholes, 1988, 1997; Montanari, 1990; David, 1995, 1997) recommend that the analysis should be broad-based, that is, it should take into consideration a broad range of factors against which the strengths and weaknesses of an organisation, and the opportunities and threats in its external environment, can be assessed. Frankel (1989), for instance, offers eight internal and external factors (competitive, adversity, technological, human relations, political/governmental, market, international relations, resources), all of which can be broken down into more specific subgroups. Hawkins (1991a, 1991b, 1993) takes a similarly broad approach, using a method called 'THE Full SCOPE' to assess an organisation's internal and external performance. 'THE Full SCOPE' is an acronym for *t*echnological, *h*ealth and safety, *e*nvironmental, *f*inancial, *s*ocial, *c*ommercial, *o*rganisational, *p*olitical, and *e*conomic factors. It is an organising framework that allows an organisation initially to take a broad view of all success factors that are likely to affect its internal and external performance, and then focus on those factors that are most relevant to its current situation. Based on this analysis of current success factors, the organisation's strategic position can then be plotted on the matrix and strategic choices identified.


## Strategic choices

What strategic choices can an organisation pursue, given its strategic position? In chapter four a comprehensive typology of strategies was developed to pull together the best-known strategies identified in the strategic management literature. The typology is meant to serve as a companion to the strategic choice model to show the range of strategies, from corporate to functional, that an organisation can pursue.

Of particular concern are the five generic corporate strategies: grow, develop, stabilise, turnaround, and harvest. Choosing the 'right' corporate strategy or strategies is essential if an organisation is serious about gaining long-term competitiveness. Such strategies set the general direction of organisational strategic activities and define the specific strategies that must be pursued at the lower levels of the organisation. They help the organisation integrate its various strategic activities so that, instead of being pursued separately, strategic efforts are able to support one another. Under the integrating framework of a corporate strategy (or set of strategies), resource allocation also becomes more effective and efficient, since the organisation has a broad understanding of the relative importance of various businesses, industries and markets in which it operates.

The five corporate strategies were discussed in detail in chapter four, hence, only a brief description of each strategy is provided here. An organisation may choose to *grow* or *develop* if it wants to compete in new high-growth areas. The two strategies differ only in that the first (grow) is used in relation to organisations that have achieved a foothold in the market while the second (develop) is used for those still in their embryonic stages. If an organisation chooses to *stabilise*, its aim is to maintain the status quo either by keeping to a tried and tested course, changing incrementally in response to environmental changes, or both. If it is in financial trouble, it is likely to choose a *turnaround* strategy to enable it to reduce or eliminate those activities that are hurting its performance and restore financial viability. If this does not work, it may move on to a *harvest* strategy where the objective is to divest of a poorly performing business or parts of it. On the strategic choice model, the five corporate strategies can be plotted into four quadrants, as shown in the preceding chapter in Figure 5.13.

As the model shows, of all the four quadrants, quadrant 1 represents the most favourable position (competitively strong, many market opportunities), closely followed by quadrant 3 (competitively strong, many threats). Quadrants 2 (competitively weak, many opportunities); and quadrant 4 (competitively weak, many threats) are undesirable. Which strategy or strategies should be pursued if an organisation falls in a given quadrant? What happens when the organisation sits very close to or on the borderline? There are no straightforward answers to these questions, just as the model does not provide 'how-to' steps to resolve them.

Earlier, it has been noted that a major assumption in the use of the model is that the user must be able to identify those success factors that apply to current conditions. There is no magic formula for determining these factors; their correct identification requires an intelligent combination of deliberate analysis and intuitive judgment. When it comes to making strategic choices, this same caveat applies. The user must be able to use good intuitive judgement in positioning the organisation, particularly when several choices may be available and the organisation (or a business) falls close to or on the borderline. This is where strategic thinking comes in: the user is expected to ask critical questions about the different strategy alternatives relative to the position of the organisation and then make decisions based on this appraisal.

Hawkins (1993, pp. 19-29) argues that the evaluation of corporate strategies should address ten key questions. Basically, these questions seek answers on the strategy's organisational compatibility (questions 1-3), commercial value (questions 4-6), and intrinsic power (questions 7-10).

1. Is the strategy consistent with the findings of the environmental assessment (internal and external) and with what the organisation intends to achieve (goals and objectives)?
2. Are the right people available to support the strategy? Are the organisational culture and managerial skills adequate for the strategy to work?
3. Are there sufficient resources (capital, facilities, managerial expertise, people) to make the strategy work?
4. Does the strategy offer a genuine competitive advantage? Is it based upon something which is important to customers, and something which the organisation can do better than its competitors?
5. Does the strategy offer an acceptable level of risk (relative to return) that the organisation is happy to live with?
6. Is the strategy socially acceptable? Would society find the strategy to be within the norms of ethical behaviour?

7.  Is there sufficient flexibility in the strategy? Is there enough 'slack' in the strategy so that if environmental conditions give the organisation a surprise, the strategy may be adapted or modified?
8.  Is the strategy clear enough for all to understand?
9.  Can the strategy be measured so that it can be compared against other alternatives and its ability to meet its target be monitored?
10. Is the strategy achievable and challenging enough so that people will be motivated to make it work, yet not so easy or conservative that they lose interest in it?

Once corporate strategies are selected, supporting specific strategies can then be identified. Specific strategies will not be discussed here as they lie outside the focus of this book.


## Testing the applicability of the model to Asia-Pacific shipping

The assumptions underlying the strategic choice model are based largely on research in areas outside commercial shipping, hence the extent to which they apply to Asia-Pacific shipowners still has to be tested. If the model is correct, that it can be assumed that Asia-Pacific shipowners will:

- Change/modify their strategies in response to changing environmental conditions.
- Base strategic changes and the time frames for these changes on their future expectations of organisational and market conditions.
- Pursue a 'grow' strategy when internal organisational competitive (internal) and market (external) factors are high[1].
- Pursue a 'stabilise' strategy when organisational competitive factors are high and market factors are low.
- Pursue a 'turnaround' or 'develop' strategy when organisational competitive factors are low and market factors are high.
- Pursue a 'harvest' strategy when organisational competitive and market factors are both low.

Since not much is known about the strategic choices that Asia-Pacific shipowners make, it is necessary to establish if these assumptions do reflect what Asia-Pacific shipowners actually do. If theory and practice do not

---

[1] i.e. Competitively strong and many market opportunities. 'High' and 'low' are used as in Figure 5.13.

match, where do the differences lie? And if there are differences, what should a strategy selection model that is specific to Asia-Pacific shipowners look like? These are questions that this book aims to answer.

Because empirical evidence supporting the strategic choice model is drawn largely from manufacturing industries, the applicability of the model to service industries like shipping, and in particular to commercial shipping within a specific geographical area, the Asia-Pacific, has yet to be determined. As noted in earlier chapters, very little is known about how Asia-Pacific shipowners make strategic choices (Reker, 1997; Barton, 1995; Wong, 1991; Hawkins, 1989). In addition, a substantial body of research highlighting significant differences between service and manufacturing industries (Armistead, 1994; Herbert and Deresky, 1987; Schellenberg, 1983; Hambrick, 1983) has cast serious doubts on what has often been assumed as the universal and uniform applicability of strategy selection models. Thus, before the model can be used both as a conceptual and practical tool to understand and aid strategic decision making by Asia-Pacific shipowners, its applicability to this particular group of users requires testing.

This chapter explains the methodology used to determine how applicable the strategic choice model is to Asia-Pacific commercial shipowners. It also provides a detailed description of the research methods used for the study, the major sources of data, and the procedures for data collection and analysis. To provide a backdrop to the discussion, a brief overview of the research methods and data sources is presented first.

## Overview of research methods

To determine how applicable is the strategic choice model to Asia-Pacific commercial shipowners, several data sources and research methods were used to guide data collection and analysis. The decision to combine several sources and methods was made to enable cross-checking of information obtained from one source or through one method with information obtained from another source or through another method. It also made possible the combined used of qualitative and quantitative approaches to data collection and analysis.

This process of systematic verification, using both qualitative and quantitative data, is called *triangulation*, which is discussed more fully later in this chapter.

*Data sources*

Data for the study was collected from three sources: shipowners, maritime experts, and maritime statistical and related documents. Shipowners were the primary source of information, with maritime experts and relevant documents used to verify, evaluate, or expand on information collected from or about shipowners. The shipowners included in the study were ship operators in the bulk and liner markets based in twelve Asia-Pacific countries: Australia, China, Hong Kong, Indonesia, Japan, Malaysia, New Zealand, the Philippines, Singapore, South Korea, Taiwan, and Thailand. Maritime experts included leading researchers and practitioners in the Asia-Pacific maritime field. Their primary role was to verify whether and to what extent the information obtained from and about shipowners was congruent with what was known about the Asia-Pacific region in general and Asia-Pacific commercial shipowners in particular. Maritime documents included available relevant material (trade journals, statistical series, annual reports, company reports, etc.) that provided information about the Asia-Pacific region in general and its commercial shipowners in particular.

A total of 748 respondents provided data for the study. Of these, 733 represented shipowners and fifteen were maritime experts. Of the 733 shipping respondents, 109 participated in the survey, 54 in the interviews, and 570 in the simulation. A total of 130 shipowning companies were represented, or about 38 per cent of the original survey population of 340. Details are provided in Table 6.1.

*Characteristics of the shipping respondents*

All shipping respondents held senior management positions in their organisations. These positions included senior executive positions (21 per cent) with responsibility for the entire organisation (e.g. chairman of the board, chief executive officer, president, managing director, executive director), senior divisional level positions (66 per cent) with responsibility for major areas or divisions within the organisation (e.g. director, senior manager, general manager), and corporate level positions (13 per cent) with responsibility for the organisation's corporate or strategic management activities (e.g. corporate or strategic manager, development & planning manager, corporate planner or strategist).

More than half of the respondents (62 per cent) had been in their current positions for one to five years; the remaining 38 per cent for six to ten years. Many (72 per cent) had been involved in strategic planning for about six to ten years but much of what they knew about it had been learned on the job. The majority (76 per cent) had no formal training (university degree or short courses) in strategic planning or management. Most were 40-49 year old males (81 per cent) who held the nationality of the country in which they worked. In terms of ethnic background, the majority was Chinese (42 per cent), European or North American (19 per cent), Indian (12 per cent), and other South Asian (11 per cent); the rest were scattered among the various nationalities represented in the study.

**Table 6.1**
**Distribution of respondents by country and research method**

|  | Survey | Interviews | Simulations | Expert Review | Total |
|---|---|---|---|---|---|
| Australia | 6 | 4 | 52 | 2 | 64 |
| China | 7 | 4 | – | – | 11 |
| Hong Kong | 13 | 6 | 165 | 3 | 187 |
| Indonesia | 10 | 7 | 91 | 1 | 109 |
| Japan | 25 | 10 | – | 3 | 38 |
| Malaysia | 7 | 4 | 88 | 1 | 100 |
| New Zealand | 5 | 4 | 41 | 1 | 51 |
| Philippines | 4 | 2 | – | 1 | 7 |
| Singapore | 13 | 6 | 133 | 2 | 154 |
| South Korea | 9 | 2 | – | – | 11 |
| Taiwan | 6 | 3 | – | 1 | 10 |
| Thailand | 4 | 2 | – | – | 6 |
| Total | 109 | 54 | 570 | 15 | 748 |

Background data on the 54 survey respondents and non-respondents who participated in the interviews showed a high level of similarity between the two groups. They differed only in that, on average, survey respondents were younger and had more formal training and experience in strategic planning than non-respondents. Data on the simulation participants followed the same set of general characteristics as those described above.

The shipowners represented by the respondents operated in two major market sectors, bulk (53 per cent ) and liner (47 per cent). Of these, 19 per cent could be classified as large operators, 46 percent as medium-sized, and 35 per cent as small. Company size was based on the number of ships and businesses or divisions in the company. A shipowner was classified as large if it had more than 35 ships and more than five businesses/divisions; medium-sized if it had between 10-35 ships and between 3-5 businesses/divisions; and small if it had 5-10 ships and 0-3 businesses/divisions.

To ensure comparability, background information was collected from all the shipping respondents. It included personal data about the respondent (position in the organisation, years in this position, experience and training in strategic planning, age, gender, nationality, ethnic background), company information (market sector and percentage of total operations, trade routes, company size), and general strategic planning practices (presence of a strategic plan, strategic planning process). Where possible, self-reports were cross-checked against information available in shipping statistical reports, trade journals, and annual company reports.

*Research methods*

To collect information from shipowners, three research methods were used: a mail survey, interviews, and simulation. To verify information collected from shipowners or to shed further light on specific issues under study, two other methods, expert review and document review, were also used.

A mail survey was initially administered to commercial shipowners in the Asia-Pacific to collect baseline information about their strategic practices. This was followed up by interviews with a sample of shipowners to allow for more in-depth examination and analysis of issues. At the same time, simulation sessions were conducted, during which shipowners made strategic decisions under computer-simulated shipping conditions. The information collected from shipowners was sent to a number of maritime experts who were asked to provide feedback on the findings based on their knowledge of the maritime industry in the Asia Pacific. Depending on the location of the person, feedback was provided either in writing, by phone, or in person. Relevant documentation that pertained to the issues investigated by the study was also reviewed to obtain further information.

Data collected was both quantitative and qualitative in nature; hence, appropriate quantitative and qualitative methods were used to analyse the data and interpret the results. Overall, a qualitative approach to analysis, which allowed for emergent patterns and trends to be identified, categorised, and described, was used to integrate and interpret results obtained through the various methods and sources into a final set of findings and conclusions.

## Triangulation as a research approach[2]

Because of its highly applied nature, strategic management research has always been dominated by field studies. Field studies are undertaken in practical settings, involve real managers and organisations, and draw from a

---

[2] Full details of the research methods and application are in Hawkins, J. (1997) *A strategic choice model for Asia-Pacific shipping*, Unpublished Ph.D. thesis, University of Plymouth, UK.

variety of research methods to examine strategic and organisational behaviour and processes (Snow and Thomas, 1994). Many of these field studies have taken a quantitative approach; in recent years however there has been a growing call for an expanded research perspective, one that reflects a better balance between theory building and testing, and between quantitative and qualitative methods. 'Multimethod approaches' to the study of strategy are particularly recommended as an alternative to the dominant quantitative paradigm because they allow the collection and analysis of quantitative and qualitative data in a variety of ways and thus provide a far richer data base (Snow and Thomas, 1994; Lyles, 1990).

**Table 6.2**
**Types of information from data sources and means of collecting it**
**(Summary table)**

| Data Source | Type of Information Sought | Means of Data Collection | | | |
| --- | --- | --- | --- | --- | --- |
| | | Mail Survey | Interview / Discussion | Simulation | Document Review |
| Shipowners | General strategic planning approach | ● | ● | ● | |
| | Selection of corporate strategies | ● | ● | ● | |
| | Background information on the shipowner | ● | ● | | ● |
| Maritime experts | General economic and maritime trends in the Asia-Pacific region | | ● | | |
| | Strategic practices of Asia-Pacific shipowners | | ● | | |
| Maritime documents | Trade information on Asia-Pacific commercial shipping | | | | ● |
| | Strategic planning, strategy selection | | | | ● |

A term typically associated with multimethod approaches is *triangulation*. This is defined as a systematic process of using several methods, perspectives, and/or sources to evaluate or validate the same idea (Baker and Ahern, 1990; Miles and Huberman, 1984; McGrath *et al*, 1982; Patton, 1980; Cook and Reichardt, 1979; Denzin, 1978; Webb *et al* 1965). Triangulation uses both qualitative and quantitative methods to arrive at one conclusion (Northurp and Kraemer, 1982). Its effectiveness is based on the premise that the weaknesses of one method can be counterbalanced by the strengths of another (Jick, 1979; Cook and Reichardt, 1979). Through this process, the methods are used to check and build on one another. Convergence is said to be reached when evidence gathered in different ways from different sources support the same conclusion (Baker and Ahern, 1990; Kerlinger, 1973).

The research methods used in the study—mail survey, interviews, computer simulation, expert review and document review—were selected on the basis of their ability to build on one another's strengths while minimising their respective weaknesses. As the following discussion shows, by triangulating findings collected through these various methods and sources, convergence, or the extent to which it is achieved, can thus be established.

A summary of data sources, the information sought from them, and the means of obtaining the information is provided in Table 6.2.

## Data collection and analysis

Figure 6.1 summarises the five stages in data collection and analysis. Initial data from shipowners was collected through a mail survey at stage 1, followed by in-depth interviews with a randomly selected group of survey respondents and non-respondents. Both types of data were analysed, and initial findings on the strategic choices made by Asia-Pacific shipowners were arrived at. At stage 2, simulation data was collected and evaluated against stage 1 findings. At stage 3, findings from the survey, interviews and simulation were integrated to produce an aggregate picture of corporate strategic choices made by shipowners.

A first iteration of the strategic choice model for shipping, based on information provided by Asia-Pacific shipowners, was prepared. At stage 4, experts were asked to review the strategic choice model for shipping. Their feedback was evaluated against shipowner-generated information, and results were incorporated into the final findings. Finally, at stage 5, the final version of the strategic choice model was prepared. At each stage, data obtained from relevant documents were also included in the analysis. These stages are discussed in further detail below.

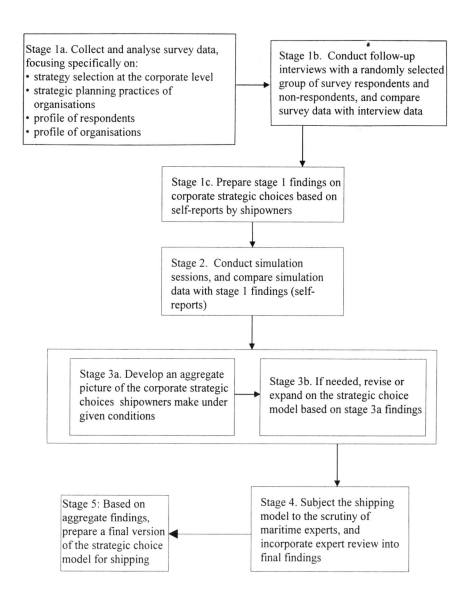

**Figure 6.1 Stages in data collection and analysis**

*Stage 1. Survey and interviews*

Using the Lloyd's Maritime Information Services, a list of all commercial shipowners for inclusion in the study was compiled. The list included all shipowners who:

113

- were based in Australia, China, Hong Kong, Indonesia, Japan, Malaysia, New Zealand, the Philippines, Singapore, South Korea, Taiwan, and Thailand (the major contributors to the economic growth of the Asia-Pacific region);
- managed and operated ships, i.e. ship operators, shipmanagers, managing agents, and disponent owners (this criterion excluded owners and leasing companies who did not directly operate ships);
- traded in liner and bulk trades (the two major shipping markets in the Asia-Pacific region);
- operated any of the four major types of commercial cargo-carrying ships, i.e. tankers, bulk carriers, container ships and general cargo ships, as these made up more than 86 per cent of the Asia-Pacific fleet and 84 per cent of the world's fleet (this criterion excluded (a) passenger, RO-RO, gas, chemical and refrigerated cargo ships which made up a small percentage of the fleet and dealt with specialised trades, and (b) non-commercial cargo-carrying ships like fish-catching, offshore supply, research, towing, dredging, ice breaking, cable and naval ships and yachts);
- engaged in regional trade within the Asia-Pacific region (this criterion excluded shipowners engaged solely in coastal trades or trades outside the region, e.g. European or American trades);
- operated more than five ships greater than 1000 grt (this criterion is widely used to identify major shipowners (e.g. Lloyd's Register), who are targetted here because they are more likely to use corporate strategies than those who only operate one to three ships).

The initial list of shipowners who met all these criteria was crosschecked against the listings in Lloyd's Electronic Maritime Directory (1995,1996) and Fairplay's World Shipping Directory (1995, 1996). A total of 340 shipowners was finally arrived at. Of these, five were selected to pre-test the survey questionnaire; the rest were included in the mail survey. The mail survey sought information on four areas: the general strategic planning practices of the shipowner; the process normally followed by the shipowner to select and evaluate corporate strategies; the type of corporate strategies the shipowner was likely to make under certain environmental conditions; and background information about the respondent and the shipowner. Questions on corporate strategy choices were based on the strategic choice model described earlier in this chapter.

To crosscheck survey information, follow-up interviews were conducted either face to face or by phone with a randomly selected group of survey respondents and non-respondents. Face-to-face interviews were conducted in Indonesia, Malaysia, Singapore, Australia and New Zealand, where simulation sessions were also held. The first three, all in East Asia, were considered the 'emerging tigers' in Asia; the last two represented western-style economies and thus served as a contrast to the Asian economies. Interviews for all other countries were conducted over the phone. A total of 54 shipowners were interviewed; half represented 25 per cent of survey respondents and the other half were non-respondents.

The survey and interviews elicited both quantitative and qualitative data. Using the quantitative data from the survey questionnaire, a descriptive statistical analysis was conducted to develop:

- a general profile of respondents (current position, years in this position, experience and training in strategic planning, age, sex, nationality, ethnic background);
- the organisations they belonged to (shipping sectors in which they operated, major Asia-Pacific trade routes, location of the head office, company size in terms of number of ships owned, revenue, and businesses or divisions operated);
- the general strategic planning practices of these organisations (whether they have a strategic plan, format and time frame of the strategic plan, importance given to strategic planning, estimated percentage of the annual budget spent on strategic planning, frequency of change, success rate); and
- their corporate strategies (whether they have specific corporate strategies, frequency of review, key factors that lead to changes in strategies, key people responsible for corporate strategy decisions, time spent on strategy selection and evaluation).

The open-ended questions in the questionnaire and the interviews focused on two aspects: the general processes followed by organisations for strategic planning and strategy selection and evaluation, and what specific corporate strategic choices they would make given certain environmental conditions. Data thus gathered was content-analysed to uncover recurrent trends and patterns. Content analysis is a method used to analyse qualitative data, systematically reducing data into understandable patterns and organising them into a compact form using narrative text, matrices, graphs, charts, etc. As a final step, findings from both the survey and the interviews were integrated into an initial set of findings.

*Stage 2.    Shipowner participation in the computer simulation*

Simulation sessions were conducted during the same period that the follow-up interviews were held. Thirty sessions were held in five countries

(Australia, New Zealand, Indonesia, Malaysia and Singapore), and a total of 570 senior managers representing 86 shipowners participated. A qualitative approach was used to analyse simulation data. This came in the form of strategic decisions made by participants over 20 quarter-year periods (future outlook, strategic objectives, corporate strategy, fleet structure decisions, and operational decisions, all of which were based on their analysis of company and market conditions). The approach also included the researcher's observations of participant or team behaviour during the simulation, and post-simulation feedback from a randomly selected group of 90 participants.

To attract shipowner interest, the simulation was conducted as an intensive one-day shipping competition. A one-page flier, which invited shipowners to test their strategic decision-making skills against those of other commercial shipowners, was circulated to shipowners through national shipowner organisations, which organised the competitions in their respective countries. No deliberate effort was taken to invite specific shipowners to the competition; instead, competitions were announced through national shipowner bodies in the various countries and shipowners were asked to respond within a given period of time. There was no direct contact between the researcher and shipowners until the commencement of the competition.

The objective of the competition was to turn a financially-troubled shipping company around and earn as much profit as possible. Whoever posted the highest company value at the end of the competition was judged the winner. A computer-based strategic planning simulation program called 'Stratship' was used for this purpose[3].

The simulation data collected consisted of three types: strategic decisions jotted down on quarterly decision sheets, researcher observations of participant and team behaviour during the simulation and post-simulation feedback from participants. Of the 190 sets of decision sheets submitted by the study teams, 174 were useable (i.e. provided all essential information); for the post-simulation evaluation, feedback from all 90 participants was used.

*Stage 3.* *First iteration of the strategic choice model for shipping*

With the data from shipowners integrated into a single set of findings, preliminary conclusions were made about the strategic choice model,

---

[3] The Stratship program used by the study was developed by the Esmee Fairbairn Research Centre as a strategic planning simulation for the maritime industry. For further information contact Esmee Fairbairn Research Centre, Heriot-Watt University, Riccarton, Edinburgh EH14 4AS, UK.

particularly in terms of the research objectives and questions. These initial conclusions were used to make any necessary modifications or changes to the generic strategic choice model and prepare a shipping-specific version of the model.

*Stage 4.    Expert review of the strategic choice model for shipping*

To test the robustness of the shipping model, fifteen leading researchers and practitioners in the maritime field within the Asia-Pacific region were asked to review the model. For this purpose, each expert was given a briefing paper that provided a full description of the strategic choice model, and was asked to provide a critique of the model based on a set of open-ended questions. Communication with the experts was mainly written, but discussions by phone or fax were also conducted to discuss any issue or provide further information. The reviews from the experts were content-analysed, evaluated against shipowner-generated information, and then incorporated into the final set of findings.

*Stage 5.    Final version of the strategic choice model for shipping*

At this last stage, the integrated set of findings from shipowners, experts, and documents was used to make final conclusions about the research assumptions. A qualitative approach, again using content analysis, was applied for this final synthesis of findings into major conclusions. Based on these conclusions, a final version of the strategic choice model for shipping was prepared.

# 7 Corporate strategy of Asia-Pacific shipowners: survey and interviews

## Introduction

In both the survey and interviews, shipowners provided clear support for the strategic choice model, either following it precisely as intended or modifying its parameters to suit their own strategic ends. Modifications typically involved disregarding environmental conditions when selecting a strategy, pursuing a strategy under conditions not called for by the model, or combining several strategies instead of limiting themselves to the one or two choices prescribed by the model. This trend consistently came up in the survey and interviews, highlighting the point that strategic choices were not as clear-cut as the model assumed.

## Results of the survey

### Strategic planning practices

As part of the background data on shipowners, shipping respondents were asked whether their organisations had strategic plans. The general picture that emerged was that the majority of shipowners (68 per cent) had no formalised strategic plans; however, most (84 per cent) did report following a systematic process of decision making. A key feature of this process involved intensive discussions among senior management during which long-term goals and objectives were set and specific means or strategies to achieve them were selected. A small minority (23 per cent) reported using specific analytical techniques (SWOT being the most frequently cited) during these discussions.

The 32 per cent who had strategic plans described them as formalised documents that normally covered a five-year period and were subject to review and change every year or every one and a half years. Strategic

119

planning was a top priority in their companies, with about an average 28 per cent of the company's annual budget being spent on strategic activities. The majority of these respondents (82 per cent) were satisfied with their plans, giving them an average of 70 per cent success rate.

**Table 7.1**
**Survey responses to the six assumptions of the strategic choice model**
**(n=109)**

| Assumptions of the Model | Categories of Responses (%) | | | | |
|---|---|---|---|---|---|
| Asia-Pacific shipowners will: | Yes | Yes, but | Unsure | No | No Reply* |
| 1 change/modify their corporate strategies in response to changing environmental conditions | 85 | 7 | 5 | – | 3 |
| 2 base strategic changes and the time frames of these changes on their future expectations of environmental conditions | 80 | – | 9 | 9 | 2 |
| 3 pursue a 'grow' strategy when internal and external environmental factors are both favourable | 76 | 8 | 4 | 9 | 3 |
| 4 pursue a 'stabilise' strategy when internal environmental factors are favourable but external factors are not | 72 | 9 | 9 | 5 | 5 |
| 5 pursue a 'develop' or 'turnaround' strategy when external factors are favourable but internal factors are not | 68 | – | 16 | 12 | 4 |
| 6 pursue a 'harvest' strategy when internal and external environmental factors are both unfavourable | 52 | 17 | 21 | 9 | 1 |

*N.b. 'no replies' are not referred to in the discussion.

*Corporate strategy selection*

Regardless of whether they had strategic plans or not, the majority of shipowners (69 per cent) reported having corporate strategies. Corporate strategies were defined as those strategies that focused on a company's mix or portfolio of businesses and determined which businesses the company should be in and how these businesses should be managed. According to the respondents, senior management was primarily responsible for selecting corporate strategies (87 per cent), which were reviewed every year (74 per cent) and changed when necessary (65 per cent). In most instances, the selection of corporate strategies did not progress into formal plans (75 per cent), mirroring the trend discerned earlier with regard to the development of strategic plans. These two trends indicated that while the majority might have followed a systematic process of setting goals and objectives and then selecting strategies in support of these goals and objectives, the overall process of strategic planning and strategy selection remained informal. This issue will be raised more fully in the section on interview data.

## Survey data

The survey data (based on 32 per cent of the survey population or 109 respondents) indicated strong support for the strategic choice model. The results are summarised in Table 7.1. Discussion of survey results is organised around the six assumptions of the strategic choice model, which were presented in the form of questions.

## Survey responses

*Will Asia-Pacific shipowners change/modify their corporate strategies in response to changing environmental conditions?*

There was strong agreement among respondents (85 per cent) that they would change their corporate strategies in response to changing environmental conditions, whether these were internal or external to the organisation. The need to remain flexible and be able to respond to changing times was high in respondents' lists, and was seen as the key to survival. A further seven per cent gave a qualified yes, saying that although they would tend to do so, they would not if the change would compromise the objectives they wanted to achieve. In such instances, some suggested that they might ignore environmental trends altogether. 'If for instance external conditions suggested lowering a freight rate objective that we'd set,' said a respondent, 'we'd be more inclined to ignore the market signals and stick to our objective.' The remaining five per cent were not prepared to commit to a definite position, saying it would depend a lot on the circumstances; in the words of a corporate strategist, 'some changes you can leave alone, others you have to act upon; so it all depends'.

*Will Asia-Pacific shipowners base strategic changes and the time frames of these changes on their future expectations of environmental conditions?*

The majority (80 per cent) agreed that they would, and did, base changes to corporate strategies and the time frames of these changes on what they perceived would be the future of their organisations and the market. Respondents indicated that such future expectations were based not only on their own perceptions but also on the preferences and priorities of primary stakeholders (shareholders, boards of directors, etc.) Some nine per cent were unsure whether they would take this course of action, saying it would depend on the magnitude of the change contemplated. A final nine per cent disagreed, saying that there were many more factors than mere future expectations to influence strategic changes. The most frequently cited factors were strategic vision (i.e. a company's long term goals and objectives), financial credit availability (i.e. ability to expand), global and regional political and economic conditions, and strength of the competition (as one managing director put it, 'if our competitors are weaker than us, why change?').

*Will Asia-Pacific shipowners pursue a 'grow' strategy when internal and external environmental conditions are both favourable?*

There was clear agreement on this question, with 76 per cent saying they would pursue a 'grow' strategy under favourable environmental conditions, that is, they would seek to expand if the organisation was competitively strong and the market offered many opportunities. Another eight per cent also said yes, but qualified their response by adding that as a matter of strategic policy, they would seek to grow regardless of external conditions, provided their organisation was capable of carrying out the strategy. Some four per cent were unsure whether they would, saying their decision depended on other factors such as the strength of their competitors and the objectives and targets set by their organisation. The remaining nine per cent disagreed, saying that environmental factors were not their primary basis for choosing a strategy; in many instances, owner or major stakeholder preferences and priorities dictated strategic choices, regardless of environmental conditions.

*Will Asia-Pacific shipowners pursue a 'stabilise' strategy when internal environmental factors are favourable but external environmental factors are not?*

There was also clear consensus on this question. The majority (72 per cent) would choose to stabilise if the organisation was strong but the market posed many threats, that is, they would aim to maintain the status quo, making minor changes only to better deal with these threats. Another nine percent also said yes but qualified their response by stating that they would do so only 'under normal circumstances'; it was not clear, however, what 'non-normal' circumstances were, as most did not elaborate on this response. However, the comment of one executive director could be an indication of likely scenarios when organisations chose not to take the safe course. According to this respondent, if their competitors were not strong, they would 'take a gamble and milk the market for as much as we could; we would decide to expand (i.e. grow), for instance, even when market conditions were supposed to be bad for business'. Around nine per cent were unsure whether they would choose this strategy, saying it would depend on current circumstances; a number opted for the 'grow' strategy as a likely alternative. A further seven per cent said that they would not choose 'stabilise' at all.

*Will Asia-Pacific shipowners pursue a 'develop' or 'turnaround' strategy when external environmental factors are favourable but internal environmental factors are not?*

The majority of respondents (68 per cent) agreed that they would choose a 'develop' or 'turnaround' strategy to take advantage of favourable market conditions particularly if their organisation was competitively weak and facing financial problems. Responses accompanying this choice indicated that a 'turnaround' strategy, which involved reducing or cutting out unprofitable activities or operations to contain the financial haemorrhage, was seen as an emergency 'do it now' measure to avoid financial failure. In contrast, the 'develop' strategy, which involved entering into profitable trades where the organisation was weak but where it could build its competitive strength, was a more deliberately planned rescue attempt. Another 16 per cent were unsure as to what strategy to pursue, opting for the typical 'depends on circumstances' reply but providing no further elaboration. The remaining respondents disagreed, saying that to escape from a bad situation one required a more innovative approach such as a 'grow' strategy, as this allowed the organisation to optimise its strengths.

*Will Asia-Pacific shipowners pursue a 'harvest' strategy when internal and external environmental factors are both unfavourable?*

Responses to this item were more dispersed. Although 69 per cent said yes to this item, their answers fell into three categories: (a) 52 per cent firmly agreed that a 'harvest' strategy, which involved selling off an unprofitable business (or parts of it), would be the preferred choice when the market held few opportunities and the organisation was weak or in financial trouble; (b) seven per cent were more tentative, saying they would do so most of the time, but would make an exception if they had strategic reasons for staying in the area (e.g. if they believed the market would improve); (c) ten per cent said that they would pursue a 'harvest' strategy regardless of environmental conditions if they found better alternatives elsewhere or if there had been a change in strategic direction.

Of the remaining respondents, 21 per cent were not certain whether to take this course of action, while nine per cent firmly disagreed, saying they would not choose a 'harvest' strategy regardless of environmental conditions, preferring a 'turnaround' strategy or occasionally a 'grow' strategy. A likely reason for the last group's reluctance could be discerned from the responses of some respondents: shipping was their business, and they would find it difficult to get out of the area unless there were better alternatives in sight. Thus it was more acceptable to try turning around the fortunes of the company (i.e. turnaround) or, to a lesser extent, seek to grow.

## Summary of survey results

Survey data provided strong support for the strategic choice model. Agreement was particularly strong with regard to the model's first four assumptions. A large majority said they would change or modify their corporate strategies in response to changing environmental conditions (85 per cent); base strategic changes and their time frames on future expectations of environmental conditions (80 per cent); pursue a 'grow' strategy when internal (or organisational) and external (or market) conditions were favourable (76 per cent); and pursue a 'stabilise' strategy when internal conditions were favourable but external conditions were not (72 per cent). However, agreement slightly weakened when it came to the use of 'develop' and 'turnaround' strategies (68 per cent) and even more with 'harvest' strategies (52 per cent).

A likely explanation for the lesser degree of agreement in the use of the 'develop', turnaround', and 'harvest' strategies lies in the nature of these strategies. All three are prescribed when the organisation is weak or in financial trouble, and they are meant to bail the organisation out to allow it to regain financial health. One involves taking a gamble by venturing into areas that are profitable, but where the organisation is not competitively strong; the other two involve excising unprofitable operations to stop further financial loss. Under these circumstances, the survey data revealed two sets of responses: one was aggressive, the other conservative. Those who took an aggressive stand preferred to gamble, opting for more risky strategies like 'grow' and 'develop' to get themselves out of trouble because while the risks were high so were the rewards; they would also try 'turnaround' before 'harvest'. Those who took a more conservative approach preferred strategies that carried less risk, such as 'stabilise', or if they were in trouble, they would opt for a 'turnaround' or 'harvest' strategy rather than pursue a 'grow' or 'develop' strategy.

Another tendency that emerged from the survey data was the link between experience in strategic management or planning and the level of uncertainty when making strategic choices. Those who said they were not sure which strategy to pursue under which environmental condition tended to be younger and less experienced. This could have been a simple lack of knowledge of the field (i.e. of shipping and strategic decision making) to enable them to make educated guesses, and as a result, a lack of confidence in providing definitive answers.

**Organisational Competitive Factors**

|  | High (Strengths) | Low (Weaknesses) |
|---|---|---|
| High (Opportunities) | Quadrant 1<br><br>Grow | Quadrant 2<br><br>Develop<br>Turnaround<br>(+ Grow) |
| (Threats) Low | Quadrant 3<br><br>Stabilise<br>(+ Grow) | Quadrant 4<br><br>Harvest<br>(+ Turnaround) |

**Market Factors**

**Figure 7.1 Matrix of strategic choices based on survey findings**

While there was overall consensus on the choice of strategies, the survey data also showed that choices were not as clear-cut as the strategic choice model assumed. Rather than restrict themselves to the choices offered by the model, respondents tended to widen the field by combining or substituting strategies. Among those who supported the model, the 'grow' strategy emerged as a popular choice, pursued regardless of environmental factors and often in combination with other strategies to give an organisation a better strategic balance. The most frequently used combinations of strategies are plotted in the four quadrants of the matrix in Figure 7.1, with those in parentheses representing shipowners' additions.

As noted earlier, environmental conditions or factors were described as 'favourable' when an organisation had many strengths and few weaknesses and the market held many opportunities and few threats; they were 'unfavourable' when the converse was true. Thus the more favourable the conditions were, that is, the more strengths the organisation had and the more opportunities the market offered, the higher was an organisation's strategic 'position'. Conversely, the less favourable the conditions, the lower its position. It should also be noted that the answers given by respondents did not always fit easily into the four quadrants of the model. In a few cases, respondents chose to pursue more of the functional-type strategies, with marketing strategies cited frequently. In other instances, the strategy could not be firmly ascertained because of poor wording. However, because such cases were very few, they had been excluded from the discussion.

A number of other findings emerged from the survey. The larger the company, the greater the likelihood that a formal strategic planning system was in place. Data showed that larger liner operators (58 per cent) were more likely to have strategic plans than small liner operators (23 per cent) and bulk operators (19 per cent).

Younger respondents (up to 50 years old) were more highly trained or educated in management but lacked experience; older respondents (older than 50 years old) were more experienced but lacked formal training. About 74 per cent of the first group had received some formal management training (short course or degree) in contrast to seventeen per cent of the second group. Only a small percentage (nine per cent) reported having both attributes. In terms of nationality, respondents from Australia, Japan, New Zealand and Singapore (68 per cent) had more training and experience in strategic planning or management and applied more resources to strategic activities than those from the other countries. They also provided more details on their survey forms.

**Interview data**

Interview data came from 54 respondents, half of whom were randomly selected from the group of survey respondents and half from the group of non-respondents. Background data collected on both groups showed a high level of comparability, both in terms of respondent and company characteristics.

During the interviews, survey non-respondents were asked why they had not responded to the questionnaire. The largest group (41 per cent) cited lack of time and 'too many commitments' at the time the questionnaire arrived. Others (22 per cent) cited difficulty in answering the questions because they were not very fluent in the use of the English language or were unfamiliar with strategic planning concepts and therefore had great difficulty putting their ideas into words. 'We do talk of strategies', one respondent said, 'but not in the terms you had them in the questionnaire, so I was not sure how to proceed.' Others (27 per cent) cited confidentiality of information. As one respondent frankly said, 'putting down in writing our ideas on how we keep our company competitive and then giving this information to some outside organisation which we don't know much about is not very prudent; it is being very foolish. For all we know you might be working for the competition'. The rest (ten per cent) preferred not to give any explanation.

In contrast to the survey, requests for personal interviews were met with interest mainly for two reasons. First, the interview was seen as a good chance to learn more about strategic planning and corporate strategy selection (44 per cent) and second, the interviews were arranged through personal contacts, who vouched for the researcher's credibility and intent (34 per cent). As one chief executive officer smilingly put it, 'If it weren't for my good friend ... putting in a good word for you, I would be somewhere else right now.' The remaining 22 per cent agreed to the interviews either because they had the time so they gave it, especially since the researcher had travelled a long way to see them, or because they were curious about what the researcher had to say.

On the main question of corporate strategy selection, interview data followed similar patterns as the survey data. However, some key differences also surfaced. In particular, the interviews revealed a greater tendency to combine strategies and that an informal approach to strategic planning and strategy selection was more widely practised than suggested by survey data. The findings are discussed below and summarised in Table 7.2.

**Table 7.2**

**Interview responses to the six assumptions of the strategic choice model (n=54)**

| Assumptions of the Strategic Choice Model | Categories of Responses (%) | | | |
|---|---|---|---|---|
| Asia-Pacific shipowners will: | Yes | Yes, but... | Unsure | No |
| 1 change/modify their corporate strategies in response to changing environmental conditions | 75 | 12 | 6 | 7 |
| 2 base strategic changes and the time frames of these changes on their future expectations of environmental conditions | 44 | 16 | 35 | 5 |
| 3 pursue a 'grow' strategy when internal and external environmental factors are both favourable | 63 | 22 | 8 | 7 |
| 4 pursue a 'stabilise' strategy when internal environmental factors are favourable but external factors are not | 61 | 19 | 15 | 5 |
| 5 pursue a 'develop' or 'turnaround' strategy when external factors are favourable but internal factors are not | 52 | 25 | 16 | 7 |
| 6 pursue a 'harvest' strategy when internal and external environmental factors are both unfavourable | 65 | – | 31 | 4 |

As with the survey, the interview results were organised around the six assumptions of the strategic choice model.

*Will Asia-Pacific shipowners change/modify their corporate strategies in response to changing environmental conditions?*

The majority (75 per cent) agreed on this item, saying flexibility was critical to long-term survival. They followed this approach as a matter of policy, but the magnitude of the change depended on the specific issues involved. Citing the financial crisis gripping East Asia at the time of the interviews, one company president said, 'So far this monetary curse has spared [our country], but our trading partners [elsewhere in the region] are in real trouble. Here [in our company] we have ongoing top-level meetings to keep a close eye on things so can plan ahead. We have two or three contingency plans on the drawing board, so we'll see what happens next.'

The other twelve per cent also said yes, but they did so on a more selective basis. 'Most of the time' they would change or modify their corporate strategies due to environmental changes but they would *not* do so if they wanted to take a gamble, or alternative strategies were not acceptable to management, or organisational politics dictated otherwise. On this last point, if a proposed change led to disagreement among the senior people, for instance, the group might decide to keep the status quo rather than change to avoid further arguments and dispute (the 'groupthink' problem).

About six per cent would not commit themselves either way, saying that any action taken would depend on the type and magnitude of the environmental changes involved. The remaining seven per cent said environmental changes, particularly external ones, would not influence their choice of corporate strategies. 'We would follow our vision and long-term objectives,' confided a general manager, 'rather than be swayed by changes in environmental conditions, which we see as mostly short term. Of course we need to take precautions when major problems hit, like this currency crisis we're having now, but it does not mean we need to change our long-term goals and strategies.' Another commented: 'We are here for the long run; we need to project what we want to be 10-15 years from now, so we must be able to take current changes in the environment within this long-term perspective.'

*Will Asia-Pacific shipowners base strategic changes and the time frames of these changes on their future expectations of environmental conditions?*

Unlike the other five assumptions, consensus on this point was weaker, with responses dispersed more widely. The largest group (44 percent) firmly agreed, saying that future expectations played a major role in their strategic choices. 'If we do not believe the market is going to be good,' said one, 'then we would have to decide whether we stay or we go.' 'That's why we need to keep on top of things,' explained another, 'and know what the market trends are. The problem though is getting the right information when you need it; if it's not there, and often it isn't, then you rely on yourself, on your own intuition, to help you make the decision.'

A smaller group (16 per cent) also agreed, but they qualified their response by saying that if there were attractive opportunities around, they would disregard future expectations and take advantage of current opportunities. Thus even if market conditions were predicted to be bad, if they could obtain credit or purchase new tonnage under highly favourable terms, they would do so. 'It will be taking a big risk,' said one respondent, 'but if we pull it off, then we gain a lot.' Others indicated favouring a similar approach, which could be aptly described as the 'gambler's choice'.

A large number of respondents (35 per cent) were not sure if they would consistently take this approach. While they agreed that future expectations of environmental conditions, particularly market conditions, were an important factor to consider, they were less certain as to whether they would actually institute strategic changes based on market expectations alone. This group preferred a broader base for their decision making so that along with market expectations, other key factor areas such as organisational goals and objectives, ship prices, financial credit availability, and current freight rate levels were also taken into consideration. How opportunities in these various areas balanced up determined the type and time frame of strategic changes.

The remaining five per cent said they would not change. For some, it was a case of 'once we make a decision, then we follow it through'; for others, it was a case of organisational politics. With senior management performance increasingly assessed against strategic plans or, in the absence of plans, against long-term goals and objectives, many senior managers in this group voiced a reluctance to advocate changes, especially major ones. They expressed a fear that this would lead to a loss of current privileges, incentives or bonuses, or to the adoption of performance criteria that would be less favourable to them. A number of respondents also said the attitudes and perceptions of the board of directors could be a deterrent to change. In some cases, changes were vetoed because influential members of the board did not like or were suspicious of major or too many changes. At other times if senior management did not express any strong views toward the need to change, the status quo prevailed.

*Will Asia-Pacific shipowners pursue a 'grow' strategy when internal and external environmental conditions are both favourable?*

About 63 per cent agreed they would pursue a 'grow' strategy when market opportunities were excellent and their organisation had the capability to push through the strategy. As one manager put it, 'In this game you can only get ahead if you are willing to take chances. When things are good and there are lots of opportunities about, you need to take swift action. If you're too cautious or indecisive, you get left behind.' A further 22 per cent also agreed but said that they would not necessarily restrict themselves to a 'grow' strategy alone but would use it in combination with other strategies such as 'develop' and 'stabilise'. This seemed to be a preferred option of larger operators who owned or operated several businesses or divisions. In areas where they were more vulnerable, they said they would choose a 'develop' strategy to improve their competitive strength. In areas that were more stable, they would choose a 'stabilise' strategy to maximise profits.

Some eight per cent were unsure, saying 'it would depend on the circumstances'. Even after reviewing previous decisions, they remained unsure as to whether environmental factors had been the single most influential factor leading to the use of a 'grow' strategy. However, a number did say that their choice of strategy often depended on the level of risk the board was prepared to accept. If pursuing a 'grow' strategy would expose their organisation to too many risks, either they would lower the target or objective they had set, or they would choose an alternative strategy to reduce the risks.

The remaining seven per cent firmly disagreed, offering arguments similar to those given by the 'unsure' group. To them a 'grow' strategy was always a risky proposition and even under favourable conditions, they would look for a less risky strategy, such as 'stabilise', that would give them consistent returns. These respondents pointed out that a lot of shipowners pursued 'grow' strategies regardless of environmental conditions. There had been too much expansion due to this indiscriminate pursuit, which was why profitability in shipping was low (i.e. 7-12 per cent return in investment was frequently cited). Rather than grow, therefore, this minority group opted to stabilise, which carried less risk.

*Will Asia-Pacific shipowners pursue a 'stabilise' strategy when internal environmental factors are favourable but external environmental factors are not?*

The majority (61 per cent) said yes to this item, particularly when they were in a position to maximise profits. This strategy was widely accepted as a short-term measure. As one strategist put it, 'If we're on top, or at least close to it, we'd milk the market for as much and for as long as we could. Then we'd change tactics.'

Another 19 per cent also said 'yes' but qualified their response by saying that they would not limit themselves to a 'stabilise' strategy alone, but would use other strategies such as 'grow', 'develop', and 'harvest' either in combination or as substitutes. According to this group, they would take this approach to balance strengths and weaknesses, spread the risks, and thus give themselves better protection from market uncertainties. Some respondents in this group (12 per cent) attested to the virtue of combining strategies, producing internal documents that showed how the use of alternative strategies had helped improve the company's financial performance.

Around 15 per cent were unsure, saying their choice of strategy would depend on circumstances, particularly on the longevity and severity of market threats. They would not categorically say a 'stabilise' strategy would be appropriate unless they knew what the specific circumstances were. The remaining five per cent said that they would not use a 'stabilise' strategy at all. They would opt for a 'grow' or 'develop' strategy instead, because these strategies would enable them to increase their market lead and allow them to achieve greater returns than was possible with the more conservative 'stabilise' strategy.

*Will Asia-Pacific shipowners pursue a 'develop' strategy or 'turnaround' strategy when external environmental factors are favourable but internal environmental factors are not?*

A slight majority (52 per cent) firmly agreed, with a further 25 per cent saying that they would do so in combination with a 'grow' strategy. Both groups gave the same line of reasoning as proffered by the strategic choice model. They would pursue a 'turnaround' strategy to get out of financial trouble. In areas where the organisation was competitively weak but had the capacity to surge ahead, they would pursue a 'develop' strategy to improve the organisation's competitive strength. The second group, however, went a step further; in addition to these two strategies, which they called short-term, they also said they would pursue a more long-term 'grow' strategy to build on their strengths. 'You really need a package of strategies,' said one respondent, 'so that you can dodge bullets here, beat the enemies there, and have a rest in between.'

Another sixteen per cent were unsure, stating no preference for either strategy or saying that they were not sure what answer to give. Even when asked further what they would do if they were weak but there were many opportunities in the market, this group showed a reluctance to commit themselves to either strategy which they saw, in the words of one respondent, as 'risky steps for an already shaky organisation'. There were several likely reasons for this reluctance: lack of confidence, particularly among the younger and less experienced managers; fear of failure, especially where the organisational climate was not very forgiving of managerial or strategic mistakes or miscalculations; or simple managerial laziness. However, none of these underlying reasons were brought into the open with this group of respondents, and because of the potential for conflict and antagonism, the researcher decided not to probe further.

The remaining seven per cent said that they would not use either strategy, opting for the 'grow' strategy instead. Because they were in an environment where there were lots of opportunities, it was better to take an aggressive approach to give them the capacity and economies of scale to improve their competitive position. To a great extent, this last group served as the counterpoint of the 'unsure' group: where the 'unsure' group dithered, the 'grow' group gambled.

*Will Asia-Pacific shipowners pursue a 'harvest' strategy when internal and external environmental factors are both unfavourable?*

The majority (65 per cent) said that they would pursue a 'harvest' strategy when internal and external environmental conditions were both unfavourable. 'Better cut your losses while you can' easily summarised the sentiments of this group. However, a large 31 per cent were unsure. The question generated a lot of emotive statements from interviewees because a 'harvest' strategy meant getting out of a business that they knew and possibly into a new unknown one. It may even mean getting out of shipping permanently unless they had a way of turning the company's fortunes around. Most said they would try as hard as they could to save the business before they would even contemplate a 'harvest' strategy. Explaining this 'do or die' approach, a chairman of the board said: 'Shipping is our business, so we will fight to the bitter end for our survival. The only acceptable strategy is one that will enable us to save the business, especially one that is focused on establishing a sound financial base within a niche area. This could mean a significant downsizing of the company, so we'll have to be prepared to get out in some areas [i.e. harvest] and improve those with greater potential for success [i.e. turnaround].'

The remaining four per cent disapproved of this strategy altogether, saying they would choose other strategies instead. Again, the 'turnaround' strategy emerged a popular choice, with the group echoing the same views and sentiments as those expressed by the 'unsure' group. However, while the 'unsure' group was willing to move to a 'harvest' strategy when all things failed, this last group was not. It was unclear, however, whether this 'last stand' approach was mere bravado or a true test of strategic grit ('defeat is not part of our vocabulary'). In the end, if efforts to save an ailing business failed, the result would still be 'harvest', except this time it would be forced upon a company that would have used up all its options.

**Summary of interview results**

Like the survey, the interviews revealed a close adherence to the strategic choice model. However, as the percentages in Table 7.2 show, agreement was less strong and responses more widely dispersed. The majority of interviewees would change or modify their corporate strategies in response to changing environmental conditions (75 per cent). They would pursue a 'grow' strategy when internal (or organisational) and external (or market) conditions were favourable (63 per cent); a 'stabilise' strategy when internal conditions were favourable but external conditions were not (61 per cent);

and a 'harvest' strategy when both internal and external conditions were unfavourable (65 per cent). However, agreement slightly weakened when it came to 'develop' and 'turnaround' strategies with a little over a half (52 per cent) giving a firm 'yes'. Agreement was even weaker regarding the use of future expectations of environmental conditions as basis for strategic changes, where less than half (44 per cent) agreed without offering any qualifications.

To a great extent, this wider dispersal of responses could be attributed to the fact that the interviews gave both the researcher and interviewees the opportunity to explore the questions in greater depth and to tease out various possible ways organisations would act under changing environmental conditions. In particular, this applied between those that gave an unqualified 'yes' response and those that also said 'yes' but attached qualifications to it. Interviewees were able to spell out the various factors that influenced their strategic choices, and these factors did not always coincide with what the model assumed. For instance, future expectations, while important, were often weighed against other considerations and they did not always end up as the primary arbiter of change; in fact there were occasions when they were disregarded in favour of higher-value factors. Interviews also provided further support for two tendencies that surfaced from the survey data. First, the uncertainty shown in choosing strategies was due to a relative lack of experience in shipping and management and a resultant lack of confidence; and second, in terms of strategy selection, shipowners fell into two streams. There were those who were prepared to gamble and thus chose aggressive proactive strategies (grow, develop), and those who took a more cautious 'tried and tested' route, opting for strategies that allowed them to reduce or spread the risks (stabilise, turnaround, harvest). Finally, the interviews also led to a fuller explanation of shipowners' reluctance to pursue a 'harvest' strategy. While they would not admit it in writing, a number of respondents saw the 'harvest' strategy not in simple hard-nosed, strategic terms but at a more emotional level. It was a sign of failure, it brought on fear of the unknown (i.e. how to compete in areas where the organisation had no requisite resources and expertise), and it posed a major threat to the respondents' own lives and careers.

As in the survey, the interviews also showed a strong tendency to 'mix and match' strategies, with the 'grow' strategy emerging as the most popular choice, its selection based more on the strategic objectives set by the organisation and its future expectations, rather than on environmental conditions. Many respondents said they would pursue a 'grow' strategy even when market conditions were not favourable or the organisation was competitively weak. To optimise opportunities and spread risks, they would combine 'grow' with (a) stabilise and/or develop, (b) stabilise, develop, and/or harvest, and (c) develop and/or turnaround. These choices are plotted in matrix form in Figure 7.2.

**Organisational Competitive Factors**

|  |  | High (Strengths) | Low (Weaknesses) |
|---|---|---|---|
| **High (Opportunities)** |  | Quadrant 1<br><br>Grow<br>(+Stabilise)<br>(+Develop) | Quadrant 2<br><br>Develop<br>Turnaround<br>(+Grow) |
| **Market Factors** |  |  |  |
| (Threats)<br>Low |  | Quadrant 3<br><br>Stabilise<br>(+ Grow)<br>(+ Develop)<br>(+ Harvest) | Quadrant 4<br><br>Harvest<br>(+ Turnaround) |

**Figure 7.2  Matrix of strategic choices based on interview findings**

It is worthwhile noting that, while most choices fell within the quadrants of the model, there were instances when categorisation was initially problematic. The respondent could not explain the strategy in a manner the researcher could comprehend, or would choose a business-type strategy such as lowest freight rate strategy (cost focus) or tailored service strategy (differentiation). Further discussion, however, clarified much of this initial confusion.

In addition to the major findings on corporate strategic choices, other secondary findings emerged from the interviews. Foremost among these were the role of the top executive in strategic decision making, the lack of external information to guide strategy selection, the lack of formal training in strategic management, and the prevalence of an incremental approach to corporate strategy selection. Differences in strategic planning practices also emerged between various sub-groups in the interview sample.

In the survey, respondents simply listed the key people involved in strategic decision making without delineating their relative importance in the decision-making process. During the interviews, however, one major difference emerged: among some shipowners the decision-making structure was more participative; among others, it was more autocratic. To a large extent this difference could be explained by national cultures. Among managers of

European descent (including those from North America, Australia, and New Zealand), decision making was seen as a participative process involving several layers of management. Senior management had primary responsibility but lower to middle level managers were also expected to contribute to the process. Even within the senior ranks, responsibility for decision making tended to be shared. Among East Asian managers, however, the top executive (e.g. CEO, President, Chairman) emerged as *the* decision maker, who decided who would contribute to the decision-making process and to what extent they were expected to do so. All other managers were expected to play a supportive role, as follower and adviser.

Interviews showed that the majority of respondents did not have access to a wide range of information sources to help guide their choice of the most appropriate corporate strategy. While most used internal financial information, very few used a lot of external information sources, especially statistical information sources and databases on market trends like Fearnley's or Lloyd's. Shipbroker reports and trade journals like Fairplay, Lloyd's Shipping Economist, Lloyd's Maritime Asia, and Asian Shipping were the most frequently cited sources of external information.

Another major issue that surfaced during the interviews was the difficulty faced by many interviewees in conceptualising and describing their strategies. To a great extent, this could be attributed to their lack of familiarity with the strategic management field. Many said they read trade journals and popular business magazines almost exclusively. Of the many journals on strategic management today, they could only cite a few (the Harvard Business Review was the most frequently cited) and admitted to having read them only once or twice or 'occasionally', or not at all.

This lack of familiarity with strategic management ideas and practices could in turn be attributed to a lack of training in the area, as evidenced by the number of respondents in senior level positions with no formal strategic management training. This is also borne out by a recent survey, conducted by the Far Eastern Economic Review, on management needs in Asia (Granitsas and Saywell, 1997). According to the Review's estimates, various Asian countries 'do not have enough skilled business managers to cope with demand over the next 10 years' (p. 2). The Review also cites another survey, conducted by the executive search firm Korn/Ferry International, which shows that all across Asia, demand for senior and middle executives is particularly acute. These executives are expected to have a good grasp of finance and marketing, understand how multinational companies do business, and demonstrate a good working knowledge of their chosen industry, management thought and practice, and commercial realities. Although steps are being taken by government and private industry alike to solve this enormous need for skilled managers, at present, demand is far outstripping supply.

Another major pattern that emerged from the interviews was that the most prevalent strategic approach used by respondents, regardless of trade (i.e. liner, tanker, dry bulk), was far more informal than that reported in the survey or prescribed by the formal planning model with its emphasis on rational and analytical planning procedures and techniques. Instead, it more closely resembled the incremental model, which saw planning as an informal, fragmented, intuitive, evolutionary, and political process. Indeed, interviewees voiced a strong reliance on what one senior manager described as 'an intuitive, trial-and-error approach' to strategy development. This approach was particularly popular among Asian senior managers who said it came naturally to them and had served them well in the past. Another reason for the popularity of the incremental approach could be that it reduced the level of risk that managers had to take. This applied particularly as the shipping environment became more globalised, more competitive, and therefore more uncertain and risky, and as managers were increasingly held accountable for strategic decisions and organisational performance.

The use of an incremental approach, however, did not necessarily mean a deliberate adherence to the incrementalist school of thought. Many respondents were as unfamiliar of this area of management thought as they were of the rational-analytical or formal planning approach. Neither had many used theoretical and/or analytical models offered by the strategic management field to assist in strategy selection. The few who showed familiarity with some models voiced a suspicion toward them. As one managing director put it, 'what we have seen so far are way up in the air; they are not practical and they don't tell you how you can actually apply them to your work.' Most senior managers, however, did reveal a need for practical evaluation tools that could help them choose and evaluate strategies more rigorously. 'Our evaluation approach,' said a company president, 'is a bit rudimentary, not sophisticated at all. We ourselves know we need a better method of finding out whether we are doing the right thing, but so far we are still working on it.'

On the question of corporate strategy selection, liner and bulk operators displayed a high level of similarity in their responses. Differences surfaced in three areas only. First, liner operators, especially container operators, used more external information sources than tanker or dry bulk operators, with dry bulk using the least amount of information. Second, the liner sector put more time and effort into strategic planning than bulk shipping, and within bulk shipping, the tanker sector did more planning than dry bulk. Third, although the liner sector did more planning than bulk shipping, this gap was closing as more and more bulk operators were being forced to take a more strategic approach and to do more planning to remain competitive in an increasingly uncertain and risky environment.

Company size emerged to be an influencing factor on the extent to which corporate strategies were formalised. Discussions with senior managers revealed that in general the larger the company, the greater the effort put into strategy selection and the more formal the approach used. Conversely, the smaller the company, the more informal the strategy selection process was, and the less likely was the strategy to be articulated into a formal plan. The strategy or plan was also less transparent to the organisation because more likely than not it was 'articulated' only in the minds of the senior managers who released key aspects to other employees on a need-to-know basis.

**Synthesis: shipowners' views on corporate strategy selection**

What then can be learned from the representatives of the shipowners' self-reports from the survey and interviews? Table 7.3 summarises the majority views that emerged from the survey and interviews with regard to the six major assumptions of the strategic choice model. The 'qualified yes' column is the same as the 'yes, but...' columns in previous tables and represents all 'yes' responses that deviated slightly from the model.

**Table 7.3**
**Comparing survey and interview findings with the strategic choice model**

| The model assumes that Asia-Pacific shipowners will: | Survey | | Interviews | |
|---|---|---|---|---|
| | Yes | Qualified Yes | Yes | Qualified Yes |
| 1 change/modify their corporate strategies in response to changing environmental conditions | 85 | 7 | 75 | 12 |
| 2 base strategic changes and the time frames of these changes on their future expectations of environmental conditions | 80 | – | 44 | 16 |
| 3 pursue a 'grow' strategy when internal and external environmental factors are both favourable | 76 | 8 | 63 | 22 |
| 4 pursue a 'stabilise' strategy when internal environmental factors are favourable but external factors are not | 72 | 9 | 61 | 19 |
| 5 pursue a 'develop' or 'turnaround' strategy when external factors are favourable but internal factors are not | 68 | – | 52 | 25 |
| 6 pursue a 'harvest' strategy when internal and external environmental factors are both unfavourable | 52 | 17 | 65 | – |

138

As Table 7.3 shows, both survey and interview data supported the assumptions of the strategic choice model. However, as the 'qualified yes' columns suggest, the choice of strategies was more dispersed and less clear-cut than the model assumed. A strategy would be pursued regardless of environmental conditions to enable an organisation to grow fast, or it would be combined with any of the other four strategies to give the organisation greater flexibility and protection from risk. A popular choice was the 'grow' strategy, which was selected even when conditions were unfavourable. The various choices are plotted in Figure 7.3, with items preceded by a plus (+) sign added by shipowners either during the survey (SQ) or interviews (I) and are therefore new to the model.

As the matrix shows, while the tendency to combine strategies was evident in both the survey and interviews, this tendency became more marked and noticeable during the interviews. To a great extent, this difference could probably be attributed to the relative merits of mail surveys and personal interviews. The latter allowed a more in-depth discussion of key issues, thus making possible a greater clarification and clearer delineation of strategic choices that otherwise would have been missed by the mail survey.

|  | **Organisational Competitive Factors** | |
|  | High (Strengths) | Low (Weaknesses) |
|---|---|---|
| High (Opportunities) | Quadrant 1 | Quadrant 2 |
|  | Grow + Stabilise (I) + Develop (I) | Develop Turnaround + Grow (SQ, I) |
| **Market Factors** | Quadrant 3 | Quadrant 4 |
| (Threats) Low | Stabilise + Grow (SQ, I) + Develop (I) + Harvest (I) | Harvest + Turnaround (SQ, I) |

**Figure 7.3 Matrix of corporate strategic choices based on survey and interview data**

In the next chapter, these views of shipowners' representatives will be compared with strategic decisions made by them under simulated conditions to determine the extent to which the different sets of findings are congruent.

# 8 Corporate strategy selection by Asia-Pacific shipowners: simulation

## Introduction

In this chapter, focus now shifts to data obtained through another research method, the simulation. Like the survey and interviews, the simulation relied upon information provided by shipowners. Unlike the first two, however, which relied primarily on self-reports, the simulation required shipowners to make strategic decisions under conditions that simulated a typical competitive shipping environment. The computer-based simulation program *Stratship* was used for this purpose[1]. To attract shipowner interest, the simulation was run as a shipping competition among commercial shipowners. A total of 570 senior managers participated, representing 86 Asia-Pacific shipowners all of whom were part of the shipowner population used for the survey. Participants worked in teams of three or four each, with members from the same company typically working together. Each team was required to complete a decision sheet for each of the twenty quarter-years that the simulation was programmed to run, with the aim of making a shipping company financially profitable.

## Simulation variables for strategic decision-making

The basic decision-making structure for the simulation was simple. Participants had to analyse the information provided by the computer program, and then make strategic decisions. Two types of quarterly information could be accessed: the company's financial status and market conditions. Information on the company's financial (or internal

---

[1] See footnote 3 of chapter six.

environmental) conditions changed according to the strategic decisions taken by participants; information on market (or external environmental) conditions changed as determined by the computer program, independent of any decision taken by participants. Changes to market conditions varied in magnitude; some were slight (e.g. interest rates) while others were major (e.g. trade indices). Such a program setup made it relatively easy to delineate the specific conditions under which a certain strategy was chosen.

**Table 8.1**
**List of quarterly variables**

| Company Information | Market Information | Strategic Decisions* |
|---|---|---|
| Total vessel operating costs | Route trends | Future outlook for quarter(s) |
| | *For each route*: | |
| Route accounts | • leg | Strategic objectives |
| *For each route*: | • market share | |
| • cash surplus/deficit | • load factor | Corporate strategies |
| • capitalised route value | | |
| | Market trends | Fleet structure decisions |
| Accounts summary | *For each route*: | • order |
| • operational cash-flow | • trade indices | • buy |
| • financial cash-flow | • liner rates | • sell |
| • net cash-flow | | • scrap |
| • current liquid assets | Vessel price | • charter in or out |
| | | • re-charter |
| Company value | Construction lag | |
| • total fleet value | | Operational decisions |
| • liquid assets | Charter rates | • add/delete routes |
| • value of routes | | • (re)allocate vessels to routes |
| | Interest rates | • decide on port set-up costs, |
| | | • vessel speed, joint ventures, |
| | Oil prices | • freight rates, marketing |
| | | • expenditures |
| | Exogenous shocks | |

* Strategic decisions were made by participants, and affected company information but not market information; market conditions were programmed to change every quarter, irrespective of strategic decisions and changes in company information.

Table 8.1 summarises the types of company and market information available to participants and the strategic decisions they were expected to make on the basis of this information. As columns one and two of the table show, information on the company's financial status included total vessel operating costs, the financial viability of each trading route (route accounts), cash-flow and liquidity status (accounts summary), and overall company value. Information on market conditions covered route trends, market trends, vessel prices, construction lags, charter rates, interest rates, oil prices, and exogenous shocks. Participating teams analysed this information, jotting their findings on their decision sheets for that quarter, and from this analysis, they made strategic decisions for the next quarter, or if they wished, for several quarters ahead. They predicted what the outlook for the next quarters would be, set what strategic objectives to pursue within this time frame, selected a specific corporate strategy, or a combination of strategies, to enable them to achieve their objectives, and translated this strategy (or set of strategies) into specific decisions. These consisted of fleet structure decisions (i.e. order, buy, sell, scrap, charter in, re-charter, or charter out) and operational decisions (i.e. add or delete routes or legs, (re)allocate vessels to routes, or decide on port set-up costs, vessel speed, joint ventures, freight rates, and marketing expenditures). These decisions were also jotted down on the quarterly decision sheet, and their effect on the company's current fleet structure and route status was also recorded.

**Main results of the simulation**

Simulation findings were arrived at using a qualitative approach to data analysis. The general approach was to identify the corporate strategies used by the teams over the simulation period (i.e. twenty quarters), check these strategies against prevailing environmental conditions, and determine the extent to which decisions followed the assumptions of the model. Key trends and patterns were identified, first at the individual team level and then at an aggregate level to arrive at more generalised and broader patterns of behaviour.

Like the survey and interview data, the discussion of simulation findings is organised around the six assumptions of the strategic choice model. For each assumption, simulation decisions are categorised according to whether they adhered to or deviated from the strategic choice model; then the nature of this adherence or deviation is explained, with emphasis given to the various modifications made to the model. Decision categories are based on the following types of decision-makers, identified during the initial analysis of simulation data:

- *Consistent followers* Those who followed the strategic choice model without deviations;
- *Eclectic users* Those who often followed the model but changed parameters when it suited them, for instance, disregarding environmental conditions to pursue strategic objectives, or combining or substituting strategies to strengthen their hand;
- *Occasional samplers* Those who followed the model occasionally; and
- *Non-users* Those who did not follow it at all.

**Table 8.2**

**Simulation responses to the six assumptions of the strategic choice model (n=570)**

| Assumptions of the Model | Categories of Responses (%) | | | |
|---|---|---|---|---|
| Asia-Pacific shipowners will: | Consistent Follower | Eclectic User | Occasional Sampler | Non-user |
| 1 change/modify their corporate strategies in response to changing environmental conditions | 58 | 18 | 15 | 9 |
| 2 base strategic changes and the time frames of these changes on their future expectations of environmental conditions | 74 | – | 14 | 12 |
| 3 pursue a 'grow' strategy when internal and external environmental factors are both favourable | 55 | 30 | 6 | 9 |
| 4 pursue a 'stabilise' strategy when internal environmental factors are favourable but external factors are not | 67 | 14 | 11 | 8 |
| 5 pursue a 'develop' or 'turnaround' strategy when external factors are favourable but internal factors are not | 44 | 32 | 19 | 5 |
| 6 pursue a 'harvest' strategy when internal and external environmental factors are both unfavourable | 79 | 7 | 5 | 9 |
| Support for the model | | | | |

Each category had a cut-off point of 75 per cent to qualify for any one category. In other words, a team should have taken the action called for at least 75 per cent of the time required to complete the entire simulation. A team would be considered a *consistent follower*, for instance, if it adhered to the model without making any modifications 75 per cent of the time. The findings are summarised in Table 8.2.

The results of the simulation were assessed by adopting the same question-based approach as for the survey and the interviews.

*Will Asia-Pacific shipowners change/modify their corporate strategies in response to changing environmental conditions?*

On this count, the majority of participants (58 per cent) strictly followed the model, that is, they changed/modified their corporate strategies in response to changing environmental conditions. However, the level of deviation was only slightly lower, with 42 per cent of respondents deciding on a different course of action. Some 18 per cent followed the model more often than not, deviating only when they wanted to speculate. Others (15 per cent) followed the model only occasionally, preferring to take a gamble the rest of the time. The remainder (9 per cent) did not make any changes at all. To a lesser degree, the deviation could also be attributed to errors or miscalculations in participants' assessments of environmental conditions.

When those who faithfully followed the model (*consistent followers*) and those who frequently followed the model but deviated occasionally (*eclectic users*) were bracketed together, their combined support for the first assumption of the model rose to a high 76 per cent. Another clear tendency to emerge was that future predictions had a significant effect on all simulation participants. That is, the firmer their future predictions of internal and external environmental conditions were, the more likely were they to change their corporate strategy even if it was not appropriate to current environmental conditions or trends. Conversely, if they expressed uncertainty as to what the future held, they were less likely to make changes to their corporate strategy.

*Will Asia-Pacific shipowners base strategic changes and the time frames of these changes on their future expectations of environmental conditions?*

The simulation program addressed the question of future expectations more narrowly than the survey and interviews. It locked participants into a narrower decision path where they had to specify their outlook for the next quarter or number of quarters, and based on this outlook, determine their strategic objectives and strategies for that time frame, and then make their decisions.

Overall, simulation data supported the second assumption of the model. The majority of decisions (74 per cent) showed that decision-makers relied a lot on their future expectations of environmental conditions when making strategic changes and selecting the time frames for these changes. The results also showed that the time frames chosen for corporate strategies were typically short term: very few went more than seven quarters ahead, with the average falling within three to six quarters. Furthermore, the longer the time frame set, the more conservative the change predicted, almost as if forecasts were averaged over the period. For example, the changes in freight rates that decision-makers would predict within five to six quarters would be half as much as what was predicted within one to three quarters.

Deviations formed a minority, with fourteen per cent following the model only occasionally and twelve per cent not doing so at all. On average those belonging to these groups were not in strong financial positions when they made their decisions. They disregarded future expectations in times of financial crisis, or when both internal (e.g. falling company value) and external (e.g. declining trade routes, dropping market share) environmental conditions were bad. Their response was to do either of two things: do nothing and just wait and see, or say they would pursue a certain strategy but not carry out changes that reflected such a strategy. For example, they might say they would pursue a 'grow', 'develop', or 'turnaround' strategy to improve their financial situation but the changes they subsequently implemented were so minor that any effect was negligible or hardly visible. Examples are lowering freight rates slightly by 5 to 8 per cent, or reducing the speed of the fleet on one or two routes from twenty to eighteen knots.

*Will Asia-Pacific shipowners pursue a 'grow' strategy when internal and external environmental factors are both favourable?*

Only a slight majority (55 per cent) followed the model without deviation. In other words, they pursued a 'grow' strategy when both internal and external environmental factors were favourable. The rest (45 per cent) deviated from the model in varying degrees. A substantial group (30 per cent) did follow the model but chose to spread risks by combining 'grow' with other strategies (18 per cent) or diverted occasionally in favour of another strategy or in spite of unfavourable conditions (12 per cent). The rest either followed the model intermittently (6 per cent) or did not do so at all (9 per cent). In spite of these deviations, however, when those who faithfully followed the model (55 per cent) and those who followed it, but at times changed directions for strategic reasons (30 per cent), were combined, support for the third assumption of the model rose to a strong 86 per cent.

The most common 'grow' strategies used by participants were expansion and diversification. Typically, participants expanded and diversified into more trade routes and/or added more ships to their most profitable trade routes.

146

Ships were mostly second-hand tonnage rather than newbuildings because of the long lead time required to build vessels (defined as 'construction lag' in the program) and the cheaper cost of purchasing relative to the availability of finance (defined as 'borrowing limit' in the program). Another popular 'grow' strategy was to diversify operations, which took four major forms: ship operating (i.e. operating trade routes only), ship chartering, playing the sale and purchase market (i.e. buying and selling ships), and joint ventures. Of these four approaches, a combination of (a) ship operating with chartering in, chartering out and rechartering was the most used, followed equally by (b) chartering and sale and purchase, and (c) chartering, sale and purchase, and a limited amount of ship operating. Joint ventures were the least preferred form of diversification.

A trend that clearly emerged from the data was the dominance of external environmental factors over internal factors. While both external and internal factors had to be favourable before a 'grow' strategy was pursued, more 'grow' choices were made when external factors were stronger than internal factors. For instance, if participants thought that the market held many opportunities that were simply too good to miss, they would choose to grow even if they might not be as competitively strong or ready as they needed to be.

For those who combined 'grow' with other strategies (eighteen per cent), the most popular choices were 'develop' and 'stabilise'. The 'develop' strategy was to help the company expand and diversify into new and existing high growth areas such as new trade routes, reallocation of vessels to routes, charter-in vessels for high market share or demand routes. The 'stabilise' strategy was to maximise the revenue value of a profitable trade route or charter without increasing costs. To a much lesser degree a 'harvest' strategy was also used in conjunction with 'grow' to divest of routes which were still profitable but did not show as much potential as other routes, or to divest of charters, ships, and occasionally joint venture arrangements to maximise opportunities.

Those who deviated from the model only occasionally (twelve per cent) did either of two things: they pursued a 'grow' strategy even when conditions were not favourable or they substituted another strategy. A 'stabilise' strategy was the most frequently used. The aim was to maximise profits by minimising costs and maximising revenue opportunities. This typically involved making minor adjustments like increasing or decreasing ship speeds (on average a two knot change), marketing expenditures (on average a seven per cent change) and freight rates (on average an eight per cent change).

With the remaining fifteen per cent of the population, who represented significant deviations from the model, some six per cent used a 'grow' strategy only occasionally, giving greater preference to a 'stabilise' strategy to minimise operating costs, maximise revenue, and thus increase overall profits. The other nine per cent did not use it at all. With this last group, responses were so widely dispersed and varied that no clear pattern emerged as to why a 'grow' strategy was not pursued under favourable conditions or what alternative strategies would have been acceptable under these conditions.

*Will Asia-Pacific shipowners pursue a 'stabilise' strategy when internal environmental factors are favourable but external factors are not?*

A majority of shipowners (67 per cent) pursued a 'stabilise' strategy under the conditions assumed by the model, that is, when internal environmental factors were favourable and external environmental factors were not. Most used this strategy to maximise profits by maintaining their internal operating structure (e.g. maintain the same trade routes or charters as in previous time frames) and reducing costs. With a stable, albeit slightly declining, revenue base and reduced costs, they were able to increase route performance and profits. Typically, costs were decreased by reducing vessel speeds (on average a four knot reduction), marketing expenditure (on average a 16 per cent cut), and route size. Route size was normally decreased by removing route legs (on average one leg removed) and indirect routes.

Trading route operators and charterers mostly used the 'stabilise' strategy, with those in the sale and purchase markets using it the least. All three groups used the 'stabilise' strategy as a short-term measure. Most participants used it over an average of three quarters; very few used it continuously beyond five quarters. The 'stabilise' strategy proved to be most used during times of relatively high freight rates and when participants perceived the market demand to be high but the threat of decline imminent. One team described this as when 'the freight rate is at or near the peak of the business/shipping cycle and likely to decline soon—next one to two quarters'.

Of those who deviated from the model, fourteen per cent also used the 'stabilise' strategy under conditions stipulated by the model, but rather than restrict themselves to this one choice, they usually combined it with other strategies. 'Grow' and 'develop' were the most commonly used; 'harvest' the least. The most typical approach of this group was to:

- maintain an existing route with a 'stabilise' strategy (either change nothing or make minor adjustments to vessel speeds, freight rates, marketing expenditure, and vessel allocation to routes);
- pursue a 'develop' strategy to expand or diversify into new trade routes or scope of operation (i.e. instead of just operating vessels, increase scope of operation by adding more charters, pursuing the sale and purchase market and/or less frequently, setting up joint ventures); and

- pursue a 'grow' strategy to expand or diversify into existing routes (i.e. by increasing the number of legs or vessels on a route, marketing expenditure, and freight rate adjustments).

When the 'harvest' strategy was used, the most typical approach was to use:

- the 'stabilise' strategy in the most profitable areas;
- a limited amount of the 'grow' strategy in existing areas that were predicted to be profitable; and
- a 'harvest' strategy in the most threatened areas or when poor trading conditions were predicted.

By using a combination approach, this group of eclectic users aimed to maximise internal strengths while the market still gave acceptable returns. Like the majority group of consistent followers, they used the 'stabilise' strategy as a short term measure, rarely going beyond seven quarters but using it for about one to two quarters longer than the former.

With the remaining 19 per cent of the population, which represented significant deviations from the model, a number followed the model only occasionally (11 per cent) while the rest (8 per cent) did not do so at all. Instead of the 'stabilise' strategy, other strategies, notably 'harvest', 'grow' and 'develop' were preferred. The 'harvest' strategy was most used in the sale and purchase market where participants sold vessels while ship prices were still high to strengthen their cash flow and financial and operating positions. At the opposite end, others pursued 'grow' and 'develop' strategies to take advantage of strong internal environmental factors amidst what they perceived to be a declining market. Under these circumstances, chartering in vessels over longer time periods (four to six quarters ahead was the norm) to take advantage of reduced charter rates was the most frequently used approach.

In spite of these deviations from the model, when those who faithfully followed the model (67 per cent) were added to those who followed the model frequently (14 per cent), a strong support for the model's fourth assumption emerged (81 per cent).

*Will Asia-Pacific shipowners pursue a 'develop' or 'turnaround' strategy when external environmental factors are favourable but internal factors are not?*

On this assumption, strict adherence to the model was lower, with less than half of the participants (44 per cent) using a 'develop' or 'turnaround' strategy under the assumed conditions, that is, when external environmental factors were favourable and internal factors were not. Of this group, 'turnaround' was more widely used than 'develop', and each strategy tended to be used differently. The 'develop' strategy was used more on a rising market (i.e. increasing freight rates and trade demand), where the approach was to go into new high profit areas and earn good revenue so that a company's competitiveness, particularly its financial position, could be strengthened. The 'turnaround' strategy on the other hand was used mostly on existing areas of operations, and it did not matter whether market conditions had been on the rise or stable for a period of time (i.e. three to four quarters of strong market conditions). The turnaround approach was to reduce internal costs and market exposure as much as possible while maximising good revenues. This was usually done by reallocating the majority of the fleet to the most profitable routes, reducing route size by deleting indirect and some direct but unprofitable ports of call on a particular route (e.g. reducing four ports of call or legs to two). It was also done by reducing vessel speed and marketing expenditure, and forming joint ventures on routes where they perceived there would not be high growth in the longer term (seven to ten quarters ahead normally).

Another important distinction in the way the two strategies were used was that 'turnaround' involved a greater degree of change than 'develop'. However, this was to be expected. A 'develop' strategy normally required a major infusion of resources to become viable, but companies in such circumstances typically lacked the financial capacity. They had insufficient cash flow to purchase or charter vessels and buy into new trade routes to realise fully the strategy's potential.

Among those who deviated from the model (56 per cent), two categories emerged:

- those who also followed the model but modified its parameters as they saw fit, either by occasionally substituting another strategy (13 per cent) or regularly using other strategies in combination with a develop/turnaround strategy (19 per cent); and
- those who showed the least support for the model, either by following it only intermittently (19 per cent) or not doing so at all (5 per cent).

The two groups in the first category followed a similar approach. The first group substituted a 'grow' strategy on occasion, while the second group frequently combined 'grow' with 'develop/turnaround'. To a far lesser extent, the second group also used a 'harvest' strategy to divest of trade routes that still showed earning potential and were less of a financial drain on internal operations. The 'grow' strategy was popular with both groups in the first category because it helped them expand and diversify into existing areas of strength without creating significant increases in costs, which was often the limitation of the 'develop' strategy. The typical growth approach was to increase the capacity of existing operations by purchasing and/or chartering in more vessels. These were mostly second-hand, as new vessels were more expensive. Wherever possible, positioning costs (i.e. the cost of getting a vessel allocated to a particular route) were minimised by allocating vessels to their closest route. This was an area where many made good cost savings.

For those in the second category, which deviated from the model the most, their general tendency was not to make any strategic changes to take advantage of favourable external conditions and halt worsening internal conditions. While the first group in the second category would occasionally try a 'grow' or 'harvest' strategy to improve financial health or avoid a financial crisis, more often that not both groups did nothing more than maintain their current strategies and wait and see if internal operations improved.

Of all of the strategies used when external conditions were favourable but internal conditions were not, 'turnaround' proved to be the most successful. It provided the greatest increase in company value in the shortest period of time. It was successful because it was better able to pit market opportunities (i.e. high levels of revenue) against internal weaknesses (lack of capacity and finance). Unlike 'grow' and 'develop' strategies, for instance, it did not require a major infusion of funds and other resources. This was one of the major problems that financially weakened companies typically met when they tried to implement 'grow' or 'develop' strategies. They simply did not have the internal capacity (lack of cash flow, limited access to charters and finance due to poor route values) to improve operations (number of trade routes, vessels on routes and chartered vessels) and take full advantage of good market opportunities.

Although a slight majority did deviate from the model (56 per cent), support for this assumption still proved to be strong when the numbers of those who approximately followed the model were added to those who faithfully followed it (44 per cent). Those approximately following the model occasionally substituted another strategy (13 per cent) or frequently combined strategies (19 per cent). Accepting this interpretation, a healthy majority (76 per cent) emerged in support of the model.

*Will Asia-Pacific shipowners pursue a 'harvest' strategy when internal and external environmental factors are both unfavourable?*

A large percentage of decisions (79 per cent) showed strict adherence to the model, pursuing a harvest strategy under the assumed conditions, that is, when both internal and external environmental conditions were unfavourable. The most common approaches were to abandon poorly performing trade routes and sell off vessels to improve internal conditions. In contrast with the 'grow' strategy where external factors tended to dominate over internal factors, internal factors tended to prevail in 'harvest' decisions. Indeed, the weaker the organisation, as shown by poor cash flow and liquidity, or declining company value, the greater the magnitude of divestment.

Within this majority group of consistent followers, there were two main groupings: diversified operators and sole ship operators. The diversified group, which operated in various trade routes and were major charterers as well, divested most of their trading operations by abandoning routes and selling off vessels. At the same time, they maintained their charter operations as their new core base. The ship operating group, on the other hand, divested either most of their trade routes and vessels (e.g. from four trade routes down to one and from a fleet size of 25 down to seven) or pursued selective trade routes, ports of call and vessel divestments. A typical approach of this second group was to divest of one trade route, make direct port calls only on the remaining routes, and sell off most of the fleet and maintain the minimum level of vessels on routes. This was normally two vessels per route.

Deviations from the model (21 per cent) fell into three groups: those who frequently combined 'harvest' with other strategies (seven per cent), those who followed the model only occasionally (five per cent), and those who did not do so at all (nine per cent). The most popular combination pursued by the first group was 'harvest' and 'turnaround'. A 'harvest' strategy was applied for areas or operations perceived to have limited future value or were most vulnerable to worsening conditions, and a 'turnaround' strategy for areas that could be improved if costs could be better controlled relative to revenue earning potential. For those who used 'harvest' occasionally or not at all, the most commonly used substitute was the 'turnaround' strategy. The typical approach was to reduce costs and the scope of operations as much as possible to improve cash flow and liquidity. This was achieved by reducing vessel speed to the minimum, significantly cutting freight rates and marketing expenditure, reducing ports of call, and carefully balancing vessel allocation to routes which minimised their exposure to high operating costs on routes. For this last group, they often had no choice but to pursue a 'turnaround' strategy if they wanted to continue with the simulation. Choosing to harvest when they were running out of options would have meant not having any vessels, charters, or trade routes with which to carry on with the simulation. Under these conditions some tried the 'grow' strategy but they were generally unsuccessful because they did not have the financial capacity to grow significantly enough to halt their worsening fortunes. Those who chose the 'turnaround' strategy often produced better results, which allowed them to stay in the simulation longer than those who chose the 'grow' strategy.

Of all the strategies used here, the selective combination of 'harvest' and 'turnaround' strategies proved to be the most successful in increasing company value. An example of this was a selective 'harvest' strategy on trade routes and areas of operation showing limited future potential (i.e. getting out of joint ventures, charters or trade routes; selling vessels at the appropriate time) and a 'turnaround' strategy on those areas perceived to show good future potential. Pursuing a 'turnaround' strategy on its own was the next most successful strategy.

Overall, when both the majority group of consistent followers (79 per cent) and those who also used 'harvest' but in combination with other strategies (seven per cent) were bracketed together, a very strong level of support (86 per cent) for this final assumption of the model emerged.

As the preceding discussion has shown, like the survey and interviews, simulation data strongly supported all six assumptions of the model. The general pattern of response was also the same. Support came from two main groups: those who followed the model without making any changes to it, and those often followed the model but modified its parameters for strategic reasons. Again, as in the survey and interviews, modifications typically involved disregarding environmental conditions when strategic considerations required it. This was achieved by using a strategy under environmental conditions not called for by the model, or combining several strategies to spread risk, instead of just limiting themselves to the one or two choices offered by the model.

The most frequently used combinations of strategies during the simulation are shown in Figure 8.1. Those in parentheses indicate other choices made by shipowners in addition to the strategies assumed by the model. When compared with Figure 7.3, which shows the results from shipowners' self-reports, the high degree of congruence becomes easily noticeable. Choices were the same except in quadrants 1 and 2, where the 'harvest' strategy appeared as another choice. It should be stressed here, however, that 'harvest' was only chosen on a few occasions.

**Organisational Competitive Factors**

| | High (Strengths) | Low (Weaknesses) |
|---|---|---|
| High (Opportunities) | Quadrant 1<br><br>Grow<br>(+Develop)<br>(+Stabilise)<br>(+Harvest) | Quadrant 2<br><br>Develop<br>Turnaround<br>(+Grow)<br>(+Harvest) |
| Low (Threats) | Quadrant 3<br><br>Stabilise<br>(+Grow)<br>(+Develop)<br>(+Harvest) | Quadrant 4<br><br>Harvest<br>(+Turnaround) |

(External Environmental Factors)

**Figure 8.1  Corporate strategic choices based on simulation data**

In addition to the main findings on corporate strategy selection, a number of key secondary findings were also identified. These involved decision-making styles, patterns of information use, environmental focus, competitive performance of participating teams, and cultural differences. The first was based on the researcher's observations of team behaviour during the simulation sessions, the next three on data provided by participants on their decision sheets, and the last on a combination of researcher observations and participant data.

*Decision-making styles*

Four major styles of strategic analysis and decision-making were displayed by the participating teams: autocratic, democratic, delegating, and adaptive.

In the *autocratic team*, the most senior person in the team took control and became the key strategist while other members became the implementers and followers. It was a very hierarchical approach, with the most senior people having the greatest input. This was the preferred style of many East Asian senior managers, particularly those from a Chinese ethnic background with Hong Kong, Singapore, and Indonesia the main countries of domicile.

In the *democratic team*, everyone got equally involved in the team's strategy analysis, strategy development, and decision-making. Each team

154

member was expected to be equally participative, and as a result, there was a lot more discussion and debate than in other teams. The main negative aspect of this type of decision-making was lack of leadership; there were occasions when no one was in charge. This style was observed most frequently in teams whose members were of East Asian and European origins (with Singapore, Malaysia, and Australia as main countries of domicile).

In the *delegating team*, team members allocated the various tasks among themselves and each became responsible for their own area. They did not do much collective brainstorming or decision-making. Instead responsibility was delegated over three areas: assessing and providing key information on major environmental trends, making strategic policy and setting strategic directions, and policy implementation and operational decision-making. In terms of ethnic makeup, unlike the previous two teams (autocratic and democratic), no clear trend emerged, with the ethnic backgrounds of team members too varied to allow general patterns to be observed.

In the last group, the *adaptive team*, the roles of individual team members changed as the simulation progressed. Like the delegating team, members assumed any of three key responsibilities: information providers, strategic policy makers, and operational decision-makers. During the simulation, they rotated their roles to remain motivated and creative. Brainstorming and decision-making was always done as a group. The team leader was much more participative than those in the other groups, and it was also not uncommon for the leader to change during the simulation to improve group dynamics. Members of adaptive teams were of East Asian and European descent, with a slight dominance of the latter where the main countries of domicile were Hong Kong, Singapore, Indonesia, and New Zealand.

Of the four groups, adaptive teams were observed to be the most empowered and highly motivated. On average they also achieved the highest levels of performance measured in terms of the highest company value. However, autocratic teams tended to be just as successful due to the high level of individual competence of their team leaders. The big difference between the two was in the degree of team spirit. As a rule, members of adaptive teams were highly participative; in contrast, there were occasions when members of autocratic teams appeared not to be involved or interested due to dominant team leaders. The other two team types, *delegating* and *democratic*, did not perform as well as the first two. Members in these teams often lacked the strong commitment and enthusiasm displayed by other teams, and team leadership was often lacking to set key strategic directions and get the best out of team members. In terms of the simulation's objective, they performed the worst, achieving the lowest company values.

A key finding to emerge from the simulation data was the way participating teams used the information provided by the simulation program. Three main user types were identified: those whose use of external information was limited to the trades in which they operated (limited external information users), those who overemphasised internal information (internal information users), and those who made extensive use of both external and internal information (extensive information users).

The first group, the *limited external information users*, generally used all available internal information (i.e. route accounts, cash flow, fleet value, liquid assets, value of routes and company value), and as much external information as was available to them *but only* on those areas in which they were operating. Seldom did they venture beyond their trade routes. For example, if they were involved in Europe-Japan-USA routes, they only looked for information pertaining to these routes and ignored other routes. As a result, they often missed the opportunities that lay in these areas. If they did look at other routes, they did so haphazardly or intermittently, rather than consistently and proactively, with an eye for new opportunities. Among the key external environmental factors they usually overlooked were trade indices and freight rates for routes in which they were not involved. Surprisingly, there were more risk takers than conservative decision-makers in this group; there were also more dry bulk operators.

The second group, the *internal information users*, spent most of their time analysing internal information, often at the expense of external information. The group tended to view internal trends more by the percentage difference between quarters than by changes in external conditions such as changing trade indices. It focused primarily on the 'bottom-line' approach: How much profit are we making on routes? What is our company value relative to previous quarters? Financial information (i.e. route profit, cash flow, company value) was also given more emphasis than operational information (i.e. number of vessels on routes, vessel speed, ports of call). Interestingly enough, this group also made more internal graphs than any other group to assist decision-making. While all participants took advantage of the option of viewing key variables in graph form, as preset by the simulation program, this group made more graphs than other groups to plot their key internal variables. Because of their preoccupation with internal variables, like the first group, they missed a lot of key external trends. Unlike the first group, however, this second user group was dominated by conservative decision-makers. It was also made up of a wide range of industry sector operators with no one sector dominating.

The third and last user group, the *extensive information users*, made extensive use of all external and internal information provided in the simulation. This group often spent more time analysing information than the other two groups. As a result, it took them longer to progress through the quarters. While this group included conservative and risk-taking decision-makers, the latter slightly outnumbered the former. In terms of industry sectors, there were also more liner and tanker operators.

Of the three user groups, the last group, which spent more time analysing information and made more extensive use of both internal and external information, achieved the highest levels of performance by obtaining higher company values. They were followed by the first group, which limited its use of external information to what was relevant to its areas of operation.

*Environmental focus*

Another finding to emerge from the simulation data was the dominance of either an external or internal environmental focus among participating teams. *Externally focused teams* analysed both external and internal environmental factors in their decision-making, but they tended to align their corporate strategies more closely with external factors than internal factors. For instance, if external environmental conditions were good, they would pursue a 'grow' strategy even if they lacked the cash flow to fund adequately the growth that such a strategy called for. Externally focused teams were found to be more responsive to market conditions. They were able to change faster than internally focused teams or maintain strategies that were flexible enough to adapt to changing market conditions. In most cases, because of their external focus, these teams were able to maintain the intent of the selected strategy while retaining their ability to respond to changing external conditions.

In contrast, *internally focused teams* tended to be a lot less flexible and adaptable in the face of changing market conditions, and were thus slower to respond to such changes. They tended to wait until external trends started affecting internal trends (e.g. declining trade route revenues and profits) before acting. Often this was two quarters later than the externally focused teams. They also tended to be more conservative in their decision-making, preferring minor changes to major ones. In many ways, internally focused teams were also the internal information users, the second group of information users identified in the preceding sub-section, who put undue reliance on internal information.

Among the various participating teams, three definite categories of performers emerged: *high performers*, *average performers*, and *low performers*. The objective of the simulation was to make an ailing company become financially profitable, hence, the higher the company value that a team posted at the end of the simulation, the more successful it was deemed to be. At the beginning of the simulation, the company value stood at $614.74 million. At the end of the competition, the high performers (nineteen per cent) climbed to a company value of greater than $1 billion, the average performers (53 per cent) reached between $600 million to $1 billion, and the low performers (28 per cent) reached less than $600 million.

Major differences between the higher and lower performers are highlighted below. Comparisons with the average group proved much more difficult because most teams in this group straddled both ends, making comparisons less reliable. Thus, no comparisons are made for this group.

*High performers* were the most successful teams, defined as having a company value of greater than $1 billion. They consistently came up with corporate strategies that achieved their objectives, and more importantly, *within the limits of what the environmental conditions dictated*. These teams succeeded by matching external environmental conditions with the best internal or organisational attributes (healthy cash flows, high growth trade routes), and came up with corporate strategies that captured the organisation's best future opportunities and also defended its most vulnerable areas from external threats.

There was, however, no one approach used by this group that was clearly superior to others. Approaches included having a high market share (large number of vessels and trade routes), playing the sale and purchase market, being a major charterer, or combining all three. All led to profitable results depending on environmental conditions. While some used some of these methods more than others, the data showed no clear pattern as to which method led to higher performance. Each of them worked well provided environmental factors were appropriate.

High performers also consistently chose more longer-term strategies (four to seven quarters ahead) and modified them to suit environmental conditions, particularly external conditions, as opposed to others who had short-term strategies and changed them a lot more frequently. Longer-term strategies were also more strategic in outlook thus enabling high performers to better predict broader trends and prepare for change. They also spent far greater time analysing information than any other group. Amongst the highest performers were those from the liner sector of the shipping industry. In terms of country or ethnic background, results showed that high performers represented a good mix of different countries and ethnic backgrounds.

*Low performers* were the least successful performers whose company value went below $600 million, which was lower than what they started with. Their hallmark was chronic lack of resources and capabilities. The least successful teams went into new trade routes or new areas of business (e.g. from ship operating to ship chartering) without the requisite capabilities such as good liquidity. They failed to live within their means, often trying to expand without the requisite resources, such as buying new vessels with poor cash flow. They often did not make much profit from such changes and their performance was generally mediocre.

For many within this group, their corporate strategies were too short-term (one to three quarters ahead) and operational. They frequently changed their strategies before they had a chance to work. For example, they might have been pursuing a 'grow' strategy when external trends were good but as soon as the market showed any signs of decline, they dropped that strategy for another (e.g. 'stabilise').

This group also spent more time in reactive, rather than proactive, mode. They often played the simulation from quarter to quarter, always reacting to circumstances that happened in the previous quarter. They also lagged behind changes in market conditions. Their main rationale for this short-term approach was to take advantage of short-term gains or opportunities, but this was often at the expense of long-term performance. However, there was too much concentration on short periods of high profits, which were either not repeatable in the longer term or affected longer term performance. For example, they might have made good profits from selling vessels when prices were high, but then they did not have the capacity to earn good profits when the route had improved due to the reduced fleet.

Low performers tended to put too much emphasis on internal information and paid inadequate attention to external trends. Indeed they showed a strong tendency to underestimate or overestimate market conditions, resulting in poor performance. In this group were a lot of conservative decision-makers who were slow to act—and react—and did so only when external conditions affected internal conditions, for example loss of revenue on trade routes, falling ship prices, or reduced charter rates. Their corporate strategies were middle-of-the-road play-safe strategies, which rarely produced high results. For many, performance throughout the simulation progressively declined, with some eventually going bankrupt.

The greatest number of bankruptcies came from three types of decision-makers:

- those who pursued rigid and inflexible strategies, and who, in the face of changing environmental conditions, were either very slow to respond or did not respond at all, sticking to what they had previously decided to do;
- those who took on too much risk at the wrong time and had inadequate financial resources and capability to recover from overexposure; and
- those who pursued very short-term (quarter by quarter) strategies and were highly conservative and reactive in their decision-making.

Most bankruptcies were the results of wrongly timed joint ventures, which led to heavy financial losses and severe reduction of operating flexibility. For example, some had to use valuable fleet capacity on a loss-making route when they could have used them on a route that was making high profits. In terms of industry sector, country or ethnic background, no discernible trends were observed. This group could perhaps be best described as an unfortunate mix of all types.

To summarise, top performers had clearly articulated strategies, which conveyed what was to be achieved and how it was to be achieved. These strategies were usually long-term but they were also flexible. In many instances, they included several types (e.g. grow, develop, stabilise) for greater strategic balance. These allowed top performers to map out long-term plans for growth while at the same time maintaining the ability to adapt to changing conditions. High performers were proactive; they were sensitive to environmental information, especially on external conditions; and they were quick to adapt to environmental changes.

Low performers on the other hand often had unclear or confusing strategies, either as a result of sloppy presentation or because the changes they implemented did not match with the selected strategy. Their strategies were usually short term, but they were also inflexible. Once chosen they were kept, even if environmental conditions called for a change. As reflected in this approach, performers were reactive and conservative, slow to react, even slower to change. While they did look at external factors, they put more emphasis to internal factors.

*Cultural differences*

To a great extent, the four decision-making styles discussed earlier were indicative of a range of behavioural differences between East Asian managers from Malaysia, Singapore, Indonesia, and managers of European ethnic descent from Australia, New Zealand, and a few European countries. For ease in reference, the latter group will simply be called 'European'. In general, East Asian shipowners took more risks but suffered the most bankruptcies. They made decisions more quickly, were slower to change strategies, displayed a more autocratic team management style, were more aggressive and competitive, and were less likely to revisit previous decisions when deliberating on new decisions. In contrast, European shipowners tended to be a lot more conservative. Those East Asian shipowners who took the greatest risks came from the bulk sector of the industry, both dry bulk and tanker, while the majority of European shipowners were from the liner sector. Among East Asian shipowners, the level of risk taken did not appear to relate to market conditions. With European shipowners, the level of risk taken tended to increase as their performance declined, measured by a fall in company value.

East Asian shipowners made their decisions much faster than European shipowners. Based on time differences noted in posting quarterly results, on average, they were close to a quarter of an hour faster (thirteen minutes) at making quarter by quarter decisions. In contrast, European shipowners spent more time analysing information before making a decision, which accounted for the time difference. Those from the liner sector tended to spend more time analysing information than from the bulk sector.

The simulation structured more periods of environmental changes than stable conditions. While this led European shipowners to change strategies more frequently, the same could not be said of East Asian shipowners. On average East Asian shipowners tended to keep the same strategic objectives for a longer period of time than their European counterparts. However, this did not mean that East Asian shipowners had longer-term objectives and European shipowners had shorter-term ones. More correctly, the latter made changes depending on what the environmental conditions were. When conditions were stable, they kept their strategic objectives for a longer period of time; when conditions were unstable or rapidly changed, the more frequently were these objectives changed. Shipowners from the dry bulk and tanker sectors were quicker to change their objectives than those from the liner sector, especially those from container trades who were usually the last to change.

As was found during the interviews, both East Asian and European shipowners stressed the need for teamwork. However, while the Europeans tended to maintain team harmony and cohesiveness through greater individual participation, East Asian shipowners in contrast leaned toward a more autocratic and hierarchical approach. Either approach was observed to work well when the members of a team, regardless of cultural origin, had the same mindset (i.e. supporting either a democratic or an autocratic style); however, conflict arose when members had differing mindsets, especially in the area of decision-making and leadership.

Despite these differences, data and observations from the simulation provided no clear evidence that one particular approach or style led to a higher level of performance. While it was probable that different approaches or styles could lead to different levels of performance, the simulation was unable to determine categorically the influence of these factors on performance.

## Post-simulation evaluation

A limitation of simulation is that the format and the information provided were different from what is normally found in the participants' work environment. As one shipping CEO commented, 'This is not the way we present information in our company or even in the previous companies I have worked for. But once I adapted to it, it was no problem.'

Nevertheless, it must be accepted that it has limitations, which have an influence on the quality of the decisions and approaches taken during the simulation. The following are some of the criticisms made by participants. Too much or too little information was provided; the simulation was too structured; the range of strategic choices available was too narrow; there was too much time pressure; the temptation to experiment was never far away; and the market statistics provided were not current. Furthermore, some participants found it difficult to set strategic objectives, had difficulty in articulating a corporate strategy and in using time frames.

Counterbalancing these limitations there were several strengths of the simulation, which participants agreed made up for the program's weaknesses. Competing with peers was a big incentive. Because of time pressure, their behaviour during the simulation approximated their normal behaviour and working in teams made decision-making more realistic.

The simulation showed strong support for all six assumptions of the strategic choice model, indicating the model's applicability to Asia-Pacific shipping. However, slight modifications to the model were needed to reflect a general tendency among shipowners to use other strategies in combination with those offered by the model. The findings highlighted differences in team decision-making styles, use of information, environmental focus, and competitive performance. Cultural differences were also identified. However, despite the limitations and difficulties encountered during the simulation, the overall majority view was that the simulation was a realistic assessment of shipowners' strategic behaviour. In particular, participants found that the simulation represented a fair assessment of their performance. The simulation environment was just as competitive, tough and hard to foresee as reality was, and the strategies they pursued, and the conditions upon which these strategies were based, reflected what they would have actually done in real life. Overall, participants found the simulation a useful and stimulating learning tool for honing strategic decision-making skills. For many of them, unfortunately, such simulation programs or similar tools to assist strategy selection were not available in their organisations.

# 9 A new shipping-based strategic choice model

## Introduction

This chapter commences with a synthesis of the shipowner-generated information and the revision of the strategic choice model into a shipping-based model[1]. Then feedback from shipping experts who reviewed this shipping model is presented, and, finally, a revised version of the model for use in Asia-Pacific commercial shipping is offered.

The strategic choice model assumes that under certain environmental conditions, certain generic corporate strategies are more appropriate to pursue than others. The model provides a system by which environmental conditions are assessed on the basis of market (or external) and organisational competitive (or internal) factors that are relevant to the organisation at the particular time when strategic choices are made. As noted earlier, internal or organisational competitive factors refer to an organisation's strengths and weaknesses vis-à-vis competitors; external or market factors refer to the opportunities and threats in the environment in which the organisation competes. On the strategic choice model, the overall strategic position of a business or organisation is ranked on a sliding scale, with a 'high' or a 'low' rating marking either end of the continuum. The more strengths and opportunities a business organisation has, the higher is its strategic position; the more weaknesses and threats, the lower the position. Judgements on such strategic positions are typically qualitative, based on the decision-maker's knowledge, experience and intuition, bolstered by access to good external information.

---

[1] Some of the findings were originally published in Hawkins, J.E and Gray, R (1999) Making strategic choices for Asia-Pacific shipping, *International Journal of Maritime Economics*, 1, 2, 57-71.

The original model was shown in Figure 5.13. As the model shows, when an organisation rates highly on both organisational and market factors, which means it is competitively strong and the market offers many opportunities, its best course of action is to 'grow' (quadrant 1). If it is competitively strong but there are many threats in the market, a better alternative is to 'stabilise', that is, to keep the status quo (quadrant 3). If an organisation is competitively weak but the market offers many opportunities, it should take advantage of these opportunities by pursuing a 'develop' strategy in new areas or a 'turnaround' strategy in existing areas (quadrant 2). However, if the organisation is weak and there are more threats than opportunities in the market, a 'harvest' strategy is more appropriate (quadrant 4).

Because the assumptions underlying the strategic choice model had been drawn largely from non-shipping areas, the extent to which they applied to Asia-Pacific shipowners required testing. To what extent did shipowner data support the model's assumptions? Table 9.1 summarises the majority views obtained from the survey, interviews and simulation. The 'yes' columns represent those who strictly adhered to the model, that is, without any deviations; the 'qualified yes' columns, those who also followed the model but modified it occasionally or regularly for strategic reasons.

From the table, several key patterns can be observed. Data obtained through the three research methods (survey, interviews and simulation) revealed a similar pattern of response. Shipping respondents supported all six assumptions of the strategic choice model, with survey respondents giving an overall support rating of 79 per cent; interviewees, 75 per cent; and simulation participants, 79 per cent. The aggregate majority vote averaged around 78 per cent.

As the 'qualified yes' columns indicate, strategic choices were not always limited to those assumed by the model. In both self-reports (survey and interviews) and simulation data, the tendency to modify the model's parameters for strategic purposes was evident. Shipowners either changed direction occasionally to pursue a strategic objective (e.g. disregarding future expectation of market conditions or pursuing a particular strategy under conditions not called for in the model) or regularly combined the strategy specified in the model with other strategies (e.g. 'grow' with 'develop' and/or 'stabilise').

The 'mix and match' practice by shipowners initially emerged from the survey data, but the extent to which it was done, and how it was done, did not become clearer until during the interviews and simulation. To a great extent, this process of gradual clarification was to be expected given the relative merits of the research methods used. The mail survey provided initial baseline information about the shipping respondents, but it relied solely on the ability and willingness of individual respondents to provide the necessary information. In contrast, interviews allowed further probes into interviewees' thoughts and practices so that the nature and frequency of modifications made to the model, as well as the reasons behind them, were more clearly explained. The simulation also made a high degree of clarification possible because participants were required to make specific strategic decisions under changing environmental conditions, thereby allowing specific linkages to be established between strategies and environmental conditions. That all three methods led to a similar pattern of responses confirmed their convergence as called for by the triangulation approach.

**Table 9.1**

**A summary of shipowners' feedback on the strategic choice model**

| The model assumes that Asia-Pacific shipowners will: | Survey | | | Interviews | | | Simulation | | |
|---|---|---|---|---|---|---|---|---|---|
| | Yes | Yes Qualified | | Yes | Yes Qualified | | Yes | Yes Qualified | |
| 1 change/modify their corporate strategies in response to changing environmental conditions | 85 | 7 | | 75 | 1 2 | | 58 | 1 8 | |
| 2 base strategic changes and the time frames of these changes on their future expectations of environmental conditions | 80 | – | | 44 | 1 6 | | 74 | – | |
| 3 pursue a 'grow' strategy when internal and external environmental factors are both favourable | 76 | 8 | | 63 | 2 2 | | 55 | 3 0 | |
| 4 pursue a 'stabilise' strategy when internal environmental factors are favourable but external factors are not | 72 | 9 | | 61 | 1 9 | | 67 | 1 4 | |
| 5 pursue a 'develop' or 'turnaround' strategy when external factors are favourable but internal factors are not | 68 | – | | 52 | 2 5 | | 44 | 3 2 | |
| 6 pursue a 'harvest' strategy when internal and external environmental factors are both unfavourable | 52 | 1 7 | | 65 | – | | 79 | 7 | |

## An Asia-Pacific shipping strategic choice model: initial version

Based on the analysis of data from representatives of shipowners' data, the following conclusions could thus be drawn regarding strategy selection among the Asia-Pacific shipowners who participated in the study:

- The generic strategic choice model was applicable to Asia-Pacific commercial shipping, but certain modifications were required.
- As a rule, Asia-Pacific shipowners changed or modified their corporate strategies in response to changing environmental conditions. Where strategic objectives or other organisational considerations, notably preferences of major stakeholders and internal politics, ran counter to market conditions, the former took precedence and changes were not always implemented even if called for by the model.
- Asia-Pacific shipowners based strategic changes and the time frames of these changes on their future expectations of environmental conditions; however, there were occasions when such expectations, particularly of market conditions, were subordinated to other, more significant, strategic considerations.
- When organisational competitive (or internal) and market (or external) factors or conditions were both favourable (competitively strong, many market opportunities), a 'grow' strategy was the preferred choice, pursued alone or in combination with 'develop' and 'stabilise' strategies.
- When organisational competitive factors were favourable but market factors were not (competitively strong, many market threats), a 'stabilise' strategy was the preferred choice, pursued alone or in combination with 'grow' and 'develop' strategies, and to a much lesser extent, with a 'harvest' strategy.
- When market factors were favourable but organisational competitive factors were not (competitively weak, many market opportunities), 'develop' and 'turnaround' strategies were the preferred choices, pursued jointly or independently of each other, or in combination with a 'grow' strategy.
- When organisational competitive factors and market factors were both unfavourable (competitively weak, many market threats), a 'harvest' strategy was the preferred choice, either pursued alone or in combination with a 'turnaround' strategy.

These preferred strategy choices are plotted in matrix form in Figure 9.1. This figure now represents the revised version of the original strategic choice model and is the first iteration of a shipping-specific strategic choice model. Strategies preceded with a plus (+) sign are the additions made by shipowners. It should be noted that in the simulation data, the 'harvest' strategy appeared as another choice; however, because it was not as widely and as frequently used as the other strategies, it has been excluded from the model.

| | **Organisational Competitive Factors** | |
| | High (Strengths) | Low (Weaknesses) |
|---|---|---|
| High (Opportunities) | Quadrant 1<br><br>Grow<br>(+Develop)<br>(+Stabilise) | Quadrant 2<br><br>Develop<br>Turnaround<br>(+Grow) |
| Low (Threats) | Quadrant 3<br><br>Stabilise<br>(+Grow)<br>(+Develop)<br>(+Harvest) | Quadrant 4<br><br>Harvest<br>(+Turnaround) |

(left axis label: **Market factors**)

**Figure 9.1  Asia-Pacific shipping strategic choice model: first iteration**

**Expert review of the shipping model**

A final aspect of the research approach was to subject the shipping-based model to an expert review. The objective was to compare results obtained from shipowners with another data source, in this case, a combination of academics and practitioners who knew Asia-Pacific commercial shipping and were experienced in corporate strategy selection. The expert panel used for this purpose consisted of six maritime management and two strategy consultants, two maritime academics, three shipowner associations' representatives, and two shipping research institutes' representatives. All were based in the Asia-Pacific region.

A briefing paper describing the strategic choice model for Asia-Pacific commercial shipping was sent to each expert for review. They were asked to comment on the model's realism. In their opinion did it represent what Asia-Pacific shipowners actually did? They were also asked to comment on its utility as an analytical or evaluation tool to help shipowners in their strategic analysis and strategy choices, and to recommend specific ways by which the model's applicability to Asia-Pacific shipowners could be enhanced. Comments received were compared against shipowner data so that a final version of the strategic choice model for Asia-Pacific shipping could be drawn up.

## Table 9.2
### Expert feedback on the strategic choice model for Asia-Pacific shipping (%)

| | Very realistic | Realistic | Unsure | Somewhat realistic | Not at all |
|---|---|---|---|---|---|
| How realistic is the model, that is, to what extent does it reflect what you know about Asia-Pacific shipowners? | 20 | 67 | 13 | 0 | 0 |

| | Very useful | Useful | Unsure | Somewhat useful | Not at all |
|---|---|---|---|---|---|
| How useful would Asia-Pacific shipowners find the model as a tool for analysing and selecting corporate strategies? | 20 | 47 | 20 | 13 | 0 |

| | Suggestion | Times cited |
|---|---|---|
| In what specific ways can the model be improved to enhance its realism and utility? | *Improve the rating scale:*<br>• Add a rating scale to the model<br>• Use % for rating scale | 4 |
| | *Improve terminology:*<br>• Add the word 'shipping' to 'market factors'<br>• Delete the word 'competitive' from 'organisational factors'<br>• Add 'key success factors' to each variable name | 6 |
| | *Provide training in the proper use of the model* | 3 |

As Table 9.2 shows, support for the model's realism was strong (87 per percent), and the majority (67 per cent) agreed it was a useful tool for strategic decision making. However, in both areas, a number of issues were raised which could diminish the model's realism and utility unless adequately addressed. These are discussed below under their respective headings. Several specific suggestions to improve the model were also offered.

*Realism of the model*

A big majority agreed that the model was realistic (87 per cent); that is, that its six assumptions represented what Asia-Pacific shipowners generally did in real life. However, two experts expressed some uncertainty. While they may represent a minority view, their comments are worth noting because they reflect concerns also aired in the strategic management literature. Both experts were concerned that the model might be too simplistic because of its reliance on the matrix approach to strategy selection and evaluation. They thought the use of a two-dimensional scale was too narrow a view and queried what would happen when strategies or factors fell right on the borderline between quadrants. While they were not able to offer any alternative approach, leading one expert to add that 'this model was better than none at all', both emphasised the need for 'better guidance or some means of measurement otherwise the model would become unrealistic'.

A few other experts also queried the model's assumption that the user would be competent to define key environmental factors. According to one, the model would be realistic only to the extent that users knew how to use it. He stated, 'This would be difficult for some shipowners who are not skilled in strategic analysis; I wouldn't put much store on its realism if put in the hands of an unskilled user'. Suggested another: 'Detailed instructions should accompany the model so that even the novice could follow it; either that or give them some training.'

*Utility of the model as an evaluation tool*

Opinion on this question was more dispersed, with a smaller majority (67 per cent) seeing the model as a useful evaluation tool. Some of these experts likened the model to a strategic map on which strategic alternatives could be viewed and plotted, providing a broad-picture perspective of the strategic terrain. One expert explained:

[Asia Pacific] shipowners get so caught up in day-to-day operational decisions that it is often very difficult to get them to step back and take a look at the broader picture of how they intend to achieve their objectives and what corporate strategies they will use to guide the organisation. As a result, their decisions are more likely to be operational and short term rather than strategic. They also often miss the broader emerging trends. This is where the model can help them if they use it. It will force them to look beyond their narrow operational focus because of the emphasis given to thinking about and identifying key environmental information.

Among those who were unsure of the model's usefulness as an analytical or evaluation tool (33 per cent), the lack of training and expertise in strategic analysis was cited as a major hindrance in the use of the model. A typical comment was that 'because of the lack of training in [strategic] management and the usual approach by a lot of shipping people to make decisions based upon intuition as opposed to using planning tools like this one, it may not be useful simply because they won't know how to use it properly. Only if they are trained in its use and can appreciate the benefits of using it will it truly be useful to them.'

Another threat to the model's utility is the tendency of many people to follow it blindly, instead of making intelligent use of it as an analytical model to aid in the selection and evaluation of corporate strategies. As one expert described it, 'There is always the danger of these sorts of models being used as some sort of 'cookbook'. Some people will expect it to provide all the answers to their prayers and tell them exactly what to do. They don't have to think because the model will provide all the answers and a step-by-step recipe to success. Then when they find out that it doesn't work like that, the model is branded as useless.' Another expert added, 'If the model is used properly, it will tend to raise a lot more questions that it attempts to answer. However, that is a big if!'

*Suggestions for improvement*

Given these concerns, what improvements should be made to the model? According to the few experts who provided specific suggestions, changes could be made in two areas: the use of a rating scale and changes to the terminology.

*Rating scale* A frequently cited limitation of the model is its lack of a rating scale for plotting the strategic position of a business or organisation. While judgmental calls were essential, commented one, it would help if there were some standard basis for decision making: 'Everybody around the table should have the same yardstick.' Such a scale should also overcome the problem of 'fence-sitters', that is, those businesses or organisations that sit on or close to quadrant borders because it would make it easier to plot a business's or organisation's position relative to its strengths and weaknesses and to the opportunities and threats it faces.

It was also suggested that an effective rating scale would be expressed in percentage points, rather than the usual numeric scales (e.g. 1-5, 1-10), even though conceptually they were the same thing. According to one expert, 'shipowners are so used to dealing with percentage figures that it would be much easier for them to rate their business(es) in this manner. The moment you changed this to a 1-10 scale, which is saying the same thing, you will have problems because this will require a change in mindset for some.'

*Terminology* Three changes to the terminology were suggested to tighten up the meaning of variables: add the word 'shipping' to market factors to emphasise the model's shipping orientation, delete the word 'competitive' from 'organisational competitive factors' since competitive factors depended on overall organisational health ('if the organisation isn't fit, it can't compete'), and rename each set of variables to 'shipping market success factors' and 'organisational success factors'.

As the preceding discussion shows, shipping experts lent their support to the model, both in terms of its realism and utility as an evaluation model. No major conceptual criticism was made, with suggestions focusing more on technical areas, e.g. the rating scale and terminology. As the next section shows, these suggestions were incorporated into the final version of the model.

## A strategic choice model for Asia-Pacific shipping: final version

Figure 9.2 represents the final version of the strategic choice model for Asia-Pacific commercial shipping. It synthesises findings based on three research methods (survey, interviews, and simulation) and from two data sources (shipowners, shipping experts). A review of relevant documents and observations of simulation activities also provided additional data. Throughout, a qualitative approach to data analysis was used, except where the data lent itself to statistical analysis, as was the case with some survey data. The high degree of congruence among the various sets of findings establishes strong support for the model's applicability to Asia-Pacific commercial shipping.

*Description of the model*

The model can be used to analyse the strategic position of a single business unit, or the relative positions of different business units operated by an organisation, or the relative position of an organisation vis-à-vis its main competitors.

|  |  | **Key Organisational Success Factors** | | | |
|---|---|---|---|---|---|
|  |  | High (Strengths) | | Low (Weaknesses) | |
|  |  | 100%    75% | | 50%    25%    0% | |
| High (Opportunities) | 100% | Quadrant 1<br><br>Grow<br>Develop<br>Stabilise | | Quadrant 2<br><br>Turnaround<br>Develop<br>Grow | |
|  | 75% |  | |  | |
| Key shipping market factors | 50% | Quadrant 3<br><br>Stabilise<br>Grow<br>Develop<br>Harvest | | Quadrant 4<br><br>Turnaround<br>Harvest | |
|  | 25% |  | |  | |
| Low (Threats) | 0% |  | |  | |

**Figure 9.2  Asia-Pacific shipping strategic choice model**

The model bases strategy selection on an assessment of an organisation's internal and external environment. The internal environment is described on the horizontal axis in terms of organisational success factors; the external environment on the vertical axis in terms of shipping market success factors. Organisational success factors refer to an organisation's strengths and weaknesses relative to its major competitors; shipping market factors refer to the opportunities and threats in the particular area(s) in which the organisation competes. This type of analysis is popularly known in the literature as the SWOT approach, with SWOT being an acronym for strengths, weaknesses, opportunities, and threats.

The rating scale is used to plot the relative position of an organisation on the two dimensions discussed above, that is, in terms of organisational success factors (strengths and weaknesses) and shipping market success factors (opportunities and threats). The scale has 5 cut-off points, expressed as percentages, with 0 per cent representing the 'low' end of the continuum and 100 per cent the 'high' end. The more strengths an organisation has and the more opportunities there are in the market, the higher is the organisation's strategic position. Conversely, the more weaknesses an organisation has and the more threats there are in the market, the lower is the organisation's strategic position. The 5 cut-off points on the scale are interpreted as follows:

|  | Organisational Success Factors | Shipping Market Success Factors |
| --- | --- | --- |
| 100% | many strengths and no weaknesses | many opportunities and no threats |
| 75% | many strengths but a few weaknesses | many opportunities but a few threats |
| 50% | strengths and weaknesses balance out | opportunities and threats balance out |
| 25% | many weaknesses with a few strengths | many threats but a few opportunities |
| 0% | many weaknesses and no strengths | many threats and no opportunities |

A qualitative or quantitative approach can equally be used to plot an organisation's position on the matrix. However, a combination of both is advisable as this provides a more solid basis for decision making. Qualitative assessment involves the use of judgement, intuition or 'gut sense', and experience to gauge the relative position of the organisation. Quantitative assessment involves a more systematic measurement of success factors by assigning specific weights and ranks to each success factor and calculating an overall ranking. The combined use of judgement calls and systematic measurement serves as an effective check-and-balance tool during decision making, with one method informing and enriching the other.

*Strategic choices*

Figure 9.2 shows the different combinations of corporate strategies that Asia-Pacific shipowners are likely to pursue within each quadrant of the matrix. This 'mix and match' approach is preferred to the one or two choices offered by the original strategic choice model because it makes it easier for organisations to achieve strategic balance and reduce the risks to the organisation.

In quadrant 1, where there are many market opportunities and the organisation is competitively strong, a 'grow' strategy is typically pursued to further strengthen an organisation's position in highly profitable areas where it already operates. However, it may also pursue a 'develop' strategy to enter into new high-profit areas and/or a 'stabilise' strategy to maintain its strong position in more mature markets.

In quadrant 2, where there are many market opportunities but the organisation is competitively weak, the more appropriate approach is to pursue a 'develop' and/or 'turnaround' strategy, and to a lesser extent, a 'grow' strategy. The first and last are both aggressive approaches, aimed at building the organisation's competitiveness in, respectively, new and existing highly profitable areas of operation; the second is an emergency measure, designed to overcome serious financial problems and restore financial health and viability. Whether these strategies are pursued singly or in combination with one another depends on the shipowner's number of businesses and the level of risk it is prepared to take.

In quadrant 3, where there are many market threats but the organisation is competitively strong, the main strategy pursued is 'stabilise', where the objective is to maintain the status quo, with changes kept to a minimal and incremental level. However, 'grow', 'develop', and to a lesser extent, 'harvest' strategies may also be pursued, either as a substitute to or in combination with 'stabilise', to offset market threats and spread the risks. 'Grow' and 'develop' are normally pursued when the organisation decides to speculate; 'stabilise' is chosen when the organisation decides to sell up and get out of the business while it is still highly marketable.

In quadrant 4, where the organisation is competitively weak and faces many market threats, a 'harvest' strategy is usually pursued, with the organisation selling up and getting out of the unprofitable area. It may also be substituted or combined with a 'turnaround' strategy in an attempt to turn the organisation's fortunes around and make it financially viable again.

*Using the model*

The process of analysing an organisation's environment to determine its strategic position and subsequently choose the most appropriate strategy or combination of strategies involves three main steps.

*Step 1* Identify key organisational and shipping market success factors of particular relevance to the organisation at the time the analysis is conducted.

This step requires a broad outlook, rather than a myopic or parochial one, because there are no set factors to draw on. Factors differ according to shipowner and market segment, and they change over time. It is important, therefore, for the organisation to look both inside, which is relatively easy, and out to spot new and potential opportunities and threats, and select those strategies that will optimise the organisation's strengths and reduce its weaknesses. With a reasonably wide scan of the external environment, balanced by a realistic estimate of the organisation's competitiveness, strategic decision makers would be better placed to gauge their organisation's relative strength and profitability in the market.

*Step 2* Using the rating scale, rate and plot the relative position of each business area of the organisation on the matrix.

This can be based on 'gut sense' and judgement calls, with decision makers using their knowledge of the organisation's various business areas to position them along the horizontal and vertical axes of the matrix. An alternative approach is to assign weights to specific success factors to standardise the rating process. However, since there is no standard set of weights available; every organisation would have to decide on these themselves, depending on the relative importance they attach to the environmental factors they have identified in step 1. A third approach is to take a combined qualitative and quantitative approach to enhance confidence in the decisions made.

*Step 3* With the relative position of each business area plotted on the matrix, evaluate whether all or which of the strategies recommended by the model are appropriate to pursue, given the organisation's strategic objectives and environmental assessment. Again, there is no magic formula to reach the 'right' answer. When selecting strategies, particularly when several choices are available and the organisation falls close to or on the borderline, decision-makers would need to depend on intuitive judgement, to ask critical questions, to think strategically, so they can make wise choices.

**Strategy selection as part of a process**

While selecting the 'right' corporate strategy is essential to survival in an increasingly competitive and globalised shipping market, it is also wise to reiterate what has been stated earlier. Strategy selection is but one aspect of the broader strategic management process and corporate strategies are but one level of strategies that an organisation should be concerned with. Thus, while this book has focused on strategy selection, in practice, there is a need for a constant zooming in and out. The first is to focus on the fine details on any one aspect of the environment, the second is to take in the broader picture and the various opportunities and threats it holds.

# 10 Conclusions

This book had three objectives: to analyse the strategic choices that Asia-Pacific shipowners pursued at the corporate level; to compare actual shipowners' behaviour with strategic management theory on strategy selection; and to develop a strategy selection model that was applicable to Asia-Pacific shipowners and consistent with strategy management theory.

## Corporate strategy selection by Asia-Pacific shipowners

Who is responsible for corporate strategic choices? On this question, the book echoed what is widely acknowledged in the strategic management literature; that is, that senior management is primarily responsible for making corporate strategic choices. Senior management in this case represents three levels: the top executives who are responsible for the entire organisation, divisional managers responsible for major areas or divisions within the organisation, and managers responsible for providing corporate-level advice and assistance on strategic planning and strategic management. All three groups are expected to contribute to the decision-making process, but to a great degree, culture dictates the way their respective roles are interpreted.

The study, based on a survey, questionnaires and a simulation, showed that senior managers did not necessarily behave as assumed by the strategic choice model or the dominant rationalist school of strategic management thought. Strategies were selected regardless of environmental conditions to pursue strategic objectives, or they were maintained even when changes were called for by environmental conditions because of management conflict, inertia, fear, or inexperience. The study also found that Asia-Pacific shipowners in general did not follow a formalised approach to strategic planning and/or strategy selection; strategic planning was carried out, but it did not necessarily lead to formal documentation. Rather, the preferred process emerged to be informal, intuitive, and incremental. Further, while discussions and consultations were held to make strategic choices, formalised approaches to analysing the environment and evaluating strategic alternatives, such as scenario analysis and computer simulation, were not widely used. Neither, it seemed, was there an extensive use of external information sources; these, to many, were too unreliable and costly to warrant usage. Much of the decision making was based on personal knowledge, experience, and intuition.

To a great extent, managerial frames of reference (Hamel and Pralahad, 1993), or what are more colloquially known as 'mindsets', determine an organisation's strategic choices. The study found that where senior managers were more willing to take risks and speculate, an organisation was more likely to choose aggressive strategies and disregard prevailing environmental conditions to pursue strategic objectives. Where senior managers were more cautious, preferring to stay within safe margins, the organisation was more likely to pursue less risky strategies and keep within the parameters of the strategic choice model. Where senior managers were more conservative, the organisation was also more likely to have in place formalised strategic planning systems.

Such organisational differences surfaced between bulk and liner trades, and between large and small operators. Shipowners in the bulk trades pursued more aggressive strategies and took more risks. In contrast, their counterparts in the liner trades opted for 'safer' choices that would reduce financial risks. More shipowners in the liner trades were also found to have strategic plans than their counterparts in the bulk trades. This was true as well with large operators, who tended to follow more formalised strategic planning processes than smaller operators. Differences also extended to national cultures. East Asian shipowners were found to take more risks, pursue more aggressive strategies, adopt a more autocratic approach, and follow a more informal process than their European counterparts.

Within Asia-Pacific shipping, there is a prevailing lack of familiarity with the theories and models of strategy selection, and strategic management as a whole, and with recent developments in this field of study. Although Asia-Pacific shipowners did pursue corporate strategies, a large majority did not show much familiarity with the mainstream literature on strategy selection. This literature includes types and levels of strategies, strategy selection models, strategy selection processes, analytical and evaluation tools, and the relationship between strategy selection and overall strategic management. To a great degree, this could be traced to a lack of training in general management and/or strategic management, and a subsequent lack of exposure to current developments in these fields. Throughout East Asia especially, the explosive growth of the various economies in the region over the last two to three decades has significantly increased demand for managers at middle and senior levels who knew how to do business in a highly competitive and increasingly globalised market. Unfortunately, as recent surveys show (Granitsas and Saywell, 1997), this demand has so far been largely unmet.

Similar figures specifically for shipping are not available, and the financial crisis gripping the region at the turn of the century may well have dampened some of this demand. Nevertheless, it would still be fair to assume that the demand for experienced and well-trained senior managers is still acutely felt in the Asia-Pacific shipping industry. The industry has grown rapidly in recent decades to meet regional and world transport needs; it now controls about 38 per cent of the world fleet, second only to Europe, which controls 44 per cent. Owners of a fleet this large, whose growth has been compressed into a remarkably short period of time, would not have had the time to groom managers with the training, experience, and expertise in both intra-regional and global trading. Neither would it have found a ready pool of qualified managers from long-established shipping countries in Europe, as there has been a steady decline in their numbers in the last two decades (Bennett, 1996). Current efforts by international organisations now focus on the need to provide strategic management training. UNCTAD (1995), for instance, has conducted various formal and on-the-job training programs to upgrade strategic planning and management skills within the maritime industry. In recent years, seminars on strategic planning for senior shipping management in the Asia-Pacific region have been conducted, and strategic planning courses for shipping managers have been developed under UNCTAD's TRAINMAR programme.

The general profile of the Asia-Pacific shipowner that emerges bears strong resemblance to what studies outside the maritime field have found (e.g. Lasserre and Schutte, 1995; Napier and Albert, 1990; Hofstede, 1980). Because East Asian economies have grown rapidly in the last two to three decades, the market environment has generally been unstable and turbulent, marked by rapid change and uncertainty. Under these conditions, it is not surprising why a fluid and flexible planning and decision-making process, unfettered by formalistic rules of planning and analysis, is viewed as critical to competitive survival, and why there is strong concern for secrecy and a general reluctance to share or seek for information widely. Napier and Albert (1990) also suggest that the devaluing of planning among East Asian managers might be an offshoot of deliberate government intervention. They argue that, when an industry is targeted for growth in the interest of the national economy, grow it will regardless of whether senior managers within the industry engage in strategic thinking and decision making. The presence of government support is substantiated by the World Bank (1993), which has reported on the extent to which most governments in East Asia have assisted local businesses to grow through a range of supportive and protective measures. However, there is no evidence that this has led to less reliance on planning. Indeed, it is just as likely that strategic planning did occur but not in the way assumed by Western models and researchers (i.e. formalised and accompanied by documentation) and hence was less transparent. This alternative explanation certainly emerged from data obtained by this study from Asia-Pacific shipowners.

Lasserre and Schutte (1995) also offer the view, based on their studies of Hong Kong Chinese, that an incremental approach to business lessens the need for strategic decision making. Business owners seize opportunities only as they come and pursue these opportunities with a fatalist's expectation of both success *and* failure; to reduce risks, therefore, one need not plan, one need only to diversify into multiple ventures with the expectation that some of these will succeed and some will not. This view, however, runs counter to what our study has found about East Asian shipowners. Firm-level strategic planning did occur, albeit informally and often without recourse to formalised procedures and documentation. At the same time, incremental steps were favoured to give the organisation greater flexibility. This was why a combination of strategies was highly popular among shipowners. It helped them maintain a better strategic balance and reduce their exposure to market risks. To some extent, this approach is reminiscent of Hamel and Pralahad's (1993) idea of strategy as stretch and leverage where the organisation manoeuvres to get the best out of its assets and resources through a creative combination of strategies.

These broad similarities between Asia-Pacific shipowners and other businesses or industries in the Asia-Pacific region and elsewhere have significant implications for the maritime industry because they help chisel away at a prevailing industry view of 'differentness', typified by the oft-quoted statement 'it may apply to them, but we're different'. Often this view of being different becomes an active deterrent against experimentation and adaptation in the field. Thus, while important differences do distinguish the maritime industry from others, it is essential that similarities are also identified and acknowledged to advance both shipping strategy theory and practice.

**Value of the strategic choice model**

The generic strategic choice model has been modified to reflect more accurately what Asia-Pacific shipowners do, but even in its original form, the model has wide applicability across industries and businesses, *provided* it is used as a 'thinking' tool and not as a step-by-step recipe to success. The strategic choice model does not lend itself well to formula management. It is not a set of specific instructions that can be manipulated to arrive at some specific decision. Rather, as Lewis *et al* (1993) put it, it is a tool for asking questions, and when used for this purpose, it can be an effective aid to strategy analysis and selection, irrespective of business or industry. The best use of the model is as a template that provides the general structure and parameters for analysis, but leaves the rest to the decision maker: what to look for in the environment, which success factors to use, which strategies to pursue. This latitude in decision making is critical because of significant inter-industry differences that have already been documented both in the maritime industry (Brooks, 1995) and elsewhere (e.g. Campbell and Verbeke, 1994; Barlett and Goshall, 1989; see also Armistead, 1994).

The model also puts discipline into an otherwise informal and intuitive strategy selection process by requiring the decision-maker to:

- maintain a close watch over the organisation's internal and external environment;
- identify key success factors in this environment that are of particular relevance to the organisation at the time the analysis is made;
- decide on the relative importance of each factor;
- gauge the strategic position of the organisation based on these success factors (by plotting it on the model, which comes in matrix form); and
- evaluate whether the strategies offered by the model will support this strategic position, and if they do not, what alternative strategies should be pursued.

The mere act of following this process adds greater transparency to strategy selection, and makes decision makers more aware of what they need to do to enhance confidence and reliability in strategic choices made.

When used in this manner, the model facilitates wider applicability of strategy selection concepts and principles because it allows individual users to tailor their analysis to their specific organisations, businesses, market sectors, or industries as well as to the specific time periods during which the analysis is conducted. However, the model does require a reasonable amount of knowledge, experience, and expertise on the part of the user, particularly in the identification of relevant success factors in an organisation's internal and external environment and in the evaluation of the relative merits and appropriateness of various strategic alternatives. In this respect therefore the model's utility relies a lot on the user's ability to make an intelligent assessment of the environment and use this assessment to make wise strategic choices.

While the generic strategic choice model can be applied widely in its original form, its applicability to specific businesses or industries still has to be proven to broaden its usage and enhance confidence in its applicability.

Industry validation is necessary for two reasons. As the study has found, there is very little evidence to suggest that strategy selection theory and models are widely used in Asia-Pacific commercial shipping. Shipping practitioners in the region therefore still have to be convinced that the strategic choice model does apply to their specific circumstance. Giving them a model that has been tested in other industries is not good enough. They may say they need evaluation or analytical tools to help them with strategic decision making, as was the case with the shipowners who participated in the study. However, they are likely to be more suspicious of models 'tried elsewhere' and more accepting of models that have been applied to their own industry and subsequently 'validated' by prevailing industry practice. The second reason is academic. Theorists and researchers need to work with a substantial store of empirical evidence so that they can continue extending the boundaries of existing theories and models, and in so doing enhance the descriptive, prescriptive, or predictive power of these theories and models. The more evidence there is that the generic strategic choice model works in a variety of industrial and business contexts, the more robust and useful it becomes. Such evidence leads to a better understanding of differences and similarities between and within industries, and adds more precision and detail to theoretical discussions of corporate strategy selection.

By examining the strategy selection practices of commercial shipowners in the Asia-Pacific region, a topic about which very little has been written, this book has attempted to add further evidence of the robustness of the strategic choice model. As we have shown, Asia-Pacific shipowners support the model, but they prefer to combine strategies rather than be restricted to the one or two choices assumed by the model. Further, of the five corporate strategies, the 'grow' strategy is by far the most popular choice, often or regularly combined with the other corporate strategies to spread risks and improve strategic balance. There is evidence to show that this pattern of strategic choices made by Asia-Pacific shipowners is similar to that observed throughout the region (leading Lasserre and Schutte (1995) to call the region the most growth-obsessed region in the world) and elsewhere in the world (Harvey, 1988). Synthesising the results of earlier studies, Harvey (1988) has drawn up a table showing the relative frequency with which corporate strategies have been used. Harvey's figures are reproduced in Table 10.1. To highlight similarities in the pattern of responses, the results obtained from Asia-Pacific shipowners are also provided.

Confirmation from various industries and geographical regions is essential for the continuous improvement of the field. It enhances confidence in the strategic choice model because it shows that the model works both within the shipping industry and elsewhere; at the same time, it advances theory building and testing because it allows researchers to fine tune the concepts, principles, and assumptions of the model. Obviously further research is needed to gain a better understanding of strategy selection in commercial shipping, particularly in relation to the Asia-Pacific.

**Table 10.1**
**Frequency of use of corporate strategies (%)**

| Corporate Strategies | Frequency of Use | |
| --- | --- | --- |
| | **Other Industries** (Harvey, 1988) | **Asia-Pacific Shipowners** |
| Grow/Develop | 54.4 | 61 |
| Stabilise | 9.2 | 12 |
| Turnaround/Harvest | 7.5 | 9 |
| Combination | 28.7 | 18 |

## A need for an integrative review of shipping strategy research

As this book has indicated, much more research into shipping strategy (strategic management, strategic planning, strategy selection) both in relation to the industry in general and the Asia-Pacific shipping in particular, is badly needed.

Strategy research in shipping is a fairly nascent field, with very little written about it. As discussed in chapter two on Asia-Pacific shipping, much of what is available in the literature is unsubstantiated by empirical evidence (Frankel, 1989). A quick perusal of leading shipping management journals published in recent years would show that contributions to the subject comprise mainly of essays, arguments, or commentaries that draw on personal views and anecdotal evidence rather than on structured inquiry. Management texts also devote minimal attention to the subject or base their discussion mainly on general strategic management literature. There has also been a general lack of training in strategic management. This is true in the Asia-Pacific, as this study has found, and there is some evidence that this may also be true elsewhere in the shipping industry (Chapman, 1989).

Given the importance of strategy and strategic planning to competitive success, particularly in the turbulent environments where shipping is typically found, more and better information about strategy and its application to the shipping industry is obviously needed (Miller and Cardinal, 1994). Studies are sorely needed to analyse, evaluate, and synthesise what has been done so far in shipping strategy research. This will enable an agenda for future research to be drawn up to give both researchers and practitioners a general picture of the field's development. It should show how it began, where it has been, what it has accomplished, what major schools of thought have emerged, where it is headed. Through such integrative reviews, collective knowledge about the field can be significantly enhanced. This is something that more established fields of inquiry (e.g. the general strategic management literature) regularly do, and from which shipping strategy research would greatly benefit.

## Applicability of Western strategy models to Asia-Pacific shipping

An evaluation of different approaches to strategy development and strategic planning is needed to determine their appropriateness to Asia-Pacific shipping.

In 1983, Lasserre (1983) argued that a formal approach to strategy formulation, as propounded and practised in the West (mainly North Europe, and North America), is inappropriate for the Asia-Pacific region, particularly in relation to East Asian countries. In a more recent publication, Lasserre and Schutte (1995) again stressed the same argument, pointing to major differences between Asians and Westerners in the way they think, live their lives, and conduct their businesses.

Evidence frequently cited of this cultural divide is the way these two groups approach strategic planning. Asians are said to prefer an informal, inductive, and incremental approach to planning, while Westerners use a more formalised and systematic approach. Writers of popular books (e.g. Chu, 1995; Naisbitt, 1995) essentially say the same thing. In shipping, there is some evidence to show that the intuitive and informal approach to decision making is prevalent within the industry (Datz, 1971; Aries, 1989). If this is the case, then the argument that Asia-Pacific shipowners follow an informal approach would be stronger, because it has both cultural and industry backing.

Because most of the widely used analytical tools and models reflect a rational-analytical perspective, which contrast with an informal and incremental approach, their applicability to Asia-Pacific decision makers thus becomes suspect. If they are to be of use to shipowners, their appropriateness has to be determined. To what extent are they applicable? To what extent would they have to be changed or modified to make them relevant to Asia-Pacific (especially East Asian) users? Research must be able to provide answers to these questions.

Another area of investigation should focus on the actual strategic process taken by Asia-Pacific shipowners. While this study gives support to an Asian preference for informal planning and strategy selection, it does not necessarily accept the argument that, ergo, little or no planning is needed or done. What is probably more correct is something in between. As noted earlier, an equally likely explanation is that East Asian shipowners do plan, but they are more likely to keep these plans, and the planning process, informal and hence less transparent to outsiders. To determine whether this is indeed the case, longitudinal and observational studies of workplace behaviour would be needed.

## A typology of shipping strategies

The development of a research-based typology of shipping strategies, particularly at the corporate and business levels, is needed to better understand similarities and diversities in shipowners' strategic choices.

A typology of strategies, covering the corporate, business, and functional levels, has been developed as part of this study (see Table 4.7). Of these, however, only the five generic corporate strategies were tested on a sample of Asia-Pacific shipowners. The next task is to extend this test to other shipowners. Would other shipowners in the region behave similarly? Would the model be equally applicable to another geographical region, say, Europe, which holds the largest percentage of the world fleet (44 per cent in 1997)? Only further research will answer this question.

Research is also needed on business strategies in shipping. Porter (1980, 1985) is the dominant authority in business strategy, and his work is widely cited in the shipping literature and is taught to executives studying shipping business management. However, a number of studies have questioned his business strategy models, particularly their applicability to other industries (Miller and Dess, 1993; Grimm et al, 1988; Wright, 1987; Mathur, 1986) and to the Asia-Pacific region (Fitzgerald, 1994), and are calling for more research into the area. In light of Porter's popularity in shipping, it would be useful to test whether it is well deserved. To what extent do Porter's models apply to shipowners' strategic choices? One effective way of finding out is through simulation, as this will require shipowners to select specific business strategies under given environmental conditions. Data from such simulation can also be backed by self-reports, obtained through surveys and/or interviews from shipowners, for greater confidence in the data.

With more research into corporate and business shipping strategies, the link between the two can be established more reliably, which should significantly improve current shipping strategy theory and practice. The need for an integrating framework is becoming particularly acute because of the growing number of studies looking at specific strategies in individual shipping trades or markets (e.g. Glen, 1997; Knudsen, 1997; Ballis et al, 1997; Cho and Perakis, 1996; Lee, 1996; Bendall and Stent, 1996; Ariel, 1989). Thus far, no serious attempt has been made to link these specific strategies to the broader categories of business or corporate strategies, which can greatly hamper the development of our understanding of shipping strategy. As one writer on creative thinking (de Bono, 1993) puts it, a general strategy is needed to direct the choice of specific strategies. The first sets the strategic direction of the organisation; the second provides more precise measures of achieving the first.

## Strategic decision making

There are two areas in strategic decision making that provide a rich ground for research: the role and influence of individual strategic decision makers, and intra-industry differences.

Strategic decision making is the primary responsibility of senior managers. However, what is not so clear is what these senior managers actually do during the decision-making process and how much influence or power they wield to affect the outcome. Who actually does the 'strategising'? Would they all have the same influence or power or would one area or level have greater power than the others? While research on these and related issues has been done elsewhere (e.g. Whittington, 1996; Schilit, 1990; Hegarty and Hoffman, 1987), the same cannot be said with the shipping industry. In an industry that is known to be secretive and conservative, would strategic decision-making powers be broad-based or would they be, as apparently in the case of East Asian shipowners, vested in the chief executive and a few trusted subordinates? Would distinctions in decision-making styles be made on the basis of culture, or would other industry-specific variables have greater influence? In today's highly globalised and competitive markets, these are timely questions to address, particularly for those who intend to compete in the Asia-Pacific region, where decision-making styles, processes, and structures are said to differ drastically from those used in the West. There is a definite attractiveness in the idea that if one knew how the chief strategists of a competitor thought and worked, one would be in a better position to gauge the steps that the competitor would take.

Differences in decision-making patterns and processes can also be extended to various sectors of the shipping industry. This study has highlighted some differences in approach between the liner, dry bulk, and tanker sectors of the industry. In general, the liner trades were found to be more conservative and risk-averse than the bulk trades, opting for strategies that exposed them to less risk. Areas of research on this and related issues already exist. Most notable are those investigating the risk preferences of shipowners (Cullinane, 1991; Harvey, 1987; Hope and Boe, 1981; Lorange and Norman, 1972), but these bodies of knowledge do not yet cohere to provide a comprehensive picture of intra-industry differences in strategic decision making. Clearly, more work is needed to integrate and extend what is currently known about differential approaches to strategic decision making within the shipping industry.


## Competing for the future

Strategy, according to a survey of management executives, consultants and academics, is considered the current single most important management issue (Bryne, 1996). As markets become globally interconnected and as business environments become more turbulent and competitive, organisations are increasingly urged to be more proactive and creative in their use of strategy to compete effectively for the future (Hamel and Pralahad, 1994). Synthesising recent management trends, Taylor (1997) says that greater stress is being placed on ongoing strategic discussions, not only among senior people but also between senior managers and all relevant parts of the organisation. There is also increasing emphasis on networks, alliances, and joint ventures to gain access to new markets or technologies. Finally and perhaps most importantly, there is a strong shift toward changing managerial mindsets, so that those responsible for leading organisations into the future will be better equipped to meet the challenges of the new century.

These trends carry immense implications for Asia-Pacific shipowners. Although many economies in the region remain fragile following the 1997 market devastation, as a whole the region is moving steadily toward economic recovery. Over the long term, the prognosis for growth is highly promising. For Asia-Pacific shipowners to take advantage of this growing resurgence, they would need new mindsets to devise better strategies for competing and maintaining their dominance in world shipping.

# Bibliography

Adler, N.J. England, G.W. Hofstede, G. Olie, R. and Smith, P.B. (1995). *Cross-cultural Management*. Oxford: Butterworth-Heinemann.

Alkhafaji, A.F. (1995). *Competitive Global Management: Principles and Strategies*. Delray Beach, FLA: St Lucie Press.

Allaire, Y. and Firsirotu, M. (1985). 'How to implement radical strategies in large organisations', *Sloan Management Review*, **26**(3), 19-35.

Allen, M. (1985). 'Strategic management hits its stride', *Planning Review*, **13**(5), 6-9, 45.

Anderson, C.R. (1984). *Management Skills, Functions, and Organisation Performance*. Dubuque, IA: William Brown.

Anderson, J.C. Jain, D.C. and Chintagunta, P.K. (1993). 'Customer value assessment in business markets', *Journal of Business-to-Business Marketing*, **1**(1), 3-29.

Andrews, K.R. (1971, revised 1980). *The Concept of Corporate Strategy*. Homewood, IL: Irwin.

Andrews, K.R. Learned, E.P. Christensen, R.C. and Guth, W. (1965). *Business Policy: Text and Cases*. Homewood, IL: Richard Irwin.

Ansoff, H.I. (1965). *Corporate Strategy: An Analytic Approach to Business Policy for Growth and Expansion*. New York: McGraw-Hill.

Ansoff, H.I. (1984). *Implanting Strategic Management*. Englewood Cliffs, NJ: Prentice-Hall.

Ansoff, H.I. (1987). *Corporate Strategy: An Analytic Approach To Business Policy For Growth And Expansion* (revised edition). New York: McGraw-Hill.

Ansoff, H..I. Avner, J. Brandenberg, R. Portner, F and Radosevitch, R. (1971). *Acquisition Behaviour of U.S. Manufacturing Firms, 1946-65*. Nashville, TN: Vanderbilt University Press.

Ansoff, H.I. Declerck, R.P. and Hayes, R.L. (1976). *From Strategic Planning to Strategic Management*. New York: John Wiley and Sons.

Argenti, J. (1974). *Systematic Corporate Planning*. London: Thomas Nelson and Sons.

Ariel, A. (1989). 'Delphi forecast of the dry bulk shipping industry in the year 2000', *Maritime Policy and Management*, **16**(4), 305-336.

Ariff, M. (ed.) (1991). *The Pacific Economy: Growth and External Stability*. Sydney: Allen and Unwin.

Arlt, W.H. (1987). 'Information requirements in strategic planning in the ports industry: Specification and management of a data base', *Maritime Policy and Management*, **14**(1), 49-61.

Armistead, C. (ed.) (1994). *Future of Services Management*. Kogan Page.

Aspinwall, M.D. (1995). *Moveable Feat: Pressure Group Conflict and the European Shipping Policy*. Aldershot: Avebury.

Asseldonk, A.G.M. (1988). *'Porter Quantified' [Summary]*. Eight Annual Strategic Management Society Conference: Winning strategies for the 1990s, Amsterdam.

Bailey, A. and Johnson, G. (1995). 'The process of strategy development', in J. Thompson (ed.), *The CIMA Handbook of Strategic Management*. Oxford: Butterworth-Heinemann.

Baker, G.E. and Ahern, T.M. (1990). 'Triangulation: Strengthening your best guess', *Performance Improvement Quarterly*, **3**(3), 27-35.

Ballis, A. Golias, J. and Abakoumkim, C. (1997). 'A comparison between conventional and advanced handling systems for low volume container maritime terminals', *Maritime Policy and Management*, **24**(1), 73-92.

Bartol, K. Martin, D.Tein, M. and Matthews, G. (1998). *Management: A Pacific Rim Focus*. Sydney: McGraw-Hill.

Barton, M. (1995). *Australian Liner Shipping in Southeast Asia: Is it Competitive? Does it Meet Exporter Demands?* Unpublished diploma thesis. Australian Maritime College, Australia.

BCG (1976). *The Rule of Three and Four*. The Boston Consulting Group Perspectives. Boston: BCG.

Bendall, H.B. and Stent, A.F. (1996) 'Hatchcoverless container ships: Productivity gains from a new technology', *Maritime Policy and Management*, **23**(2), 187-199.

Bennett, S. (1996). 'The global maritime marine market: Solutions for coping with the long-term shortage of skilled maritime personnel'. IIR Shipping Series Conference: *Strategies for Achieving Profitability Through Competence in Shipping*, London.

Bergsten, C.F. (1997), 'American politics, global trade', *The Economist* (September 27), 23-25.

Bower, J.L. (1970). *Managing the Resource Allocation Process*. Cambridge: Harvard University Press.

Bowman, C. and Asch, D. (1996). *Managing Strategy*. London: MacMillan.

Bowman, E.H. (1974). 'Epistomology, corporate strategy, and academe', *Sloan Management Review*, **15**(2), 35-50.

Branch, A.E. (1982). *Economics of Shipping Practice and Management*. London: Chapman and Hall.

Brooks, M.R. (1985). *Fleet Development and the Control of Shipping In Southeast Asia*. Occasional Paper No. 77. Singapore: Institute of Southeast Asian Studies.

Brooks, M.R. (1995). 'Understanding the ocean container market—a seven country study', *Maritime Policy And Management*, **22**(1), 39-49.

Bryne, J.A. (1996). 'Strategic planning', *Business Week* (2 September).

Business Week, (1975, April). 'Piercing the future fog', 49.

Buzzell, R.D. (1983). 'Is vertical integration profitable?', *Harvard Business Review* (January-February), 92-102.

Buzzell, R.D. Gale, B.T. and Sultan, R.G.M. (1975). Market share: A key to profitability. *Harvard Business Review* (January-February), 97-106.

Campbell, A.J. and Verbeke, A. (1994). 'The globalization of service multinationals', *Long Range Planning*, **27**(2), 95-102.

Carlson, D.J. (1989). 'Developing a business strategy for a port', Session No. 3, *AAPMA Management Course* No. 8.

Chandler, A.D. Jr. (1962). *Strategy and Structure: Chapters in the History of the Industrial Enterprise*. Boston: MIT Press.

Chapman, S.E. (1989). *A Global Analysis of Ship Ownership and Ship Management*. Colchester: Lloyd's of London Press.

Chevalier, M. and Catry, B. (1974). 'Don't misuse your market share goal', *European Business* (Winter/Spring), 43-50.

Child, J. (1972). 'Organisational structure, environment and performance: The role of strategic choice', *Sociology*, **6**(1), 1-22.

Child, J. (1974). 'Managerial and organisational factors associated with company performance—Part I', *Journal Of Management Studies*, **11**, 175-189.

Child, J. (1975). 'Managerial and organisational factors associated with company performance—Part II: A contingency analysis', *Journal Of Management Studies*, **12**, 12-27.

Cho, S.C. and Perakis, A.N. (1996). 'Optimal liner fleet routeing strategies', *Maritime Policy And Management*, **23**(3), 249-259.

Chow, I. Holbert, N. Kelley, L. and Yu, J. (1997). *Business Strategy: An Asia-Pacific Focus.* Singapore: Prentice Hall.

Chryssochoidis, G., Millar, C. and Clegg, J. (eds.) (1997). *Internationalisation Strategies* London: MacMillan.

Chu, C. (1995). *The Asian Mind Game: A Western's Survival Manual.* St. Ives, NSW: Stealth Productions.

Collis, D.J. and Montgomery, C.A. (1995). 'Competing on resources: Strategy in the 1990s', *Harvard Business Review* (July-August), 118-128.

Collis, D.J. and Montgomery, C.A. (1997). *Corporate Strategy: Resources And The Scope Of The Firm.* Chicago: Irwin.

Containerisation International (1996a, April). 'The future of global strategic alliances', 81-85.

Containerisation International (1996b, April). 'OOCL's brave new world', 65-68.

Containerisation International (1996c, April). 'The Asian offensive', 15-19.

Containerisation International (1996d, May). 'The K-Line way', 53-55.

Containerisation International (1996e, December). 'Cosco's global crusade', 45-49.

Containerisation International (1997a, January). 'Korean carriers branch out', 66-69.

Containerisation International (1997b, May). 'The millenium's energy boost', 44-95.

Containerisation International (1997c, June). 'Heating up', 49-53.

Cook, D. and Ferris, G. (1986). 'Strategic human resource management and firm effectiveness in industries experiencing decline', *Human Resource Management Journal*, **25**(3).

Cook, T.D. and Reichardt, C.S. (1979). *Qualitative And Quantative Methods In Evaluation Research.* Beverly Hills, CA: Sage.

Cullinane, K. (1991). 'The utility analysis of risk attitudes in shipping', *Maritime Policy And Management*, **18**(3), 157-169.

Cyert, R.M. and March, J.G. (1954, reprinted 1963). *A Behavioural Theory of the Firm.* Englewood Cliffs, NJ: Prentice-Hall.

Datz, I.M. (1971). *Planning Tools for Ocean Transportation.* Cambridge: Cornell Maritime Press.

David, F.R. (1993, 1997). *Strategic Management.* Upper Saddle River, NJ: Prentice Hall.

Day, G.S. (1984). *Strategic Market Planning: The Pursuit of Competitive Advantage.* St. Paul, MN: West.

Day, G.S. (1986). *Analysis for Strategic Market Decisions.* St. Paul, MN: West.

de Bono, E. (1993). *Tactics and the Art and Science of Success.* London: HarperCollins.

Denzin, N.K. (1978). *Sociological Methods.* New York: McGraw Hill.

Dess, G.G. and Davis, P.S. (1982). *An Empirical Examination Of Porter's Generic Strategies.* National Academy of Management Proceedings.

Doz, Y.L. (1980). 'International joint ventures: A framework for analysis,' *Journal Of General Management*, **14**(2), 78-91.

Drewry (1991). *Strategy and Profitability in Global Container Shipping.* London: Drewry Shipping Consultants.

Drewry (1992). *Container Market Profitability to 1997: Will Stabilisation Agreements Save Carriers from Checkmate?* London: Drewry Shipping Consultants.

Drewry (1993). *Pacific Rim Trade and Shipping: The Powerhouse of World Shipping in the 21st Century.* London: Drewry Shipping Consultants.

Drewry (1995). *Market Outlook for Bulk Carriers: Supply, Demand, Employment Prospects and Profitability*. London: Drewry Shipping Consultants.

Drewry (1995). *North-South Container Trades: Will Global Carriers Destroy the Market?* London: Drewry Shipping Consultants.

Drewry (1996a). *Container Shipping: The South East Asian Market*. London: Drewry Shipping Consultants.

Drewry (1996b). *Dry Bulk Freight Rates and Chartering: Players, Strategy and The Market*. London: Drewry Shipping Consultants.

Drewry (1996c). *Global Container Markets: Prospects and Profitability in a High Growth Era*. London: Drewry Shipping Consultants.

Dyson, R.G. (1990). 'Strategic planning', in R.G. Dyson (ed.), *Strategic Planning: Models and Analytical Techniques*. Chichester: John Wiley and Sons.

Eastlack, J. Jr. and MacDonald, P. (1970). 'CEO's role in corporate growth', *Harvard Business Review* (May-June), 150-163.

Elek, A. (1991). 'Asia Pacific Economic Cooperation (APEC)', *Southeast Asian Affairs 1991*. Singapore: Institute of Southeast Asian Studies.

ESCAP (1985a). *PORTMIS: Port Management Information System*. New York: United Nations.

ESCAP (1985b). *Report of a Country-Level Workshop on Ocean Transport Planning and Adequacy of Shipping Services*. Calcutta: United Nations.

ESCAP (1986). *Use of Maritime Transport: A Guide for Shippers, Freight Forwarders and Ship Operators. Vol. 1*. Bangkok: United Nations.

Fairplay (1997). *World Shipping Statistics 1997*. In collaboration with the Institute of Shipping Analysis. London: Fairplay.

Fairplay World Shipping Directory, 1995, 1996.

Farthing, B. (1993). *International Shipping: An Introduction to the Policies, Politics and Institutions of the Maritime World*. London: Lloyd's of London Press.

Fearnleys (1996a). *Review 1996*. Oslo: Fearnsearch.

Fearnleys (1996b). *World Bulk Trades 1996*. Oslo: Fearnsearch.

Fitzgerald, R. (ed.) (1994). *The Competitive Advantage of Far Eastern Business*. Ilford: Frank Cass.

Fitzgerald, S. (1997). *Is Australia an Asian Country? Can Australia Survive in an East Asian Future?*. St. Leonards, NSW: Allen and Unwin.

Frankel, E.G. (1982). *Management and Operations of American Shipping*. Boston: Auburn House.

Frankel, E.G. (1989). 'Strategic planning applied to shipping and ports', *Maritime Policy and Management*, 16(2), 123-132.

Fredrickson, J.W. (1984). 'The comprehensiveness of strategic decision processes: Extension, observations, future directions', *Academy of Management Journal*, 27, 445-466.

Fredrickson, J.W. and Mitchell, T.R. (1984). 'Strategic decision processes: Comprehensiveness and performance in an industry within an unstable environment', *Academy of Management Journal*, 27, 399-423.

Gaddis, P.O. (1997). 'Strategy under attack', *Long Range Planning*, 30(1), 38-45.

Galbraith, C. and Schendel, D. (1983). 'Am empirical analysis of strategy types', *Strategic Management Journal*, 4, 154-173.

Garnaut, R. (1997). 'Plenty of growth to come in Southeast Asia', *The Australian Financial Review* (September 23), 17 (a presentation made to the IMF/World Bank annual meeting in Hong Kong).

Garnaut, R. and Drysdale, P. (eds.) (1994). *Asia Pacific Regionalism: Readings in International Economic Relations*. Sydney: HarperEducational.

Glen, D.R. (1997). 'The market for second-hand ships: Further results on efficiency using cointegration analysis', *Maritime Policy and Management*, **24**(3), 245-260.

Glueck, W. (1976, revised 1980). *Business Policy, Strategy Formation and Management Action*. New York: McGraw-Hill.

Goold, M. and Campbell, A. (1987). *Strategies and Styles: The Role of the Centre in Managing Diversified Corporations*. Oxford: Basil Blackwell.

Goold, M., Campbell, A., and Alexander, M. (1994). *Corporate-Level Strategy: Creating Value in the Multibusiness Company*. New York: John Wiley and Sons.

Gopinath, C. and Hoffman, R.C. (1995). 'The relevance of strategy research: Practitioner and academic viewpoints', *Journal of Management Studies*, **32**, 575-594

Goss, R.O. and Marlow, P.B. (1993). 'Internationalism, protectionism and intervention in shipping', in K.M. Gwilliam (ed.), *Current Issues in Maritime Economics*. Dordrecht: Kluwer Academic Publishers.

Granitsas, A. and Saywell, T. (1997). 'Managing, barely', *Far Eastern Economic Review* (August 28), 54-58.

Greenley, G.E. (1986). 'Does strategic planning improve company performance?', *Long Range Planning*, **19**(2), 101-109.

Grimm, C.M. Smith, K.G. and Gannon, M.J. (1988). 'Applying Porter's (1980) strategy typology to small high-tech firms [Summary]'. Eighth Annual Strategic Management Society Conference: *Winning Strategies for the 1990's*, Amsterdam.

Grinyer, P.H. and Norburn, D. (1975). 'Planning for existing markets: Perceptions of executives and financial performance', *Journal Of The Royal Statistical Society*, **138**(1), 70-98.

Gutman, P. (1964). 'Strategies for growth', *California Management Review*, **6**(4).

Hambrick, D.C. (1980). 'Operationalising the concept of business level strategy in research', *Academy Of Management Review*, **5**(4), 567-576.

Hambrick, D.C. (1983). 'Some tests of the effectiveness and functional attributes of Miles and Snow's strategic types', *Academy Of Management Review*, **26**(1), 5-26.

Hambrick, D.C. MacMillan, I.C. and Day, D. (1982). 'Strategic attributes and performance in the four cells of the BCG matrix—A PIMS-based analysis of individual product businesses', *Academy Of Management Journal*, **25**, 510-530.

Hamel, G. and Pralahad, C.K. (1985). 'Do you really have a global strategy?', *Harvard Business Review* (July-August), 139-148.

Hamel, G. and Pralahad, C.K. (1993). 'Strategy as stretch and leverage', *Harvard Business Review* (March-April), 75-84.

Hamel, G. and Pralahad, C.K. (1994). 'Competing for the future', *Harvard Business Review* (July-August), 122-128.

Hamermesh, R.G. (1983). 'Making planning strategic', *Harvard Business Review* (July-August).

Hamermesh, R.G. (ed.) (1983). *Strategic Management*. Harvard Business Review Executive Book Series. New York: Wiley and Sons.

Hamermesh, R.G. (1986). *Making Strategy Work*. New York: Wiley.

Hansen, O.D. (1989). 'How can Norway's maritime industry ensure long-term profits from international shipping?'. *The Nor-Shipping '89 Conference Papers*. London: Lloyd's of London Press.

Harvey, D.A. (1987). *The Analysis and Financing of Capital Projects in Shipping*. Unpublished doctoral dissertation. University of Bath, England.

Harvey, D.E. (1988). *Strategic Management and Business Policy*. Columbus, OH: Merrill.

Haspeslagh, P. (1982). 'Portfolio planning: uses and limits', *Harvard Business Review* (January-February), 58-73.

Hawkins, J.E. (1989). *Shipping Subsidies and the Balance of Payments*. London: Lloyd's of London Press.

Hawkins, J.E. (1991a), 'Port investment appraisals for the 1990s', *Maritime Policy and Management*, **18**(3), 225-232.

Hawkins, J.E. (1991b), 'Strategically managing port investments'. *National Transport Conference 1991 Proceedings*. Canberra: Institution of Engineers Australia.

Hawkins, J.E. (1993). *Strategic Management for Maritime Transport*. Adelaide: University of South Australia.

Hawkins, J.E. (1996). 'Strategic management'. *Conference for Senior Shipping Executives in the South Pacific*. Maritime Division, Forum Secretariat, Suva, Fiji.

Hax, A.C. and Majluf, N.S. (1983a). 'The use of the growth-share matrix in strategic planning', *Interfaces*, **13**(1), 46-60.

Hax, A.C. and Majluf, N.S. (1983b). 'The use of the industry attractiveness-business strength matrix in strategic planning', *Interfaces*, **13**(2), 54-71.

Hedley, B. (1976). 'A fundamental approach to strategy development', Long Range Planning, **9**(12), 2-11.

Hedley, B. (1977). 'Strategy and the business portfolio', *Long Range Planning* **10**(2), 9-15.

Hegarty, W.H. and Hoffman, R.C. (1987). 'Who influences strategic decisions?', *Long Range Planning*, **20**(2), 76-85.

Henderson, B.D. (1979). *Henderson on Corporate Strategy*. Cambridge: Abt Books.

Herbert, T.T. and Deresky, H. (1987). 'Generic strategies: An empirical investigation of typology validity and strategy content', *Strategic Management Journal*, **8**, 135-147.

Herold, D.M. (1972). 'Long range planning and organisational performance', *Academy Of Management Journal*, **15**, 91-102.

Hibbert, E.P. (1997). *International Business: Strategy And Operations*. London: MacMillan.

Higgott, R. Cooper, A.F. and Bonnor, J. (1991). 'Cooperation-building in the Asia-Pacific region: APEC and the new institutionalism', Pacific Economic Papers No. 199, Australia-Japan Research Centre, Australian National University, Canberra.

Hofer, C.W. (1975). 'Toward a contingency theory of business strategy', *Academy Of Management Journal*, 784-810.

Hofer, C.W and Schendel, D. (1978). *Strategy Formulation: Analytical Concepts*. St. Paul, MN: West.

Hofer, C.W. and Davoust, M.J. (1977). *Successful Strategic Management*. Chicago: Kearney.

Hofstede, G. (1980). *Culture's Consequences: International Differences in Work-Related Values*. Beverly Hills: Sage.

Holste, S. (1993). *Liner Shipping in a Quality-Oriented World Economy*. Institute of Shipping Economics and Logistics.

Hope, E. and Boe, O. (1981). *Investment Behaviour in Norwegian Bulk Shipping*. A report from the Center for Applied Research, Norwegian School of Economics and Business Administration.

Howe, W.S. (1986). *Corporate Strategy*. London: MacMillan.

Hussey, D.E. (1994). *Strategic Management: Theory and Practice*. Oxford: Elsevier.

Ignatius, A. (1996). 'Future Shock', *Far Eastern Economic Review* (October 31), 54-56.

ISL (1996). *Shipping Statistics Yearbook 1996*. Bremen: Institute of Shipping Economics and Logistics.

ISL (1997). *Shipping Statistics and Market Review*. No.1/2 (January-February), No. 3 (March), No. 4 (April), No. 5 (May), No. 6 (June). Bremen: Institute of Shipping Economics and Logistics.

James, B.G. (1974). 'The theory of the corporate life cycle', *Long Range Planning*, 7, 49-57.

JAMRI (1987). *The Pacific Rim Era and Shipping*. JAMRI Report No. 19. Tokyo: Japan Maritime Research Institute.

Jick, T.D. (1979). 'Mixing qualitative and quantitative methods: Triangulation in action', *Administrative Science Quarterly*, **24**(4), 602-611. Reprinted in J. Van Maanen (ed.) (1984), *Qualitative Methodology*. Beverly Hills, CA: Sage.

Johnson, G. and Scholes, K. (1997). *Exploring Corporate Strategy*. Hemel Hempstead: Prentice Hall.

Jon, J-S. (1986). *Development of Shipping in Korea in the Containerisation Era*. Unpublished doctoral dissertation. University of Wales, Cardiff.

Karger, D.W. and Malik, Z.A. (1975). 'Long range planning and organisational performance', *Long Range Planning*, **8**, 60-64.

Katz, R.L. (1970). *Management of the Total Enterprise*. Englewood Cliffs, NJ: Prentice-Hall.

Kay, J. (1995). *Foundations of Corporate Success. How Business Strategies Add Value*. Oxford: Oxford University Press.

Kerlinger, F.N. (1973). *Foundations of Behavioral Research*. New York: Holt, Rinehart and Winston.

Kim, G-S. (1992). ''Government preference' and its influence on the shipping industry in Korea', *Maritime Policy and Management*, **19**(4), 265-277.

Knudsen, K. (1997). 'The economics of zero taxation of the world shipping industry', *Maritime Policy and Management*, **24**(1), 45-54.

Kotler, P. (1978). 'Harvesting strategies for weak products', *Business Horizons* (August), 17-18.

Kruger, W. (1989). 'Patterns of success in German businesses', *Long Range Planning*, **22**(2), 106-113.

Krugman, P. (1994), 'The myth of Asia's miracle', *Foreign Affairs* (November/ December), 62-78.

Kudla, R.J. (1980). 'The effects of strategic planning on common stock returns', *Academy of Management Journal*, **23**, 5-20.

Kunkel, J. (1995). 'US trade policy towards the Asia Pacific region in the 1990s', *Pacific Economic Papers* No. 241, Australia-Japan Research Centre, Australian National University, Canberra.

Lasserre, P. (1983). 'Strategic planning in South East Asia: Does it work?', *Euro-Asia Business Review*, **2**(2), 37-41.

Lasserre, P. and Schutte, H. (1995). *Strategies for Asia Pacific*. Melbourne: MacMillan.

Ledger, G. and Roe, M. (1992). 'The decline of the UK merchant fleet: An assessment of government policies in recent years', *Maritime Policy and Management*, **19**(3), 239-251.

Lee, T-W. (1996). *Shipping Developments in Far East Asia: The Korean Experience*. Aldershot: Avebury.

Leger, J.M. (1995). 'Rags to riches. Come together: investment and trade links are growing rapidly in Asia', *Far Eastern Economic Review* (October 12), 46-58.

Leinbach, T.R. and Sien, C.L. (1989). *South-East Asian Transport: Issues in Development*. Singapore: Oxford University Press.

Leontiades, J.C. (1985). *Multinational Corporate Strategy: Planning For World Markets*. Lexington, MA: Heath.

Lewarn, B. and Hawkins, J. (1994). The need for a comprehensive shipping policy. *Proceedings of the Aus-Ship 94 Seminar*. Launceston, TAS: Australian Maritime College.

Lewis, G. Morkel, A. and Hubbard, G. (1993). *Australian Strategic Management Concepts, Context and Cases*. Sydney: Prentice Hall.

Lindblom, C. (1959). 'The science of muddling through', *Public Administration Review* (Spring), **19**, 120-128.

Lingle, C. (1997). 'Toothless tigers?', *The Weekend Australian* (September 13-14), 34.

Lloyd's Maritime Asia 1997. London: Lloyd's Register of Shipping.

Lloyd's Maritime Information Service 1997. London: Lloyd's Register of Shipping.

197

Lloyd's Maritime Directory 1997. London: Lloyd's Register of Shipping.

Lloyd's Electronic Maritime Directory 1995, 1996. London: Lloyd's Register of Shipping.

Lloyd's Shipping Economist (1996a). 'Growth through diversity at MISC', *Lloyd's Shipping Economist*, **18**(8), 23-26.

Lloyd's Shipping Economist (1996b). 'Vehicle trades depending on economic stability', *Lloyd's Shipping Economist*, **18**(8), 16-19.

Lloyd's Shipping Economist (1997). 'Evergreen's show of strength', *Lloyd's Shipping Economist*, **19**(2), 19-22.

Lorange, P. and Norman, V.D. (1972). 'Portfolio planning in bulk shipping companies', in P. Lorange and V.D. Norman (eds.), *Shipping Management, Proceedings From a Seminar in Bergen*, August 23-26, 1972. Institute for Shipping Research, Bergen, Norway and Maritime Research Centre, the Hague, Netherlands.

Lyles, M.A. (1990). 'A research agenda for strategic management in the 1990s', *Journal of Management Studies*, **27**, 363-375.

MacMillan, K. (1986). 'Strategy: An introduction', *Journal of General Management*, **11**(3), 75-95.

March, J.G. and Simon, H.A. (1958). *Organisations*. New York: Wiley.

Marcus, H.S. (1987). *Marine Transportation Management*. North Ryde, NSW: Croom Helm.

Mathur, S.S. (1986). 'Strategy: Framing business intentions', *Journal of General Management*, **12**(1), 77-97.

McGrath, J.E., Martin, J., and Kulka, R.A. (1982). *Judgment Calls in Research*. Beverly Hills: Sage.

McKinsey Consulting Firm (1985). *Excellence in Norwegian Shipping*. Unpublished consultants report to the Norwegian Shipowners Association, Oslo.

Melcher, B.H. and Kerzner, H. (1988). *Strategic Planning: Development and Implementation*. Blue Ridge Summit, PA: TAB Books.

Menon, J. (1996). 'Intra-industry trade and the ASEAN free trade area', *Pacific Economic Papers* No. 251, Australia-Japan Research Centre, Australian National University, Canberra.

Miles, M.B. and Huberman, A.M. (1984). *Qualitative Data Analysis: A Sourcebook of New Methods*, Beverly Hills: Sage.

Miles, R.E. and Snow, C. (1978). *Organisational Strategy, Structure, and Process*. New York: McGraw-Hill.

Miller, A. and Dess, G.G. (1993). 'Assessing Porter's (1980) model in terms of its generalizability, accuracy and simplicity', *Journal of Management Studies*, **30**, 553-585.

Miller, C.C. and Cardinal, L.B. (1994). 'Strategic planning and firm performance: A synthesis of more than two decades of research', *Academy of Management Journal*, **37**, 1649-1665.

Miller, D. and Friesen, D.H. (1977). 'Strategy making in context: Ten empirical archetypes', *Journal of Management Studies*, **14**, 253-280.

Miller, D. and Friesen, D.H. (1986). 'Porter's (1980) generic strategies and performance: An empirical examination with American data. Part 2: Performance implications', *Organisational Studies*, **7**(3), 37-55.

Miller, D. and Mintzberg, H. (1983). 'The case for configuration', in G. Morgan (ed.), *Beyond Method: Strategies for Social Research*. Beverly Hills: CA: Sage.

Mintzberg, H. (1972). Research on strategy making. *Academy of Management Proceedings*, 90-94.

Mintzberg, H. (1973, revised 1980). *The Nature of Managerial Work*. New York: Harper and Row.

Mintzberg, H. (1976). 'Planning on the left side and managing on the right', *Harvard Business Review* (July-August), 49-58.

Mintzberg, H. (1978). 'Patterns of strategy formation', *Management Science*, **24**(9), 934-948.

Mintzberg, H. (1987). 'Crafting strategy', *Harvard Business Review* (July-August), 66-77.

Mintzberg, H. (1994). *The Rise and Fall of Strategic Planning*. Hemel Hempstead: Prentice Hall.

Mintzberg, H. (1996a). 'Generic business strategies', in H. Mintzberg and J.B. Quinn (eds.), *The Strategy Process: Concepts, Contexts, Cases*. Upper Saddle River, NJ: Prentice Hall. Extracted from H. Mintzberg (1988), 'Generic strategies: Toward a comprehensive framework', *Advances in Strategic Management*, v.5. Greenwich, CT: JAI Press), 1-67.

Mintzberg, H. (1996b). 'Generic corporate strategies', in H. Mintzberg and J.B. Quinn (eds.), *The Strategy Process: Concepts, Contexts, Cases*. Upper Saddle River, NJ: Prentice Hall. Extracted from H. Mintzberg (1988), 'Generic strategies: Toward a comprehensive framework', *Advances In Strategic Management*, v.5. Greenwich, CT:

Mintzberg, H. and Waters, J.A. (1985). 'Of strategies, deliberate and emergent', *Strategic Management Journal*, **6**, 257-272.

Montanari, J.R. Morgan, C.P. and Bracker, J.S. (1990). *Strategic Management: A Choice Approach*. Chicago: Dryden.

Morris, T. (1987a). 'Management update: Strategy and organisation' (relationship between strategy, organisational structures, and decision processes), *Journal of General Management*, **12**(3), 75-82.

Morris, T. (1987b). 'Management update: Strategy and organisation' (competitive strategies and portfolio analysis), *Journal of General Management*, **13**(1), 82-91.

Morris, T. (1988). 'Management update: Strategy and organisation' (strategy behaviour), *Journal of General Management*, **13**(3), 87-93.

Naisbitt, J. (1997). *Megatrends Asia: The Eight Asian Megatrends that are Changing the World*. London: Nicholas Brealey.

Napier, N.K. and Albert M.S. (1990). 'East Asian and American perspectives on thinking strategically: The leopard and his spots', *Asia Pacific Human Resource Management Journal* (November), 40-50.

Naylor, T.H. (ed.) (1982). *Corporate Strategy*. Amsterdam: North-Holland.

Northrup, A. and Kraemer, K.L. (1982). 'Contributions of political science and public administration to qualitative research methods', in E. Kuhns and S. Martorana (eds.), *Qualitative Methods for Institutional Research*. San Francisco: Jossey-Bass.

OECD (1994). *Maritime Transport 1993*. Paris: OECD.

OECD (1996). *Development Cooperation: 1995 Report*. Paris: OECD.

OECD (1997). Maritime transport 1995. Paris: OECD.

Park, Y.C. (1991). 'Macroeconomic developments and prospects in East Asia', in M. Ariff, M. (ed.), *The Pacific Economy: Growth and External Stability*. Sydney: Allen and Unwin.

Patton, M.Q. (1980). Qualitative evaluation methods. Beverly Hills: Sage.

Pearce, J.A. II and Robinson, R.B. Jr. (1988, 1997). *Strategic Management: Formulation, Implementation, and Control*. Chicago: Irwin.

Pelecanos, S. (1992). *Seafaring Skill Requirements for Australia's Maritime Infrastructure: Case Study*. Unpublished master's thesis. Australian Maritime College, Launceston.

Peters, H.J. (1986). *Trends in Global and Pacific Trades and Shipping and their Implications for National Maritime Sector Development in Asia's Pacific Rim Countries*. Bremen: Institute of Shipping Economics and Logistics.

Peters, T.J. and Waterman, R.H. Jr. (1982). *In Search of Excellence. Lessons from America's Best-Run Companies*. Artarmon, NSW: Harper and Row.

Pfeffer, J. (1976). 'Beyond management and the worker: The institutional function of management', *Academy of Management Journal*, **25**, 80-93.

Porter, M.E. (1980). *Competitive Strategy: Techniques for Analysing Industries and Competitors*. New York: Free Press.

Porter, M.E. (1985). *Competitive Advantage: Creating and Sustaining Superior Performance.* New York: Free Press.

Porter, M.E. (1990). *The Competitive Advantage of Nations.* London: MacMillan.

Quinn, J.B. (1978). 'Strategic change: Logical incrementalism', *Sloan Management Review,* **20**(1), 7-21.

Quinn, J.B. (1988). 'Problems with Porter's paradigm [Summary]'. Eighth Annual Strategic Management Society Conference: *Winning Strategies For The 1990s,* Amsterdam.

Quinn, J.B. Mintzberg, H. and James, R.M. (eds.) (1988). *The Strategy Process: Concepts, Contexts and Cases.* Englewood Cliffs: Prentice-Hall.

Ramanujam, V. and Venkatraman, N. (1987). 'Planning and performance: A new look at an old question', *Business Horizons,* **30**(3), 19-25.

Reker, R.A. (1997). *Logistics and the Maritime Industry. An Opportunity to Enhance Trade between Australia and East Asia.* Unpublished master's thesis. Australian Maritime College, Launceston.

Rich, C.A. (1978). 'Corporate planning in shipping: relating theory to practice. Part 2: Corporate strategy', *Maritime Policy and Management,* **5**, 39-50.

Rimmer, P.J. (1997). 'Global network firms in transport and communication: Japan's NYK, KDD and JAL?', in P.J. Rimmer (ed.), *Pacific Rim Development: Integration and Globalisation in the Asia-Pacific Economy.* St. Leonards, NSW: Allen and Unwin.

Robinson, R.B. and Pearce, J.A. (1988). 'Planned patterns of strategic behaviour and their relationship to business unit performance', *Strategic Management Journal,* **9**, 43-60.

Rohwer, J. (1996). *Asia Rising: How History's Biggest Middle Class Will Change the World.* London: Nicholas Brealey.

Rothschild, W.E. (1976). *Putting It All Together: A Guide to Strategic Thinking.* New York: Amacom.

Rothschild, W.E. (1979). *Strategic Alternatives: Selection, Development and Implementation.* New York: Amacom.

Rugman, A. and Verbeke, A. (eds.) (1992). Research in global strategic management. *A Research Annual. Corporate Response To Global Change.* Vol. 3. London: JAI Press.

Rumelt, R.P. (1974). *Strategy, Structure and Economic Performance.* Cambridge: Harvard University Press.

Rumelt, R.P. (1984). 'Toward a strategic theory of the firm', in R.B. Lamb, (ed.) *Competitive Strategic Management.* Englewood Cliffs, NJ: Prentice-Hall.

Rumelt, R.P. (1991). 'How much does industry matter?', *Strategic Management Journal,* **12**, 167-185.

Rhyne, L. (1986). 'The relationship of strategic planning to financial performance', *Strategic Management Journal,* 7, 423-436.

Saxena, K.B.C. and Joshi, P.B. (1992). 'Motivating ship managers to use management support technology', *Maritime Policy and Management,* **19**(1), 55-62.

Schellenberg, D.S. (1983). *Issues in Strategy Implementation: The Effect of Congruence among Strategy, Structure, and Managerial Performance Criteria on Organisational Performance.* Unpublished doctoral dissertation. Indiana University Graduate School of Business.

Schilit, W.K. (1990). 'A comparative analysis of strategic decisions', *Journal of Management Studies,* **27**, 442-444.

Schoeffler, S. Buzzell, R. and Heany, D.F. (1974). 'Impact of strategic planning on profit performance', *Harvard Business Review* (March-April), 137-145.

Shanks, D. (1985). 'Strategic planning for global competition', *Journal of Business Strategy,* **5**(3), 78-97.

Shibusawa, M. Ahmad, Z.H. and Bridges, B. (1992). *Pacific Asia in the 1990s.* London: Routledge.

Simon, H.A. (1976). *Administrative Behaviour.* New York: Free Press.

Slack, B. Comtois, C. and Sletmo, G. (1996). 'Shipping lines as agents of change in the port industry', *Maritime Policy and Management*, **23**(3), 289-300.

Sletmo, G.K. and Holste, S. (1993). Shipping and the competitive advantage of nations: the role of international ship registers. *Maritime Policy and Management*, **20**(3), 243-255.

Smith, G.D. Arnold, D.R. and Bizzell, B.G. (1985). *Business Strategy and Policy*. Boston: Houghton Mifflin.

Smith, J.G. (1985). *Business Strategy: An Introduction*. Oxford: Basil Blackwell.

Snow, C.C. and Thomas, J.B. (1994). 'Field research methods in strategic management: Contributions to theory building and testing', *Journal of Management Studies*, **31**, 457-480.

Soper, R.T. (1979). 'Corporate planning in liner shipping', in H.A. Beth (ed.), *Liner Shipping in the Eighties. Report on the International Symposium*. Bremen: Institute of Shipping Economics.

Spruyt, J. (1994). *Ship Management*. London: Lloyd's of London Press.

Steiner, G.A. and Miner, J.B. (1977). *Management Policy and Strategy: Text, Readings and Cases*. New York: MacMillan.

Stopford, M. (1988). *Maritime Economics*. London: Unwin Hyman.

Strategic Planning Associates (1984). 'Strategy and the shareholder: The value curve', in Lamb, R. (ed.), *Competitive Strategic Management*. Englewood Cliffs, NJ: Prentice Hall.

Svendsen, A.S. (1989). 'Shipping as human achievement and culture in economic and ecological context'. *Proceedings of the International Shipping Seminar*, Bergen.

Tan, K.Y. and Wee, C.H. (1995). 'A scenario for East Asia: Recent trends and future challenges', *Long Range Planning*, **28**(1), 41-53.

Tanaka, N. (1993). *Container Shipping and Container Ports of the World in Recent Times*. Unpublished paper, NYK Research Division, Tokyo.

Taylor, B. (1997). 'The return of strategic planning—once more with feeling', *Long Range Planning*, **30**(3), 334-344.

Thanopolou, H.A. (1995). 'The growth of fleets registered in the newly-emerging maritime countries and maritime crises', *Maritime Policy and Management*, **22**(1), 51-62.

Thomas, D.E. (1979). 'Strategy is different in service businesses', in Sasser, W.E. (ed.), *Service Management*. Cambridge:. Harvard Business Review.

Thompson, A.A. Jr. and Strickland, A.J. III (1983). *Strategy Formulation and Implementation: Tasks for the General Manager*. Plano, TX: Business Publications.

Thompson, A.A. Jr. and Strickland, A.J. III (1998). *Strategic Management: Concepts and Cases*. Boston: Irwin/McGraw-Hill.

Thune, S. and House, R. (1970), 'Where long range planning pays off', *Business Horizons* **13**(8), 81-87.

UNCTAD (1995). *Review of Maritime Transport 1994*. Geneva: United Nations.

UNCTAD (1996a). *Handbook of International Trade and Development Statistics*. Geneva: United Nations.

UNCTAD (1996b). *Review of Maritime Transport 1995*. Geneva: United Nations.

US Maritime Administration (1982). *A Guide to Strategic Planning for the US Liner Industry*. Washington, DC: USMA.

Vancil, R.F. and Lorange, P. (1975). 'Strategic planning in diversified companies', *Harvard Business Review* (January-February), 81-90.

von Neumann, J. and Morgenstern, O. (1948). *Theory of Games and Economic Behaviour*. Princeton: University Press.

Warner, A. and Arnold, D. (1986). 'Navigating the strategic maze', *Management Decisions*, **24**(6).

Webb, E.J., Campbell, T.D., Schwartz, R.D. and Sechrest, L. (1965). *Unobtrusive Measures: Non-Reactive Research in the Social Sciences*. Chicago: Rand McNally.

Wernerfelt, B. (1984). 'A resource based view of the firm', *Strategic Management Journal*, **5**, 171-180.

Whittington, R. (1996). 'Strategy as practice', *Long Range Planning*, **29**, 731-736.

Wind, Y. and Mahajan, V. (1981). 'Designing product and business portfolios', *Harvard Business Review* (January-February), 155-165.

Wissema, J.G. Van Der Pol, H.W. and Messer, H.M. (1980). 'Strategic management archetypes', *Strategic Management Journal*, **1**, 37-47.

Wong, M. (1991). *Strategic Planning Techniques for Liner Shipping Scheduling Operations*. Unpublished graduate diploma thesis. Australian Maritime College, Launceston.

Wood, D.R. and La Forge, R.L. (1979). 'The impact of comprehensive planning on financial performance', *Academy of Management Journal*, **22**, 516-526.

World Bank (1993). *The East Asian Miracle: Economic Growth and Public Policy*. Oxford: Oxford University Press.

World Bank (1994). *East Asia's Trade and Investment: Regional and Global Gains from Liberalization*. Washington, D.C.

World Bank (1997). *Regional Brief: East Asia*. The World Bank Group, Washington, D.C.

Wright, P. (1987). 'A refinement of Porter's strategies', *Strategic Management Journal*, **8**, 93-101.

Wrigley, L. (1970). *Divisional Autonomy and Diversification*. Unpublished doctoral dissertation. Harvard Business School.

Xingyuan, R. (1991). 'A perspective of Pacific-Asia regional shipping market in the 1990s'. *Proceedings of the International MARINTEC China 91 Conference*, China.

Yip, G. (1995). *Total Global Strategy*. Englewood Cliffs, NJ: Prentice Hall.

Yoo, S. and Digman, L.A. (1987). 'Decision support system: A new tool for strategic management', *Long Range Planning*, **20**(2), 114-124.

Yue, C.S. and Yuan, L.T. (1994). 'Subregional economic zones in Southeast Asia', in R. Garnaut and P. Drysdale (eds.), *Asia Pacific Regionalism: Readings in International Economic Relations*. Sydney: HarperEducational.

Yui, T. and Nakagawa, K. (eds.) (1985). 'Business history of shipping: Strategy and structure'. *Proceedings Of The Fuji International Conference On Business History 11*, Tokyo.

202

# Index